Rethinking Citizenship

For my Mum and Dad,
Frances and Michael Roche

Rethinking Citizenship

Welfare, Ideology and Change in Modern Society

Maurice Roche

POLITY PRESS

Copyright © Maurice Roche 1992

The right of Maurice Roche to be identified as author of
this work has been asserted in accordance with the
Copyright, Designs and Patents Act 1988.

First published in 1992 by Polity Press
in association with Blackwell Publishers

Editorial office:
Polity Press
65 Bridge Street
Cambridge CB2 1UR, UK

Marketing and production:
Blackwell Publishers
108 Cowley Road
Oxford OX4 1JF, UK

238 Main Street
Suite 501
Cambridge, MA 02142, USA

ISBN 0 7456 0306 8
ISBN 0 7456 0307-6 (pbk)

A CIP catalogue record for this book is available
from the British Library and from the Library of Congress.

Typeset in 11 on 13 pt Times
by Best-set Typesetter Ltd., Hong Kong
Printed in Great Britain by T.J. Press (Padstow) Ltd, Padstow, Cornwall

This book is printed on acid-free paper.

Contents

Acknowledgements

Colleagues in Sheffield University have given advice and/or support on various parts of this study and the following should be mentioned: Andrew Gamble, Alan Walker, Ankie Hoogvelt, Dave Phillips, Mike Nellis, Stephen George and, in particular, Neil Sellors. Thanks are also due to our new colleague Bill Jordan and to Tony Giddens for their helpful comments on this project. In addition I owe a long-standing intellectual debt to my one-time teacher Ernest Gellner which I would like to acknowledge here. None of these named has any responsibility for the analyses, opinions and limitations of this study. Val Heap did a fine job producing the manuscript, together with assistance from typists in the Department of Sociological Studies and support from the University's Policy Studies Centre. The apparently social act of writing depends on a lot of unsociable isolation. For their patience and support over a number of years on this and related projects I would like to thank my wife Jan Roche and our children Stephen and Helen Roche.

Introduction

I

Citizenship is a strategically important idea in late twentieth-century Western society. It is important both in contemporary politics and also in contemporary intellectual life. Its strategic significance in contemporary *politics* can hardly be over-estimated. Whether in the form of democratic movements, or of nationalist movements, or both, the world-historical changes set in motion since the late 1980s in Eastern Europe and also in what used to be the Soviet Union have been produced largely by movements of citizens striving to realize or to redefine their citizenship rights and citizen community. In Western Europe the increasing economic, legal and political integration of the European Community is beginning to challenge national sovereignty and citizenship. In addition, it is also beginning to involve the creation of a new transnational European level and sphere of citizens' rights, institutions and community.

In North America the meaning of US citizenship is being challenged in many states, not least in California, by the massive growth of the Spanish-speaking population. Elsewhere in North America Quebec separatism continues to challenge Canadian nationhood and citizenship. In the United Kingdom there are numerous challenges to the traditional notion of British nationhood and citizenship. For instance, the Scots and others continue to challenge the 'unity' of the kingdom, while reformers (e.g. Charter 88) challenge the unwritten constitution of the 'kingdom'. In addition, citizenship has in recent years become a remarkably fashionable concern in British political discourse and debate: 'part of the zeitgeist' in the words of one commentator (Jacques 1991). Virtually all positions on the political spectrum have either constructed 'Citizens' Charters' or in other ways declared their commitment to the idea, from the radical Left (e.g. Jacques 1988; Hall and Held 1989; Benn 1991) to the Labour Left (e.g. Pimlott 1988; Travis 1991; Young 1991), to the Centre (e.g. the all-party Parliamentary Commission on Citizenship, HMSO 1990; Marquand 1989; Dahrendorf 1990; and the Liberal Democrats) to the various types of Tory Right (e.g. Patten 1988; Hurd 1988; Travis and Hencke 1991). It is worth noting here that the American Neoconservative philosophy of social citizenship, which I disuss at length in part II of this book, has served as an important model for the evolution of interest in citizenship by the British Right in recent years, in both the Thatcherite and post-Thatcher periods.

Equally, citizenship is a strategically important concept *intellectually*, not least in sociology and social theory. It is important in principle because it provides a common field (1) for the sociological study of society to meet the study of social policy and politics and (2) for social theory to meet explicitly normative analysis in political theory and moral philosophy. However, in spite of this, in practice the sociology of citizenship has remained undeveloped, certainly when compared with the vast efforts which have been expended in modern sociology on the study of related phenomena such as the state and social class. There are various possible reasons for this neglect. The modern achievement and definition of the citizen's status has been strongly associated with the 'bourgeois' class. Thus, along with related concepts such as those of 'rights', citizenship has been seen as ideologically suspect by Marxist and Left social analysis.

Alternatively, the neglect may be due to the fact that, with obvious exceptions such as immigrants, citizenship is simply taken for granted by most people in modern society. It is 'obvious', it is one of our automatic assumptions about the social world in which we live, an unproblematic part of our common sense, requiring no further reflection. The nature and terms of our general social membership are not easily brought into view whether as aspects of other people's lives or indeed of our own.

Hence the continuing importance for sociology of perspectives and methodologies which seek to study the taken-for-granted social world and the tacit assumptions of membership, such as phenomenology and ethnomethodology (Roche 1973). Citizenship refers to membership in a politico-legal community. This form of membership, along with all other forms, is always prone to being taken for granted and hence overlooked not only by ordinary people but also by social scientists, social theorists and other such 'experts' in the understanding of social life.

However, after some decades of relative indifference to the phenomenon, citizenship has recently begun to attract academic attention. In the 1980s British social and political theorists in particular (e.g. Giddens 1985a; Turner 1986, 1990; King 1987; Barbalet 1988; Hall and Held 1989; Andrews 1991) have begun to renew the social analysis of citizenship in general and to reopen debates about it. Together with this, the theme of social citizenship has become an important one in studies of the welfare state and social policy (e.g. Glennerster 1983; Jordan 1987, 1989; Plant 1988a, 1988b; Alcock 1989; Taylor 1989; Lister 1990a, 1990b; Finlayson 1990).

My general interests in this book are continuous with this revival of sociological interest in the nature of citizenship in general in modern society. However, the particular aspect of citizenship I am mainly concerned with is what the founder of the sociology of citizenship, T. H. Marshall, called its 'social dimension' (1964). My aim, then, is to present an account of some of the main ideologies, policies and problems associated with 'social citizenship' in the context of contemporary social change (see also Roche 1984, 1987).

II

'Social citizenship' refers to those rights and duties of citizenship concerned with the welfare of people as citizens, taking 'welfare' in a broad sense to include such things as work, education, health and quality of life. In the mid-twentieth century in Western capitalist society conceptions of social citizenship tend to be intimately tied up with the development of, and lately the crisis of, the welfare state. In the late 1970s and 1980s these conceptions, and the welfare state systems to which they are tied, have been seriously challenged by two sets of social forces, those of *ideological change* and those of *social structural change*. My main theme in this book is that these conceptions of social citizenship need to be rethought in terms of each of these sorts of challenge.

There have been various *ideological and political challenges* emanating from the new social movements (e.g. internationalism, ecology, feminism etc.). But undoubtedly the greatest challenge has been posed by the rise to power of the New Right and Neoconservatism in Britain, the USA and elsewhere in the 1980s. In some of its variants the Right denies the existence of social rights, while in others it displaces social rights by emphasizing social duties. But in all of its variants it aims to see public expenditure on the welfare state cut and the role of the state in welfare de-emphasized. After a decade or more of the resurgent Right's influence we need to take stock of the concept of social citizenship to see what reality and relevance it has for the 1990s and beyond.

The 1970s and 1980s were also periods of great *structural change* in the economic, political and cultural foundations and frameworks of Western society. The changes are long-term and they are set to continue as we approach the twenty-first century. Of major importance among them are: the shift from industrialism to post-industrialism and from the national level to the global level in the contemporary capitalist economy; related developments in international political institutions; and the emergence of ecological problems of awesome and unprecedented scale and complexity. In different ways these and related developments have tended to undermine the social conditions on which the welfare state and social citizenship stand, not least in areas crucial to welfare such as those of income and employment distribution. As with the ideological influences, after a decade or more of these structural influences it is reasonable to try to take stock of the concept of social citizenship, to see what condition it is in and what the future direction of Western development holds in store for it.

In my discussion I will try to show how the implications of the *ideological challenges* for social citizenship are generally those of

(1) emphasizing social duties as against rights and (2) extending social duties into previously relatively uncolonized non-state/ 'civil society' spheres, particularly the family (see chapter 5), but also into society's ecosphere (ecology, see chapter 2) and into society's historicality (inter-generationality, heritage, etc., see chapter 9). As against this, the implications of the *structural changes* for social citizenship are generally those of (1) emphasizing social rights and (2) extending social rights into new post-national political formations, of which the European Community (EC) is the leading and historically most important example (see chapter 8).

Between these two sets of implications there is at least a significant difference of emphasis (which calls for ideological dialogue and harmonization) and at worst a contradiction and source of conflict (which calls for political management and reconciliation). Evidently the roots, nature and range of the relevant long-term problems facing social citizenship need to be reviewed, clarified and rethought. This book is an attempt to provide a preliminary survey of some of the relevant issues.

III

The structure of my discussion reflects these themes of ideological and structural change and the challenges they present to our conventional wisdom about social citizenship. There are three main parts to the discussion. Part I outlines what I take to be the conventional wisdom about social citizenship, together with the necessary ingredients of any debate about it, namely its ideological limitations and also its social structural limitations in the persistence and growth of poverty. Part II discusses one of the most important wings of the Right ideological challenge to social citizenship, namely that of American Neoconservatism. Part III outlines two of the major structural challenges namely 'post-industrial' socio-economic change and 'post-national' political-economic change.

These are all large issues to attempt to discuss in a book of this length. However, in my view it is necessary to attempt to get this sort of overview if we are to see the wood for the trees about the nature and fate of contemporary social citizenship. The selection decisions this has required in practice are obviously debatable in principle. Two such decisions are worth noting to help put my discussion in perspective. First, in order to illustrate welfare rights and duties I focus mainly on work, income and family policies. This is not intended to demean the relevance of other policy areas, such as housing, health and education, to the understanding of welfare and social citizenship. Education in particular is becoming a strategically important sphere for 'social citizenship' politics and policy-making in Western societies. It is here that many of the political responses to the ideological and structural challenges I discuss in this book are likely to take shape in the coming decades. However, I take these issues no further than some remarks in my conclusion (chapter 9).

Secondly, it is clearly the case that profound problems of international social justice and 'social citizenship' exist between rich and poor nations. Nonetheless, although my discussion is intended to have a comparative and international cast to it, it is focused on the advanced capitalist societies, the welfare states of Britain, the USA and Europe. It does not attempt to consider Third World countries and their problems of second-class citizenship in the contemporary global order.

Such international, educational and other dimensions of social citizenship are undoubtedly important in their own right. However, in my view it is not necessary to attempt a comprehensive coverage of them all in order to build up a reasonable and realistic picture of the nature and prospects of contemporary social citizenship. Rationales for the various national and policy illustrations chosen are given in the course of my discussion, and the main steps in that discussion are as follows.

Part I outlines what I refer to as the 'dominant paradigm' of postwar Western social citizenship. This paradigm, which stresses social rights and the need to construct major state policies and institutions of welfare, underpins both American liberal social policy and European social democracy. In chapter 1 I illustrate it with reference to British social policy, one of the paradigm's earliest and most developed versions. The British versions of (1) social citizenship and social rights (T. H. Marshall) and of (2) economic and social welfare policy (Beveridge, Titmuss and Keynes) are outlined. Chapters 2 and 3 explore some of the main ideological and practical limits of the dominant paradigm. In chapter 2 some of the main analytical and ideological limitations of the dominant paradigm are considered, and some of the many alternative versions and visions of social citizenship are briefly reviewed, in particular those of welfare pluralism, feminism and ecology. In chapter 3, one of the main practical limits of social citizenship, namely poverty and the growth of an 'underclass' in our contemporary affluent society, is considered. The American experience of this strategically important case is outlined in this chapter. The limit case of poverty and the underclass is a recurrent theme in Parts II and III. It is on this problem that contemporary ideological and analytical perspectives on social citizenship can be most clearly distinguished and compared. Different diagnoses and policy cures for contemporary poverty are discussed in most of the subsequent chapters (chapters 5–8).

Parts II and III discuss some of the main ways in which the dominant paradigm is being reformed, rethought and reinvented in the late twentieth century, on the one hand by Neoconservative politics and on the other by structural change. Part II reviews one of the most politically influential critiques of the dominant paradigm of social citizenship in recent years, that of American Neoconservatism. Chapter 4 outlines the American welfare state and the Neoconservative critique of it. Neoconservatism emphasizes citizens' social duties rather than social rights, and in chapter 4 it is distinguished from libertarian or New Right versions of Right politics and citizenship theory. Chapter 5 examines one of Neoconservatism's major schools of thought, namely that of 'familism'. This emphasizes citizens' family duties together with social policies necessary to support the family ethic. Finally, chapter 6 examines the other major school of thought in contemporary American Neoconservatism, namely that which emphasizes citizens' work duties together with the policy of 'workfare' allegedly necessary to enforce the work ethic. There is considerable tension and conflict between these two schools of thought and part II concludes in chapter 6 with a review of this problem and its implications for the coherence and credibility of the Neoconservative conception of social citizenship.

In Part III we consider the main challenges to the dominant

paradigm presented by two of the major forms of contemporary political-economic (or 'structural') social change, namely post-industrialism and post-nationalism. In chapter 7 the focus is the nature of the contemporary shift from industrial to post-industrial capitalism, together with what its effects are likely to be on employment and on the social right to work. We consider the problem of 'post-industrial poverty' and assess 'post-industrial' income policy proposals aimed both at tackling the problem and providing a new social right of citizenship. In chapter 8 we consider the development of post-national politics, economics and citizenship through the case of the EC and contemporary trends towards European economic (and possibly political) integration in the 1990s. New social rights of European citizenship are currently being developed in the EC Social Charter, and these are a focal concern in this chapter.

Finally, in chapter 9 some of the main issues of the preceding discussion and the agenda they set for future research and politics are reviewed. First, my discussion indicates various senses in which social citizenship, particularly the dominant paradigm's version of it, might be said to be a 'myth'. These are discussed in the first part of chapter 9, while the theme of the contemporary complexity and dynamics of social rights and duties is outlined in the second part of the chapter 9. Social change is driving the experience and ideal of social citizenship beyond both the nation state and the welfare state, that is beyond the two spheres which up until now have been the principal institutional arenas of the dominant paradigm of social citizenship. Contemporary social change invariably and irrevocably raises new questions about social rights and duties, on the one hand in personal, familial and local community spheres and, on the other, in transnational and inter-generational spheres. In my concluding discussion I suggest that these issues, particularly those concerned with social obligations, are unavoidable elements of any agenda for the social theory and politics of social citizenship in the 1990s and beyond.

PART I
The Dominant Paradigm and its Limits

1
Social Citizenship and the Dominant Paradigm: the British Case

I

Citizenship assumptions and paradigms

(1) Ordinary common-sense understandings of citizenship in postwar Western societies, together, it must be said, with much of the sociology of citizenship which claims to reflect upon them, have long tended to take for granted a loose set of common assumptions both about citizenship in general and also about social citizenship in particular. The conventional wisdom about citizenship in general includes such ideas as that membership in modern society takes the form of citizenship within a notionally 'liberal' and 'democratic' nation state, that the nation state is materially based on and organizes the system of industrial capitalism which operates in its territory and that citizenship consists in a system of civil, political and social rights guaranteed by the nation state.

Although the 'welfare state' and social citizenship can be argued to have their origins in the effectively pre-democratic context of Bismarck's Germany (e.g. Rimlinger 1971), none-theless the modern assumption is that their context is typically the liberal democratic state. The set of assumptions about social citizenship which I will refer to as the dominant paradigm strongly emphasizes the legitimacy of social rights and their need to be serviced by the state. These rights are typically taken to include a range of minimum conditions and services in education, health, housing, income, employment and consumption and so on. It is assumed that they are claimable against a state organized to service them, a 'welfare state' together with that part of the modern state's organization necessary for the management and development of the national economic base. I am mainly concerned with social citizenship and thus with the welfare state and social policy in this book. But since these matters cannot be understood in isolation it will be necessary to take some account of the wider context of citizenship in general and in my discussion.

This contextual sociological view is necessary given the scale of the changes and the problems which I argue can be seen to have overtaken established postwar assumptions about citizenship in general and social citizenship, particularly in the late twentieth century. The conventional wisdom about citizenship, together with the dominant paradigm of social citizenship which is part of it, is nationally and industrially based. My general line of argument is that on the one hand it is being undermined by disorganizing developments in contemporary capitalism involving 'post-national' and 'post-industrial' restructuring, while, on the other hand, the Centre Left political ideologies which did most to generate and legitimate the dominant paradigm in early postwar Western societies (e.g. British liberalism and Labourism 1940s–1970s; American 'liberalism' 1960s–1970s) are now in recession. New forms of political and cultural radicalism and conservatism implying new (or renewed) conceptions of citizens' and human rights and duties (concerned with gender and family relations, the natural and urban environment, ethnicity, age and so on) have emerged to challenge them.

I will discuss some important aspects of these structural and political changes and their impact on our understanding of citizenship through the rest of the book. But in this chapter I aim to set the scene for this discussion by outlining the dominant paradigm of social citizenship, together with some of the wider conventional wisdom which surrounds it, in a necessarily brief and schematic way.

(2) The conventional wisdom and the dominant paradigm of social citizenship have been expressed in different ways by

centrist and Left social analysts and commentators. And of course they have been institutionalized in a variety of ways, at different times and to differing degrees in different Western countries (e.g. Rimlinger 1971; Friedmann et al. 1987; Dixon and Scheurrell 1989). There are of course great differences between longstanding and thoroughgoing 'corporatist' versions of the welfare state (e.g. Sweden, see Mishra 1984) as compared with more recent and still residual (or 'incomplete') versions (e.g. USA, see Katz 1986). These differences reflect different national cultures, different forms and outcomes of Left-Right political debates and struggles, the influence of different religious traditions (e.g. Protestantism in the USA and UK, Catholicism in many European countries) and so on. My approach in this book is by no means intended to deny the importance of these historical and national cultural differences, and during the course of my discussion many of these main differences between British, American and European approaches to social citizenship and the welfare state will be evident. But the real and apparent diversity of social policy and welfare systems in Western nations in the postwar period should not blind us to the commonness of many of the aspirations and also of the institutional and distributional patterns actually achieved (e.g. Mishra 1984; Swann 1988; Esping-Andersen 1990; Pierson 1991, chs 1, 4).

The commonalities can be seen most clearly in historical and comparative perspective (e.g. with the pre-modern West, with Stalinist societies and with modern Third World societies). They are the substance of what I believe it is useful to see as a dominant paradigm of postwar Western social citizenship. This institutional and intellectual paradigm has been battered by New Right ideology and by forces of economic change in Western society since the mid-1970s. But while its previous pre-eminence and taken-for-granted legitimacy has been irrevocably undermined, nonetheless it has so far survived a succession of legitimacy and economic crises. In the 1990s it remains largely in place (albeit in an increasingly questioned, uncertain and somewhat less dominant place) in most Western nations.

An institutional and intellectual rethinking of the dominant paradigm of welfare (e.g. Jordan 1987) and of the welfare state (e.g. Mishra 1984) in the West has been going on now for over a decade. Often (as under the Thatcher and Reagan governments in Britain and the USA) it has taken an ostensibly 'radical' New Right approach allegedly aimed at 'rolling back the state' and substituting markets for the state in the field of welfare (e.g. Murray 1984; Loney et al. 1987). However, the relative failure of the New Right project to achieve longstanding reductions in states' welfare spending suggests that the dominant paradigm, although it is being undermined, has by no means been over- turned. Rather what is happening is that some of its previously buried or ignored assumptions about the societal context of the welfare state (e.g. markets, voluntary action, family welfare etc.) are now being brought out of the darkness and made into explicit objects of policy and political debate.

Long ago Gestalt psychologists revealed a process in human visual perception which is a relevant analogy for these political perceptions. In well-known examples of 'ambiguous figures' (such as the 'vase-two faces' or the 'duck-rabbit' etc.) we can see the perceptual fact of the difference between a 'figure' and its ground. But we can also see the perceptual/cognitive fact that the construction or choice of a figure (which is thus present as 'seen' and 'inspectable') is also simultaneously a choice or construction of its ground (which is thus eerily present in an 'unseen' or 'seen-but-uninspectable' form). By analogy, for nearly three decades in the dominant paradigm of social citizen- ship the role of the state in welfare has been like a perceptual 'figure'. This has made it difficult to see the 'ground' or societal welfare context which it presupposed and on which it was built but which it tended to obscure.

The radical New Right challenge to this has involved attempts to erase the figure and to create a totally new picture out of the ground, namely a picture of a state-free welfare market. But the project has failed. For instance, public spending on welfare continued to rise as a proportion both of all public spending and of GDP in the USA and the UK under Reagan and Thatcher throughout the 1980s (on the UK, see Brindle 1990c; on the USA, see ch. 4 below; generally, Pierson 1991, p. 173).

Unlike the New Right, contemporary challenges to the dominant paradigm do not naively counterpose one simplistic picture (namely market-based welfare) to another (namely state- based welfare). Rather they tend to see the picture of social welfare as being essentially complex. They recognize that much of this complexity was seen-but-uninspected in the dominant paradigm, and that it was thus effectively hidden. Thus contemporary alternative paradigms (chs 2 and 4–6 below) tend to address themselves to the illumination and development of what was hidden within the dominant paradigm. The picture addressed by the dominant paradigm, and in particular the welfare state part of it, may well be considerably redrawn by the force of post-industrial and post-national change (as I will suggest in chs 7 and 8). But it will not be erased by force of ideology–as the New Right discovered in the 1980s.

Rather, the main ideological challenges to the paradigm in the 1980s and 1990s, whether from the Neoconservative Right (chs 4, 5 and 6 below) or the libertarian Centre and Left (ch. 2 below), have sought to put the welfare state (together with its powerful professions, unions and bureaucratic processes) 'in its place' rather than to erase it. Putting the welfare state in its place involves addressing it as a limited and contextualized figure rather than as a de-contextualized figure, a figure without a ground. Thus contemporary theories and political struggles in social policy are involved, in diverse and competing ways, in constructing more complicated and pluralistic welfare figures to address. These figures include the welfare state together with various elements of its previously marginalized ground, selected according to political preference (e.g. local communities and voluntary action in the case of the Left, markets and family in the case of the Right). We will explore the various forms of 'welfare pluralism' taken by some of these ideological challenges later. But first, at this stage of the discussion I need to introduce and illustrate some of the main features of the paradigm.

One of the most politically and institutionally influential forms of the paradigm, particularly in the 1945–75 period was that of the British 'welfare state'. Policy-makers like Beveridge and Keynes gave institutional shape to the British version, while the academic study of social policy and of social citizenship was virtually founded by Richard Titmuss and T. H. Marshall reflecting on its achievements and limitations. So, although the British case undoubtedly has its idiosyncracies, it will nonetheless provide a useful starting-point for considering some general features of the dominant paradigm of social citizenship. In this chapter, then, I will look first at the concept of citizenship in T. H. Marshall's sociology (section II). I will then consider assumptions about citizenship's social context in the thinking of Beveridge and Titmuss (section III). Finally we can consider assumptions about citizenship's nature in the work of Beveridge, Titmuss and Marshall (section IV).

I should emphasize that the aim of this discussion is illustrative and not exegetic. Through a brief review of some of the views of these key writers we can hope to bring out something about the 'figure' of social citizenship and the welfare state in the British version of the dominant paradigm. We can also bring out something of the way that its overemphasis on state welfare overshadows and marginalizes the complex of non-state welfare systems, together with some of the weaknesses and ambiguities involved in this overemphasis.

II

The dominant paradigm: T. H. Marshall and the sociology of citizenship

(1)   Citizenship has been a central theme in Western social and political thought since its origins in ancient Greek theory. Plato's and Aristotle's classic accounts of democracy, tyranny and the nature of politics remain fundamental to our understanding of human beings as 'political animals'. So too does, for instance, Sophocles' classic dramatization of the moral limits of the state and of the gendered (i.e. patriarchal) character of political power in his tragedy *Antigone*. However, very little of the modern conception of representative government and democratic citizenship was to be found in the practice of ancient Greek slave-based 'direct democracies' such as Athens. Nor was it much to be found in the theory or practice of medieval feudalism and Christian religiosity.

Rather, the practical emergence of modern understandings of citizenship in the West was associated particularly with the advent of capitalism and of centralized nation states in the sixteenth to seventeenth centuries. Citizenship was finally given voice as a massively influential political concept in the seventeenth and eighteenth centuries by the world-historical events of the English, American and French Revolutions. The 'natural rights' and 'Rights of Man' announced by these revolutions, their concepts of 'liberty, equality and fraternity' and their attempts to found the modern nation state constitutionally on the will of the people helped to construct the modern Western conception of citizenship.

Much of the political history of the twentieth century has been a story of citizens' struggles, whether to defend their rights against tyrannical governments (e.g. the struggles against fascism and Stalinism), to extend rights (e.g. the women's movement in Britain and elsewhere) or to give substance to civil and social rights (e.g. the British Labour movement, the US Black movement). However, in spite of its importance in modern political practice it is ironic that, as some commentators note, citizenship has been 'deplaced' and is a notable absence in twentieth-century political theory (Vincent and Plant 1984).

(2)   Citizenship was not a strong theme in modern social theory until the British sociologist T. H. Marshall (1963) put it on the map in his classic discussion of 'Citizenship and Social Class' contained in some lectures given in 1949 and first published the following year. His relatively brief discussion provided one of the earliest, clearest and most suggestive accounts of the historical and social reasons for the emergence of the postwar 'welfare state' and of the moral and political justifications for it.

What little sociology of citizenship there is derives to a considerable extent from Marshall's thinking on the subject. Although the bulk of Marshall's work in these lectures and elsewhere were largely focused on the British experience his terms of reference were implicitly general and capable of wide-ranging application in the sociology of Western societies. For instance, leading figures in American sociology in the 1960s and 1970s used and developed Marshall's analysis in studies of nationalism and nation-building (Bendix 1964) and of the process of Western modernization (Parsons 1970). Notable studies of the social history of welfare states (Rimlinger 1971) and of postwar German society and politics (Dahrendorf 1968) in this period also drew on Marshall's analysis. Marshall's centrist/

social democratic approach to British social policy and social citizenship along with the idealistic collectivist approach of Titmuss (1963, 1970), helped to define the study of social policy in the 1960s and 1970s (Parker 1975; Room 1979; Pinker 1981; Halsey 1986; Mishra 1984; Rees in Marshall 1985).

Given all this, it is understandable why much of the recent upsurge of interest in the sociology of citizenship has tended to take the form of an updating of and a critical dialogue with Marshall's analysis (e.g. Giddens 1985a; Mann 1987; Turner 1986, 1990; Roche 1987; Barbalet 1988; Pierson 1991, ch. 6). However a discussion of Marshall's sociological commentators, updaters and critics lies outside my terms of reference in this book. This is not least because very little of the contemporary commentary is of direct relevance for understanding the particular political ideologies, structural changes and social policy debates with which I am most concerned. However, Marshall's analysis is relevant and needs to be explored a little further.

For Marshall our understanding of what citizenship is has changed and developed over time. In his 1949 lectures he based himself on the British historical experience of it, but he also attempted to speak in general terms and thus implicitly for all modern Western societies and states. He argued that the modern concept of citizenship consists of a combination of three elements – civil, political and social. These elements can be observed to have emerged roughly in a sequence of steps from simple to complex over the course of history. Thus the simple form of exclusively civil citizenship came earliest, then the more complex forms of civil and political, and, finally, in the era of the welfare state, social citizenship emerges to more or less complete both the picture and the development. Marshall's analysis of the three elements of citizenship was, he notes, 'dictated by [British] history even more clearly than by logic' (1949, quoted from 1963, p. 73). He suggests that 'it is possible . . . to assign the formative period in the life of each to a different century – civil rights to the eighteenth, political to the nineteenth and social to the twentieth' (ibid. p. 76). On this basis he then observes that each element of citizenship consists of a set of rights together with a set of institutions in respect of which those rights are exercised or which exist to serve those rights.

The civil element is composed of the rights necessary for individual freedom – liberty of the person, freedom of speech,
thought and faith, the right to own property and to conclude
valid contracts, and the right to justice. The last is of a different
order from the others because it is the right to defend and assert
all one's rights on terms of equality with others and by due
process of law. This shows us that the institutions most directly
associated with civil rights are the courts of justice. By *the
political element* I mean the right to participate in the exercise of
political power, as a member of a body invested with political
authority or as an elector of the members of such a body. The
corresponding institutions are Parliament and councils of local
government. By *the social element* I mean the whole range from
the right to a modicum of economic welfare and security to the
right to share to the full in the social heritage and to live the life
of a civilised being according to the standards prevailing in the
society. The institutions most closely connected with it are the
education system and the social services. (ibid., p. 74; my italics,
MR)

For Marshall, citizenship in general involves an equality of
membership status and of ability to participate in a society, and
it refers to what the society collectively acknowledges as
legitimate and enforceable citizens' rights in respect of the
various elements of the concept. Marshall drew this picture in
the course of a discussion of the social inequalities, particularly
those of class, generated during the course of the development
of, and by the contemporary operation of, the modern capitalist
economy. Against this background of capitalism's tendencies to
general social inequalities and class divisions Marshall saw the
evolution of citizenship as representing something of a 'war'
between two opposed principles. With the establishment of the
welfare state he saw this war as slowly being won by citizenship
and by its egalitarian and integrative effects and implications.

This optimistic picture carried two main provisos. The first
was that new forms of inequality, such as the 'rise of the
meritocracy', which Marshall's contemporary Michael Young
(1962) observed in postwar Britain, were likely to emerge
because of, and to be legitimated by, a welfare and educational
state which succeeded in offering equality of opportunity to all
of its citizens. Equal citizenship does not involve equality of

condition for Marshall as it did for Titmuss and other Left social analysts.

The second proviso was that social rights and the welfare state must be 'paid for' literally by tax revenues from a prosperous and effectively functioning and growing economy. Thus it must be 'paid for' morally and politically by duties of 'industrial citizenship' incumbent on workers and on trade unions, for instance duties not to disrupt production by official or unofficial strikes and absenteeism. Citizenship rights, particularly social rights, are to be reciprocated and paid for by the citizens' duty to work (Roche 1987). Nonetheless, given this proviso, Marshall's picture of citizenship is a picture almost exclusively of the development of *rights rather than duties*. For instance, in one of his last writings comparing pre-modern tradition-based society with modern citizenship-based society he observes that 'the old morality stressed obligations more than rights; in the new it is the opposite. It is in the nature of the polity and of the economy to foster this change' (1981, p. 175).

This is not the place to explore Marshall's sociology of citizenship in any sort of detail (see Roche 1984, 1987; Barbalet 1988). Although it is well summed up in his 'Citizenship and Social Class' lectures he concerned himself with the theme of the citizens' 'right to welfare' throughout his work and discussed it explicitly on a number of occasions (e.g. 1981). In his later work on the theme, he touched on a variety of issues with which I will be concerned in this book. These include the problem of citizens' family and work obligations (ch. 2 and part II below; Marshall 1981 chs 3–5); the potential for depoliticization in 'welfare station' (ch. 1 section IV below; Marshall 1981, ch. 8); the need to develop citizens' income policies (ch. 7 below; Marshall 1981, p. 102); and the possible development of social citizenship rights in the EC (ch. 8 below; Marshall 1981, p. 106). So during the course of my discussion I will periodically refer to Marshall's various views on such topics as these. However the main ideas in his 'Citizenship and Social Class' remain the most relevant for the themes I wish to develop in this book. We can now summarize them together with their implications for the structure and logic of my discussion.

(3)   On the basis of what we have seen of Marshall's discussion we can derive the following principles for any prospective

sociology of citizenship. Sociological conceptions of citizenship need to provide an understanding of (or at least to contain explicit basic assumptions about) at least three sets of issues (Roche 1987, 1990b). Thus they must supply (or imply) answers to the following three sets of questions. First, what is *the nature of the citizen* and of what we might call the citizen 'world' or community? In other words what is the nature of the subjectivity and sociality involved in citizenship; what social skills, resources and powers are needed for its exercise; what are the main norms and values of life in the citizen community, and most importantly, what rights and duties regulate inter-citizen and citizen–state relations? Secondly, what is *the social structural context* of citizenship and the citizen community? That is what cultural economic and state systems underpin them and influence (both in enabling and disabling ways) their capacity to develop? Finally, *the problem of change*. How has citizenship and its community and its context come to be what it is, how is it currently changing and what are its likely future lines of development?

These three sets of issues and questions help to distinguish between modern versions of citizenship. In particular they will help us to distinguish later (in chs 2, 4–6 below) between the dominant paradigm and some of its main contemporary challengers. As we have seen, Marshall's 'Citizenship and Social Class' discussion caught the spirit of Britain's postwar welfare statism. It expresses this version of the conventional wisdom about citizenship in general together with the dominant paradigm of social citizenship clearly and well. In terms of the three dimensions, Marshall's and the dominant paradigm's picture and assumptions can be summarized under the following headings.

i   The citizen world   In his lecture Marshall proposes that citizenship consists of three types of rights, i.e. civil, political and social. He implies that the *citizen 'world' or community* is a sphere in which rights-claiming citizens have their claims serviced by the state-based institutions of the law, parliamentary democracy and the welfare state. Social rights are distinct from but nonetheless continuous with and complementary to civil and political rights. They enable people to participate in a civilized society and in some sense they 'complete' the achievement of civil and political rights.

ii   Citizenship's structural context   In Marshall's view social rights are necessary to counter the class-based inequalities deriving from the main *context of citizenship*, namely the industrial capitalist economy. Nonetheless, merit-based inequalities are essentially ineradicable from a free society in which the state can only seek to ensure equality of opportunity rather than equality of outcome. Marshall held that there is an inevitable tension between the principles and institutions of welfare and social citizenship on the one hand and those of capitalism on the other. He formulated this tension in various ways in different studies (e.g. 'welfare-capitalism' in 1963; 'the hyphenated society' in 1981). Nonetheless, the image he conveys throughout is that of the manageability of this tension and, overall, of the reciprocity and functionality of the major sectors of the modern social system, particularly the state and capitalism. I will refer to this sort of dominant paradigm assumption about social citizenship as the assumption of 'national functionalism' and we will return to problems in Marshall's version of it later in this chapter (section III).

iii   Citizenship's historicality   Overall, Marshall's (and the dominant paradigm's) conception of the history of citizenship in general is that of a fairly continuous long-term growth, formation and coalescence between processes of nation-state democratization on the one hand and the development of industrial capitalism on the other. At the same time, its conception of the history of social citizenship is that of the long-term growth of a conflictual but contained and ultimately functional relationship between the welfare state and industrial capitalism. In Marshall's view the growth of the welfare state tends to 'civilize' capitalism (e.g. 1963, p. 284; see also Turner 1986).

These, then, are the three main characteristics of the dominant paradigm with which I am concerned in this book: (1) the rights and statist emphases; (2) the 'national functionalist' assumption of the differentiation but integration of social rights and the welfare state within the context of the wider modern political economic system, and (3) the conception of citizenship's history in terms of a more or less unilinear and continuous social progress. These characteristics show up equally clearly in the studies of other significant figures working in the early postwar period. In the following sections we can look a little further at the dominant paradigm's assumptions about social citizenship's *nature* and its structural *context*, taking the latter first.

III

Citizenship's social context: Beveridge and Titmuss

The dominant paradigm's key assumptions about *context*, as we have seen so far are those of 'national functionalism' and the propriety and indeed necessity of what we can refer to as 'state-dominated welfare provision'. In this section we will illustrate these assumptions from the work of William Beveridge and Richard Titmuss, respectively a founder and a leading con-structive critic of the British welfare state. However, before considering these illustrations it is necessary to make two general points about the context of welfare and social citizenship.

(1) First, the welfare role of the state can be narrowly or broadly defined. In reality a broad range of modern state func-tions objectively bear on citizens' welfare, above and beyond those officially and narrowly designated as 'welfare' and 'health' services and policy fields. These include, for instance, edu-cation, housing, transport, environment, leisure, food, consumer policies and, perhaps above all, economic and employment policy. Indeed the interconnected problems of the recognition and management of complexity are perennial themes in the analysis of both national social policy and also of the personal social services (e.g. Townsend 1975). Welfare ministers and social work managers, at national and local state levels respect-ively, are routinely confronted with the problems of co-ordinating different departmental bureaucracies and professions involved in the welfare field. And in a complex and changing society they will increasingly be faced with such problems (e.g. Algie 1975; Walton 1982).

Secondly, in addition to the state, a range of modern society's non-state sub-systems and sectors generate 'welfare' goods and services. These sub-systems and sectors include (1) voluntary organizations, (2) the family and also (3) capitalism. 'Capitalism' refers among other things to the existence of *labour markets* which generate and distribute incomes available for consumption, and also *consumer markets*, which call up the production and distribution of goods and services. With due acknowledgement of alternative conceptions and usages (e.g. classically Hegel 1967 and Marx 1970; recently Laclau and Mouffe 1985), I will use the term 'civil society' to refer to the collection of these sometimes ill-assorted and conflictual but nonetheless vitally important sectors. We must discuss *the family sector* (ch. 5) and *the labour market sector* (chs 6–8) in more detail later. But for the moment we can sum up the situation as follows. In modern Western societies in the mid- and late twentieth century the typical societal context and arena for social citizenship consists of (1) a *state welfare complex* together with (2) a *'civil society' welfare complex*. This is relevant to understanding the nature of the dominant paradigm.

Most political positions within the dominant paradigm (from Left to Centre Right, i.e. the 'postwar consensus') concur in giving a major and a leading role in welfare provision to the welfare state (whether narrowly or broadly defined). In addition, most also claim to recognize the existence and influence (whether evaluated negatively or positively) of civil society's welfare systems. Overall, however, they tend to evaluate most of its elements negatively. This ambivalence is particularly true of the attitude to capitalism of Left positions within the dominant paradigm.

Such Left positions are typically social democratic or social liberal. As such they are as antagonistic to totalitarian socialism and the command economy as they claim to be to *laissez-faire* pro-capitalist political economy. Their conception of economics and economic policy tends to have been heavily influenced by Keynes (e.g. Lekachman 1969; ch. 2 below). So, either explicitly or tacitly, they support the existence of labour and consumer markets, albeit markets which are regulated and which may also be 'fixed' in accordance with principles of social justice by the state. Whatever their occasional appearances and claims to the contrary, most positions within the dominant paradigm from Right to Left in fact accept one or other version of 'liberal democracy' and of a 'mixed economy'. This in turn implies that they all *effectively* support the 'mixed economy of welfare' or 'welfare pluralism' outlined above. With these points in mind we can now turn to consider Beveridge and Titmuss as exemplars of the dominant paradigm.

(2)   One of the foundation stones for the postwar welfare state was laid in Beveridge's *Report on Social Insurance* published in the depths of the Second World War in 1942. The Report proposed the construction of what was effectively, although not explicitly or in principle, a new system of social rights – citizenship rights to unemployment, disability and retirement income and to health services. With few modifications this was implemented in the late 1940s along with the other main pillars of the postwar settlement, a national secondary education system and a national health service.

Beveridge was a Liberal who believed strongly in a 'free society' and a market economy (Harris 1977). So, while the education and health systems were financed mainly from general taxation and were universally accessible to all, Beveridge's social insurance system was, notionally at least, intended to be financed by compulsory contributions from workers and employers and available only to contributors (1942, p. 11, para. 20; p. 12, para. 24). Its claim to being a (relatively) universal system, then, depended upon the sustained achievement of (relatively) full employment in the labour market (1942, p. 12, para. 22; 1960, p. 117). In addition, the state-organized national insurance system was intended to provide a standard minimum income to all citizen-contributors. The minimum income was assumed to be a base on which individuals could build their own private insurance and pensions arrangements (for instance through the insurance market or through non-profit-making savings and mutual aid associations). And it was assumed to be capable of acting as an incentive rather than as a disincentive to this kind of self-provisioning (1942, p. 8, para. 6). As against this, however, it is worth noting that in the 1940s the leading Fabians Beatrice and Sidney Webb were sceptical about Beveridge's assumption of no negative effects on self-provisioning and work incentives and about the imbalance between rights and duties in his proposals:

> the fact that sick and unemployed persons were entitled to money incomes without any corresponding obligation to get well and keep well, or to seek and keep employment, seemed to us likely to encourage malingering and a disinclination to work for their livelihood. (Webb 1948, p. 479, quoted Moynihan 1989, p. 18)

We will return to this important and perennially controversial issue of the possible work-disincentive effects of the welfare state in more detail later (part II, ch. 6 in particular).

Beveridge's recognition of the relevance and role of (some) non-state welfare systems is not always understood, or if understood not always deemed worth recalling, by more Left-collectivist positions within the dominant paradigms. This is possibly because of the high public profile achieved by the 1942 Report which proposed a new state-organized system. Beveridge's two other subsequent major reports, on *Full Employment in a Free Society* (published in 1944, see Bibliography Beveridge 1960) and *Voluntary Action* (1948), which completed his picture of the organization of welfare in modern Britain, were less noticed, but they contained much more about the 'civil society' side of welfare. When taken together with the 1942 Report they give a more rounded, if at times idealistic and unrealistic, picture of Beveridge's overall conception. He clearly believed in the potential for a positive and functional system of relationships to exist between the state and civil society, in their respective welfare dimensions. They provide his version of 'welfare-pluralism' or the 'social division of welfare'.

The Full Employment Report was timely in that it was produced before the beginning of (1) the 'long postwar boom' and the growth of the 'affluent society' (or at least of mass consumerism), and of (2) the intellectual ascendancy of Keynes' approach to macro-economic analysis and national economic policy which it helped to popularize among policy-makers. Following Keynes, Beveridge believed in the power of the modern state and state expenditure (1960, p. 15) to so manage aggregate demand as to be able to avoid, or at least moderate, the economic cycle and stabilize the economy at or near full employment. In addition, he proposed policies to promote the effective functioning of the labour market and to counter regional inequalities (1960, pp. 124–5). All of this constituted an approach to social policy and to the welfare state which involved using state power to enable one of the major non-state sectors, namely the capitalist economy, to generate and distribute welfare through its labour and consumer markets. Of course capitalism would inevitably distribute welfare unequally and without reference to need or to the production of social costs and diswelfares. But it seems to have been assumed that the state could then, as a *secondary* matter, exercise some influence and control over these effects.

This relatively realistic conception in the 1944 Report of the state as enabler, regulator and moderator of non-state welfare amplified the assumptions noted earlier about private insurance and self-provision in the 1942 Report. However, this theme was developed much further, albeit in a more rhetorical and idealistic way, in the 1948 Report where Beveridge lauded the virtues and institutions of voluntary action, mutual aid and philanthropy. But the combined effects of state-organized and market-based insurance were already, by the late 1940s, fundamentally and fatally undermining the previously important role of voluntary action in the provision of welfare, a trend Beveridge seemed unable or unwilling to acknowledge (Williams and Williams 1987).

(3)   Beveridge's approach to social policy illustrates the dominant paradigm conception of the structural context and welfare arena of social citizenship. He provides a picture of a state-dominated and co-ordinated 'division of welfare' between state and non-state sources and forms of welfare provision expressed in the terms of a political and moral 'social liberal'. On the more collectivist Left wing of the dominant paradigm a comparable picture can be seen. Richard Titmuss' classic accounts of, for instance, the 'social division of welfare' (1963) and the division of labour between the state and voluntary action in blood policy (1970) are comparable to Beveridge's approach in their general thrust and in many of their general assumptions.

Like Beveridge, Titmuss clearly presents a picture of welfare dominated and led by state-organized provision. But equally it is a picture that acknowledges that non-state welfare sectors exist, that among them the voluntary sector is particularly valuable and that the existence of state welfare should be seen as enabling rather than disabling this sector (see also Wolfenden 1978). However, Beveridge and Titmuss differ about other aspects of these relationships. First, as we noted earlier, Beveridge (un-realistically as it turned out) saw no particular problem in the relation between the voluntary sector (e.g. mutual aid) and the market (e.g. private insurance). Secondly, he believed that the state sector could enable the non-state sectors providing it limited itself and did not attempt to take them over completely (e.g. state-organized social insurance policy in relation to private insurance, or state employment policy in relation to capitalist labour markets).

These two beliefs imply a positive view of the potential welfare role of capitalist markets. However, Titmuss was pro-foundly antagonistic to this sort of view and its toleration of the profit motive in the welfare sphere (Reisman 1977). As against the first belief he argued that private markets in health services undermine citizens' interests in being altruistic and philanthropic to each other. Using the example of the problem of ensuring supplies of blood for medical services he demonstrated the relative inferiority of the American blood-selling system within its context of the market-based health care system as compared with the British blood-donation system within its context of a nationalized tax-funded health care system (Titmuss 1970).

As against the second of Beveridge's beliefs, Titmuss (1963) argued that the toleration of private health and retirement insurance outside the state system created unjustifiable in-equalities in welfare. In particular the state should not use its fiscal policy to encourage private occupational health and pensions schemes through the provision of tax concessions to companies and individuals. The state's use of its fiscal policy more generally needed to be brought into line with the egalitarian ethos and thrust of its health and welfare institutions and policies.

Thus various tax concessions to the middle classes, to home owners and so on needed to be curbed. These sorts of lines of criticism effectively inaugurated by Titmuss have been de-veloped subsequently by a generation of British social policy critics and neo-Marxist political economists. The former have amplified the different ways and sectors in which the modern state tolerates and even encourages market-based and class-based inequalities in welfare (e.g. Townsend 1975, 1979; Field 1989; Le Grand 1982). The latter have argued that nonetheless such inequalities and the state's role in them are functional for the reproduction of national capitalism (Gough, 1979; Doyal and Pennell 1983).

In terms of the analysis I am proposing here these undoubted political differences between Beveridge's 'social liberal' perspective and Titmuss' and others' Left collectivist perspectives on the structural context of social citizenship conceal a large measure of commonality. All wings within the dominant paradigm tacitly and often explicitly acknowledge the existence of state–civil society welfare pluralism and the need to preserve *some* version of that pluralism. They also acknowledge the need for the state to take *some* kind of a leading role in the direct provision of welfare and also in the regulation of the non-state sectors' provision of welfare. These common assumptions about the *context* of social citizenship can be examined a little further later. We now need to consider the dominant paradigm's conception of the *nature of the citizen* and of citizen relations.

IV

Citizenship's nature: dominant paradigm problems

The main assumptions about the nature of social citizenship which need some discussion here are concerned with the following: (1) the balance between social rights and duties, (2) the categorization of different and unequal types of social citizen and (3) the relation between social citizenship and the other dimensions of citizenship. I will suggest that each of these assumptions is inherently problematic. It is likely that the working out of their weaknesses in practice in the postwar period has helped to set the stage for the development of the various ideological challenges to the dominant paradigm which have emerged since the mid-1970s. We will discuss these challenges more directly in chapter 2, but first, how does the dominant paradigm conceive of the moral character of social citizenship and of its community?

1   *The rights–duties balance and the problem of demoralization*

The dominant paradigm clearly places great emphasis on social rights. But, as we have seen earlier in Marshall's case, it would be wrong to portray it as having no conception of the role of duties, obligations and responsibilities in social citizenship and the welfare state. However, the various versions of duty that it undoubtedly has are typically either unspoken, relatively muted or underemphasized in relation to its emphasis on the new social *rights of individuals* in the postwar welfare state. Of course, since these rights mainly take the form of legitimate claims against the state, they necessarily imply *state duties* to service them. In this context Marshall notes: 'Every right to receive involves an obligation to give' (1981, p. 92). The dominant paradigm necessarily contains many such acknowledgements and assumptions about state duties to tackle as Beveridge put it, the Five Giants of Want, Ignorance, Squalor, Disease and Idleness. But this is only the logical and practical corollary of the creation of the new range of citizen's rights to the tackling of these social problems within the postwar welfare state.

This generally *rights-dominated conception* of social citizenship can be qualified by reference to such things as the 'compulsory contribution' principle built in to Beveridge's Social Insurance Plan. Or it can be qualified by the various work-related duties envisaged by Beveridge (1960), T. H. Marshall (1963) and others concerning individual and trade union responsibilities to work, to maintain collective work discipline and to use the right to strike responsibly and sparingly. Or, again, it can be qualified by the moral idealism of Beveridge's hopes for voluntary action and mutual aid to provide social insurance additional to the national system, and of Titmuss' belief that rights to NHS services cultivated citizen's fellowship and altruism. Or, finally, the whole creation of the British welfare state can be seen as a recognition of the sacrifices of the citizens in the Second World War, that is as a set of rights provided as a recognition of citizens' performance of the ultimate call to duty that a state can make on them.

But none of these qualifications undermines the substance of my claim about the general conception of social citizenship provided within the postwar welfare state. For historically and politically entirely explicable reasons this conception has been heavily angled towards rights. Thus it has tended to institutionalize a conception of *the social citizen as mainly a rights-claimer*. This is clear enough for instance in Marshall's seminal formulation of citizenship and in much subsequent debate and discussion in social policy and in the sociology of citizenship.

But having said this, however explicable it maybe, this relative one-sidedness in the conception of citizenship available within the welfare state inevitably carries costs and risks. This is particularly so when it is sustained and transmitted for a generation or two beyond the world of the founding generation. The founding generation could reasonably be said to have seen itself as owed repayment for its performance of national duties of suffering and sacrifices during the Great Depression and the Second World War. But subsequent generations have not performed such duties and cannot be said to be owed such debts.

Thus one of the clear risks with the institutionalization of a rights-dominated welfare state (*pace* Titmuss and Left collectivism) is the possible erosion of a sense of the *moral* character of participation in the welfare state by subsequent generations. Without pursuing the issue into its philosophical nooks and crannies it is sufficient here to make an observation based on common-sense moral understandings. The possibility of moral action is commonly (and philosophically) assumed to derive from the ontological given of human freedom: that is moral action involves choice and thus implies an independent agency capable of choosing. It also implies notions of (1) interactional reciprocity between people involved in moral action, and of (2) the logical and practical connection between rights and duties in moral experience (e.g. Plant et al. 1980; Weale 1983; Walzer 1985; Roche 1987; Anderson 1987; Mulgan in Andrews 1991). The welfare state can be argued to have appeared to promote a rights-based and relatively duty-free and unreciprocal conception of citizenship. If this is so, then it can also be argued that it has risked presiding over a diminution of the freedom and moral autonomy of those dependent on it (promoting 'welfare dependency' etc.).

We can refer to this risk as being that of the development of 'de-moralization' or, in sociological terms, the emergence of 'anomie' (Durkheim 1964; Merton 1968; Habermas 1987; Roche 1992a) among citizens and the citizen community. It is a risk which the welfare state and the dominant paradigm has unavoidably courted in terms both of its principles and its practice from their very inception in the early postwar period. This immanent weakness and the vulnerability to the charge of 'de-moralization' have been exploited by the main Right-wing ideological challenges to the welfare state and the dominant paradigm in recent years, those of the New Right and of Neo-conservatism. We will need consider this charge again at greater length (see part II).

2   Types of social citizenship: women and the problem of second-class citizenship

A second problem with the dominant paradigm's basic conception of social citizenship is that it tends to involve, whether explicitly or implicitly, a categorization of distinct types of citizen. These categories and types have tended to be ranked and prioritized for various purposes within social policy and the welfare state. To this extent the dominant paradigm has always risked producing 'second-class citizens' and legitimating inherent inequalities in citizenship.

This kind of charge can be made about a number of social categorizations prevailing within the dominant paradigm, such as those of occupation/class, age, disability and ethnicity. But it is perhaps clearest in the case of gender and of the paradigm's essentially patriarchal approach to women. This has been one of the inspirations of and targets for the development since the 1970s of a critical feminist analysis of social policy and the welfare state. We will look a little further at this critique in the next chapter. But for the moment it is worth illustrating some of the main patriarchal assumptions present in the dominant paradigm's discourse by reference to the social policy analysts we have been considering so far.

Earlier, the objective importance of the family as part of modern society's non-state provision of welfare services was emphasized. 'Family' along with 'community' in the context of discussions of welfare and care services are largely euphemisms for women and their work as child carers and as carers for sick and elderly relatives. We have also considered some of Beveridge's, Marshall's and Titmuss' most significant pronouncements on the welfare state and non-state sectors such as markets and voluntary action. One of the most notable features of their accounts is the degree to which they pass over and appear to take for granted what is probably the biggest and most pervasive welfare sector of any kind, state or non-state, namely the caring role of women and the institution of the family. The 'founding fathers' of the welfare state were men of their time. As such – in spite of massive wartime evidence to the contrary – they tended to see women as primarily housewives and mothers rather than workers.

When Titmuss (1963) outlined his picture of the 'social division of welfare' he restricted himself to 'collectively provided' welfare and included the differing systems of state welfare services, fiscal welfare and occupational welfare in that collective provision. This allowed him to pass over the family, presumably as a private, non-collective system. But this left a remarkably big hole in an account which otherwise appeared to strive for some historical and sociological generality and perspective. Similarly, when Marshall (1972, 1981) outlined the broad complex of social systems forming the modern context of welfare he included the trio of welfare state, democracy and capitalism in what he referred to as the 'hyphenated society', Although he was sensitive to the importance of the family as 'the original and basic' (1981, p. 69) welfare service, nonetheless in this important formulation of his view of welfare's context he makes no reference to it and takes it for granted.

Finally, Beveridge in his three major reports was somewhat more forthcoming about women and the family. In the 1942 Social Insurance Plan women as housewives were to be treated differently and less favourably than men as employees because, unlike men, they were not contributors to National Insurance. They were to get new rights to grants and benefits for marriage, maternity, separation and widowhood, and also rights to pensions and new allowances for children. But all of this (except for child allowances) was provided on the basis of their husband's National Insurance contributions – and on the assumption that husbands provided women's homes from their earnings in the labour market (1942, p. 15, para. 30; pp. 48–53, paras 107–17). This assumption of the sexual division of labour (and of the implied sexual division of welfare rights and duties) between men as 'breadwinners' and women as 'mothers' and 'home-makers' was clearly present also in the 1944 Full Employment Report. Here full employment was defined as a situation in which there were 'more vacant jobs than unemployed *men*' (1960, p. 19, my italics), while in the 1948 Voluntary Action Report Beveridge chose to exclude 'women's work' and the family from consideration by defining voluntary action as welfare 'action outside each citizen's home' (1948, p. 8). Women are said to have been 'helped to make good their claim to citizenship' through the Cooperative 'Guild' Movement (ibid., p. 112). We also learn that 'shopping is women's sphere' (ibid., p. 111) and that in this capacity 'housewives are now to a greater extent an auxiliary labour force for the distribution of consumer goods' (Seers, quoted Beveridge ibid., p. 222).

The stratification of social citizenship in gender terms implied in these sorts of views is an evident feature and an equally evident weakness of the dominant paradigm which we will need to consider further (ch. 2).

3   The distinctiveness of social citizenship: the problem of de-politicization

Finally there is the problem of the relation, in the dominant paradigm, between social citizenship and the other dimensions of citizenship, the civil and the political. The paradigm tends to see the welfare state as simply a progressive stage, even the ultimate stage, in the evolution of citizenship, and to see its associated social rights as distinct from but continuous with and complementary to civil and political rights. But, as New Right, libertarian and other commentators have long pointed out, the development of social rights creates the possibility of conflict. The provision of welfare rights requires funding by increased taxation and financial transfers to welfare recipients from the state's tax-take. Long-term inflation has undermined Beveridge's hopes for basing social insurance on the contributory principle. In an inflationary environment current social insurance claims cannot be financed by the fund accumulated through past contributions. They are instead funded by transfers from current taxation, and thus from current tax-payers' income to current claimants. Such redistribution of income and property may not actually be very effective or egalitarian in practice (as Titmuss and others, e.g. Le Grand 1982, have shown). But nonetheless the basis for conflict in principle and in practice between civil property rights and welfare rights, between different dimensions of citizenship, is clearly present in modern societies with developed welfare states.

In addition there is a deeper problem than this mainly economic conflict. The development of social rights and welfare states arguably risks a relative *de-politicization* of citizenship. The status of citizen is essentially a legal and political status of membership in a civil and political community which both makes and also abides by its own laws. It thus implies political rights and duties. In the light of this the idea of social citizenship, both as such but also particularly in the discourse of the dominant paradigm, is not at all clear and well grounded, whether in practice or in principle. In practice we know that welfare states typically service their 'clients'' welfare rights by using professional expertise and bureaucratic organization. Welfare state professionals and bureaucrats can exercise considerable power and authority over their clients, power which is often discretionary and unaccountable to the latter (e.g. Johnson 1972; Illich 1976). In these sorts of ways citizens' civil and democratic political status and rights can be avoided or infringed within the state's operationalization of social rights.

In principle this is comprehensible in the light of two points. First, there is the point made earlier about the de-moralizing and dependency risks of an overemphasis on rights. These risks carry implications for the de-politicization issue. De-moralized individuals are unlikely to be able to see themselves as being credible bearers of the civil and political powers, the identity and status, of full citizenship. Secondly, the founding formulations of the dominant discourse risked de-politicizing it by tying it too closely to the idea of 'the welfare state' – a distinctive version of the state resting on an assumed cultural consensus and committed to 'national functionalist'/corporatist integrative ideals. This is evident in the work of each of the major figures we have discussed in this chapter, not least that of T. H. Marshall.

It was Marshall, after all, who initially (1949) provided the basic formulation of social citizenship not only in rights-dominated terms but also as a historically, institutionally (and we should add logically and morally) *distinct* form of citizenship, different in kind from civil and political citizenship. The problematic implications of this segregation, together with its persistence as an assumption within the dominant paradigm, are indicated more clearly in Marshall's reflections a generation later on the 'value-problems of welfare-capitalism' (1972, in his 1981). Here he proposes that 'welfare' (he has the welfare state almost exclusively in mind) is distinguished from and potentially in conflict with both democracy and capitalism, although it exists together with them in a more or less functioning 'hyphenated' system. Unlike them 'welfare' requires and seeks to mobilize altruism and value-consensus, while its necessary reliance on the discretionary power of bureaucrats and professionals lends it distinctive authoritarian and educational dimensions.

It is significant that in this analysis Marshall restricts his use of the notion of citizenship to the characterization of democracy and fails to use it in the characterization of welfare and the welfare state. Thus he observes that 'democracy stands for equality of citizenship rights' (1981, p. 118). Welfare, however, is now something distinct from citizenship. It has the characteristics noted earlier and, in addition, whether successful or unsuccessful, it tends to legitimate various forms of (respectively justifiable or unjustifiable) inequality. He observes that 'no way has been found of equating a man's [*sic*] value in the market (capitalist value), his value as a citizen (democratic value) and his value for himself (welfare value)' (ibid., p. 119). Or again, 'welfare stresses the right to receive; democracy the duty to participate' (ibid., p. 126).

In these brief characteristics and in his analysis in general Marshall tends to disconnect welfare (the welfare state, welfare rights and values) from democracy and citizenship. It is interesting that in a 1965 lecture in India Marshall seemed to recognize the problematic character of this kind of disconnection, but only in the context of non-Western or Third World economic development. In his view, such development might be promoted by means of state planning, including the attempted creation of a welfare state and thus of social citizenship. But if this happened prior to the development of civil and political citizenship then Marshall believed that it may 'stunt the growth of liberty'. He observed, in a telling phrase, that 'That is what I call welfare without citizenship' (1981, pp. 169–70). Arguably, the observation could equally well have been made of welfare in the West, for instance of Bismarckian Germany in the nineteenth century. In the twentieth century it could be made of welfare in fascist and Stalinist societies, and to a lesser extent of state welfare provision for the poor in general in Western capitalist states. But Marshall did not explore these possibilities.

In this section we have noted that the dominant paradigm is relatively indifferent to the necessary civil-political character of citizenship. It is willing to disconnect welfare from the latter and to tolerate a relatively depoliticized conception of citizenship. In spite of the liberalism of Beveridge and Marshall and the humanistic collectivism of Titmuss, it is clear that these important formulators of the intellectual grounds of the dominant paradigm were prepared to conceive of welfare independently from civil–political citizenship. To that extent their endorsement of a concept of *social* citizenship seems to have carried a price, namely that of the promotion of a relatively depoliticized understanding of citizenship both in the practical world of social policy-making and also in the academic analysis of that practice.

VI

In this chapter I have attempted to give a brief overview of the dominant paradigm of citizenship in general and of social citizenship in particular. Using illustrations from British social policy and analysis of the welfare state we have looked at some of the main features of the paradigm's versions of and assumptions about the *nature* of social citizenship and of its structural *context*.

A number of immanent problems have been identified, particularly with the former (i.e. the risks of 'de-moralization', inferiority and 'depoliticization'), in the dominant paradigm's conception of social citizenship.

Throughout the postwar period until the mid-1970s it is significant the degree to which dominant paradigm assumptions about social citizenship and the welfare state *remained* assumptions. They tended to be taken for granted, barely reflected on or theorized – even by the leading social policy theorists we have considered in this chapter. For instance, in his account of Titmuss' work, Reisman (1977) makes the following critical assessments:

> Titmuss nowhere clearly defines the ideal scope of the welfare sector, and is content to delimit the social services in terms of what the general public (for reasons, as it happens, never fully explained) normally recognise them to be. (1977, p. 30)

> For Titmuss 'the British welfare state bubbled up from collective consciousness; but he nowhere provides a rigorous and adequate theory of causality' for it. (ibid., p. 33)

> And finally he naively accepted the existence of what T. H. Marshall describes as 'a very high degree of consensus . . . about the aims of the welfare services'. (ibid., p. 35)

Even by the late 1970s, Furniss and Tilton were still able to claim: 'To date no coherent and persuasive case for the welfare state exists. Its appeal is pretheoretical' (1979, pp. 23–4).

The dominant paradigm was evidently in poor shape to respond to, let alone to anticipate, the ideological and structural challenges which arose to batter it in the 1980s. In the next chapter we will begin to consider the nature of these challenges. The schematic analysis of challenges to the dominant paradigm's assumptions about the nature and the structural context of social citizenship developed in chapter 2 will then be applied and illustrated in more detail in parts II and III.

2
Alternative Versions of Social Citizenship

The dominant paradigm of social citizenship can be challenged on a number of fronts and in a number of ways. As was suggested in the previous chapter, it arguably has some important intrinsic limitations and weaknesses. In this chapter we will explore these limitations a bit further from the point of view of critics of the dominant paradigm, and we will also briefly explore some alternative contemporary conceptions of social citizenship.

One of the critics' main claims against the dominant paradigm is that its limitations have become all too obvious over the course of recent decades. In particular it has failed in its most fundamental aim, namely to abolish Beveridge's 'giants', particularly the giant of poverty, (e.g. Runciman 1966; Townsend 1979). Poverty has endured in spite of the welfare state, and indeed it has even grown parallel with the extension of the social rights of citizenship provided by the growth of the welfare state. Whether causally connected or not, poverty seems to shadow the welfare state and the dominant paradigm. This theme is one which we will explore in greater detail later in each of the two main parts of this book (parts II and III); in order to introduce it we will consider in chapter 3 some of the evidence relating to this obvious *practical* limitation of the dominant paradigm, the limit case of contemporary poverty.

However, in this present chapter we need to review some of the main *objective* and *ideological* limitations of the dominant paradigm in more general terms. This will also help to set the scene for the discussion in the two main parts of the book. These are concerned, on the one hand (part II), with the main Right-wing *ideological challenges* to the dominant paradigm (particularly that of Neoconservatism, but including also that of the New Right), and on the other hand (part III) with the main structural challenges posed by *structural social change* (particularly that of post-industrialism and post-nationalism). These latter 'objective' problems of functional breakdown and structural change need to be briefly previewed in this chapter. So we will consider criticisms of the dominant paradigm in terms of (1) welfare pluralism and (2) the welfare state's economic effects. These critiques present themselves as concerned with 'objective' rather than ideological criticisms and limitations of the dominant paradigm (section I below).

In this chapter we also need to preview the development of clearly ideological (i.e. explicitly normative) critique of the dominant paradigm's failures and limitations. A range of Left as well as Right critiques has developed in recent decades. Although my focus later is on Right critiques it will be useful to briefly consider some Left critiques here. So in section II below we will consider alternative normative conceptions of social citizenship implied by two of the most important new social movements in late twentieth century politics and ideological debate, namely feminism and ecology. First, then, we can turn to some of the main problems of structure and change facing the dominant paradigm.

I

Limits of the dominant paradigm I: 'objective' problems of the welfare state

The problems we need to consider here are: *the challenge of welfare pluralism* ((1) below); *the problem of the welfare state's economic effects* ((2) below); and *the problem of structural social change* ((3) below). In order to set the scene for these and later discussions it is necessary first to elaborate a little on the dominant paradigm's assumptions about the structural context and organization of the welfare state introduced in chapter 1. On what social conditions and systems does the welfare state depend, both objectively and also in the view of the dominant paradigm?

For a modern Western welfare state to be possible a number of political, economic and cultural conditions connected with nationalism and the nation state are required (cf. Gellner 1983; Giddens 1985b). First, *an effective modern nation state system* (democratic political institutions, legal institutions, effective government administration, taxation and policing systems, territorial integrity, etc.) needs to be in place. Secondly (and notwithstanding the distaste for markets and the profit motive displayed on both the patrician and socialist wings of the dominant paradigm), welfare states depend on the existence of *a successful capitalist economy* to provide, among other things, the tax-base for transfer payments and other public spending. In particular, in the postwar period they have depended upon capitalist economies which were (1) *nationally organized* (involving nation state-based currency and banking systems, trade areas, financial information systems and all of the other social and material infrastructures necessary for national markets to exist), (2) *industrial* (that is involving highly mechanized but nonetheless labour-intensive mass production systems) and (3) *politically manipulable* (that is responsive to Keynesian counter-cyclical macro-economic policy; e.g. Lekachman 1969; Skidelsky 1977; Bleaney 1985). On these assumptions, the tax-base for substantial state welfare spending is realistically capable of being generated and sustained by 'full employment' policy (e.g. Beveridge 1960).

Finally, welfare states depend on the existence of *an effective common culture* in modern societies. 'Culture' covers a variety of relevant factors including: the existence of a common language and writing system; widely distributed and accessible electronic communication systems; and common or mutually comprehensible socialization, education and value systems. Many of these are capable of either being provided or significantly supported by national government. But perhaps the most pertinent dimension of an effective and common culture in this context is the dimension most directly concerned with welfare, namely *the family*. A standardized sexual division of labour and family system has evolved over many generations in industrial capitalist societies based on male 'breadwinners' and female 'caretakers' (for male workers, children and elderly relatives).

This family system has functioned to support the welfare state in a number of ways. As a direct provider of welfare the family (i.e. mainly women) relieves the state and tax-payers of operational and financial responsibility for a vast quantity of welfare services. If the demands on them were not *structurally limited*, whether explicitly or tacitly, by the existence and effective operation of the family then arguably modern welfare states would speedily overload and collapse. In addition the family helps to 'reproduce' (rest and 'recreate') the (male) worker. This and the withholding of women from the labour market that it involves means that the family system has functioned to support both the labour market and the credibility of full employment policy. The latter in turn, through the distribution of income for general consumption in consumer markets, provides for the daily domestic satisfaction of needs and the production of welfare by and within the family. Once again, if welfare states were not *structurally limited* whether explicitly or tacitly by the existence of the *general* welfare effects of capitalist labour and consumer markets then (as the Stalinist experiment has indicated), the state system becomes overloaded, functions poorly and generates and distributes as much diswelfare as welfare.

In these and other ways, then, the existence and success (such as it is) of the welfare state is tacitly dependent upon the existence and effectiveness of modern nation states and within them, of national capitalist economies and national cultures, particularly their family systems. For a welfare state to prosper, these systems in the wider society have to be functioning effectively both individually and in concert. Western welfare states depend on such 'national functionalist' (or 'corporatist'; e.g. Cawson 1982; Harrison 1984) systems, and on the interdependencies and welfare pluralism they involve. We are now in a position to consider some of the main problems which have developed with the postwar welfare state and with its structural context and organization indicated earlier, beginning with 'welfare pluralism'.

1   The challenge of 'welfare pluralism'

'Welfare pluralism' (e.g. Judge 1987; Hatch and Hadley 1981; Friedmann et al. 1987; for a Left critique see Johnson 1987; for recent American Neoconservative versions see Glazer 1988; Novak 1987b) is an approach to *normative* social analysis and social policy which emphasizes and defends the kind of *objective* plurality of state and non-state welfare systems and the limits and conditions of welfare states outlined above. The perspective is associated with a range of centrist political positions to the right of statist and collectivist Left perspectives. Welfare pluralism is perhaps more of a challenge to the dominant paradigm's appearance and self-conception than to its reality, since arguably the dominant paradigm takes welfare pluralism for granted and tacitly assumes its existence. In Britain Left collectivist and associated statist views formulations of the dominant paradigm have led social policy debate and welfare state development throughout the postwar 'consensus' period. Given the persistence of poverty and social inequality in postwar Britain these perspectives call for further development of the welfare state.

However, we noted in chapter 1 that these sorts of views tend: (1) to overemphasize the actual and potential role of the state in welfare; (2) to underplay or ignore the importance for the welfare state of the existence of structural limits to its capacity to substitute for non-state systems; and (3) to underplay, criticize or take for granted one or other of those non-state systems, or the whole civil society sector *per se*. Thus, to some extent, 'welfare pluralism' could be said to present no real challenge to the dominant paradigm *per se*. On the contrary, it could reasonably be said to be implied by it and to be another expression and formulation of it. But arguably it *does* represent a challenge to the Left collectivist and associated statist version of the paradigm, together with its various unrealistic over-emphases and hidden assumptions. A more troublesome aspect of both centrist (welfare pluralist) and New Right critiques of the welfare state concerns its alleged economic effect.

2   *The problem of the welfare state's economic effects*

By the late 1970s both Left and Right social policy analysts had become concerned about the degree to which, because of the persistence and growth of poverty, among other reasons, the welfare state could be said to have 'failed' (e.g. Townsend 1979; Le Grand 1982; Harrington 1984; Murray 1984). We will examine this topic in more detail in the next and subsequent chapters. Here we simply note the variety of responses to this alleged failure, with the Left tending to press for greater scale and faster growth in welfare state spending and the Right pressing for lower scale, for 'cuts' if possible or, if not, at least for 'no more growth'.

Whether or not the Right's recommendations arose from 'meanness of spirit' (Block et al. 1987b) they certainly arose from a belief in the welfare-generating role of the capitalist economy and in the vital importance of its contribution to both civil society and state welfare. On this New Right analysis poverty is to some extent a product of a faltering, fading and failing capitalist economy, while high and increasing levels of public expenditure on such things as the welfare state are in turn in part responsible for the problems of the economy (e.g. Bacon and Eltis 1976). This was one of the themes of the 'tax-payer' revolts in the USA, Britain and elsewhere which brought the New Right to power in the 1980s. In addition, various Left analysts seemed to concur that (without reference to their *normative* critique of capitalism) *objectively* the expansion of public and welfare spending beyond some limit tends to under-mine economic growth and the national capitalist economy. It tends to fuel inflation and undermine entrepreneurial incentives, labour incentives, labour productivity and investment. It thus helps to induce various system crises, including crises of legitimacy and 'crises of crisis-management' particularly for the state sector and its role in the overall national functionalist system (e.g. O'Connor 1973, 1984, 1987; Habermas 1975; Mishra 1984; Offe 1984, 1985a). This seemed to be confirmed in the British case during the 1970s in particular (Gamble 1985).

According to these various lines of analysis, then, from a situation of national functionalism (i.e. relative interdependence among the welfare sectors and also between the state and

capitalism) the continuous growth of the state's tax-take
from the economy for welfare and public spending purposes
threatened to produce major dysfunctions and a breakdown of
the system as a whole. Evidently there can be disagreements
about what the appropriate limits to the state's take and the
maximum size of the welfare state might be in different nations.
But the notion that there must in principle be *some* limit is
hardly arguable. In the contemporary period the state's tax-take
in most Western nations is high in both historical and absolute
terms (e.g. around 40 per cent of GDP) and it is continuously
rising on a long-term basis. Given this, the notion that a limit
has been reached, or at least that it is being closely approached,
is not an unrealistic analysis in my view. Continuous and unrestricted growth of the welfare state does seem to threaten
the dominant paradigm with a long-term problem of overload,
and with a breakdown in the 'national functionalist' political
economic system which supports it.

3   The problem of structural social change

There are, however, other even more serious long-term problems threatening the dominant paradigm and its core institution
the welfare state. My argument in this book is that the whole
social formation on which the welfare state rests and which the
dominant paradigm assumes and takes for granted is being
subjected to major long-term change in the late twentieth
century. The changes affect the three major social systems,
namely the *economy*, the *nation state* and the *culture*, together
with their interrelationships. In my view these systems are
transforming and restructuring in major ways, and their traditional and assumed interrelationships are beginning to break
down. Taking the systems one by one, I will briefly indicate here
the general lines of the analysis which will be pursued at greater
length in subsequent chapters.

i   The 'industrial capitalist economy' assumption   We no
longer need much vision and imagination to understand that the
incessant development and application of science-based technology, among other factors, is transforming late twentieth-

century advanced economies. The evidence of a new 'Industrial Revolution', this time a 'post-industrial revolution', is beginning to accumulate around us (see ch. 7). One of the main aspects of this change relevant to social citizenship is that it is possible that post-industrial, high technology, high labour-productivity economies have fewer structural incentives and less structural ability to deliver 'full employment' in response to Keynesian economic policy than do traditional labour-intensive industrial economies. To make matters worse there is also the long-term and accelerating development of contemporary capitalism towards a global economy inhabited and organized by multi-national corporations and globalized capital and currency markets. Economic globalization spells the end of national economic sovereignty. The era in which nation states possessed the power to regulate 'their' economies by Keynesian or other means in order to achieve full employment, inflation control or any other traditional national economic and social policy goal is coming to a close. This is true even for economic superpowers like the USA and Japan, but it is demonstrably so for the European nations (see ch. 8).

ii   The 'nation state' assumption   The various implications of these post-industrial economic developments lend support to the view that in the sphere of politics the 'nation state' assumption of the dominant paradigm no longer holds. Arguably we are entering a period in which much of our politics will be conducted in 'post-national' terms and in 'post-national' spheres. The economic trends point towards important changes in levels, both above (e.g. global) and below (e.g. local) the national economy level. Similarly, the ecological problems generated by both mature industrial and newly industrializing nations are also accumulating at levels both significantly above and below nation state level, from global to local.

These ecological problems – problems of public and private health and welfare – increasingly call for continuous monitoring and effective regulation by political institutions and processes organized at appropriate levels, i.e. levels beyond or below the nation state. Such political institution-building and restructuring will necessarily infringe national sovereignty, and it will tend to undermine the power and relevance of the national level of politics and of national governments. It will thus tend to undermine some of the core structures and assumptions of traditional welfare states. Whether welfare states will mutate into complex multi-level welfare governances of some kind as we move into the twenty-first century remains an open question. We will explore these large and complex issues of post-industrial and post-national social change together with their implications for social citizenship further in chapters 7 and 8 respectively.

iii   The 'common culture' assumption   Modern societies' traditional and common cultures, particularly their family systems, are being eroded by various contemporary processes of cultural and structural fragmentation. In the field of ethnic relations, for instance, the failure of Western societies to make a reality out of their rhetorics about the legitimacy and the importance for them of 'multi-culturalism' has encouraged the growth of various sorts of separatist, nationalist and otherwise mono-culturalist attitudes and ideologies. In the field of the family there has been considerable change in response to various factors such as the women's movement, consumerist attitudes to sexuality and no doubt many other factors. A plurality of alternative and competitive family forms has begun to develop, with unclear consequences for child care, socialization, cultural transmission and much else. We will explore some of the main aspects of these important cultural and familial changes further in chapter 5, together with their relevance to the contemporary debate about social citizenship.

The general line of my argument about structural change is that the days of the postwar model welfare state and its national functional systemic context, when looked at coldly in the light of the reality of late twentieth-century social change, certainly seem to be numbered. What the future holds for social citizenship is not at all clear. But what is clear is that a serious and sustained effort is needed to begin to rethink the idea and its implications for politics and practice in the light of the structural changes I have briefly indicated here. These will be explored further in later chapters of this book, particularly chapter 5 on familial/cultural change, chapter 7 on post-industrial change and chapter 8 on post-national/European change. From these *structural* changes and challenges we can now turn to consider some of the main *ideological* challenges to the dominant paradigm of social citizenship. Here the issues are less about the structural context of social citizenship and more about its definition and nature and the kind of moral community it involves.

II

Limits of the dominant paradigm II: the ideological challenges of new social movements

The main ideological challenge to the dominant paradigm of social citizenship and the welfare state in the 1970s and 1980s has evidently come from the Right, particularly the New Right. But, equally evidently, it would be a misrepresentation of the vitality of late twentieth-century political struggles and ideological debates to assume that the New Right has had the monopoly on 'radical' or alternative thinking, whether about the state and society in general or about citizenship and welfare in particular. On the contrary, the contribution of the new social movements (internationalism, the peace movement, ecology, feminism, etc.) to political rethinking and to modernity's capacity to imagine *alternative futures* for human life and society has been enormous and continues to be so (e.g. Scott 1990). In this section I want to briefly consider some aspects of feminism and ecology in terms of the rethinking they imply for our traditional assumptions about the nature of social citizenship. But first, are there any common strands in the new ideological environment of the late twentieth century, created by the New Right together with the new social movements?

1   The Right and new social movements

The differences which separate Right-wing perspectives from the variety of new social movement perspectives and their various versions of social radicalism are clear enough. For instance, most of the new social movements are antagonistic to key New

Right conceptions and commitments – such as those involving the New Right's asocial concept of human beings, its atomistic and competitive concept of society and its strongly pro-capitalist concept of economy. But nonetheless there are some areas in which Right and radical interests appear to be common or at least closely comparable. They are both strongly in favour of reasserting and re-establishing the importance for modern politics and social life of '*civil society*' (that is, leaving capitalism aside, the role of voluntarism and the role of family and community). Also there is a comparable emphasis on peoples' *duties* to one another, particularly but not exclusively within the concept of civil society. This has major implications for the way we think about citizenship in general and social citizenship in particular in the late twentieth century.

The dominant paradigm of social citizenship with its emphasis on social *rights* had its high tide in the early postwar decades in which welfare state services were being built and developed. Since that time the politics of rights has been further expanded and enriched the development of ideologies and institutions concerned with 'human rights' of various kinds (e.g. the United Nations, the European Court of Human Rights; also see Paul 1984). But I believe that parallel to this modern development of a 'rights discourse' a '*duties discourse*' has also developed in contemporary political and ideological debate. And both the Right and the new social movements have made equal, if distinct and different, contributions to this duties discourse. The Right's contribution will be examined later (chs 4, 5 and 6). For the moment I want to briefly consider two new social movement contributions to the new 'duties discourse', namely those of feminism and ecology (see also Pierson 1991, ch. 3).

It may at first glance appear to be something of a misrepresentation of feminism and ecology to present them as being political ideologies and discourses centrally concerned with promoting concepts of duty. They are surely quintessential modern rights-claiming discourses. They are surely about the extension of moral and citizenship-based rights claims into the relatively uncharted territories of (1) the 'personal', the 'private' and the 'body' in the case of the women's movement, and (2) animals, plants, land, air, sea – in a word 'nature' – in the case of the ecological movement. This is no doubt true, up to a point.

But there is *also* in these movements undoubtedly a stronger, more explicit and more sophisticated understanding than is to be found in one-sided rights movements of the fact that *rights imply duties*. What is more, ecology and feminism understand better than many rights movements do that the duties that rights imply are not all *state* duties. They understand that these duties are also, importantly, claims against other members of civil society and/or claims against ourselves.

2   Feminism and citizenship

Feminism evidently involves claims for women's rights – and many of these rights claims are indeed claims against the state, for instance claims for the satisfaction of basic welfare needs. But many are also claims to assistance and support from the state in order to take an equal part with men in civil society, i.e. claims for the state to support equal citizenship (e.g. Lister 1990a, 1990b; also Phillips, Benton and Ellis in Andrews 1991). However, equally evidently, the primary thrust of women's rights claims is intended to be felt directly by *men* rather than by the *state*. Feminism challenges men in modern society to recognize the existence of patriarchal order and of the manifold ways in which they both dominate women's lives and benefit from so doing. Advancing the cause of women's rights challenges men to accept a duty to change themselves and to change their ways of relating to women in order to honour those rights. In effect feminism challenges men to accept a duty to act against the patriarchal order in which women are second-class citizens and to act for equality, a society of equal citizenship.

The key sphere in which the issue of women's rights and men's duties needs to be pressed and is being pressed is that of the family, although the same sort of problems are at issue in the spheres of employment, education, leisure/public space etc. As far as the family goes, the promotion of women's rights first of all requires a major and difficult reordering of the unequal social citizenship involved in the typical pattern of the social division of labour, with female specialization in housework, child care and other carework and male specialization in employment (e.g. Oakley 1974; Pahl 1984). Men in modern societies are challenged by the claims of women's rights to acknowledge equal social citizenship in the division of labour and to do something about it. One step in the right direction is undoubtedly for men to accept a greater share of the duties and burdens of housework, child care and other carework. Another is for men to treat the main division of labour between domestic/care work and employment as at least a joint decision with their partner, jointly reviewed and jointly changeable. This latter step is obviously bigger and more difficult for individual men than the former because of the influence of prevailing labour market conditions and their structural biases in favour of men. However, these biases look likely to ease significantly into the 1990s, albeit under the influence of economic (capitalist) rather than ideological (feminist) factors.

The personal politics involved in attempts to redistribute work duties in this way presupposes at least relatively civilized and civil (not to mention affectionate) relationships between male and female partners and any children they may be responsible for. One of the achievements of the feminist movement has been to reveal the significant degree to which, both historically and currently, such civil norms and values have historically been dishonoured and are currently dishonoured in families. The minimal duties of respect and civility which are required in public society are equally required in order for the private realm of the family to exist in a healthy and just way. But the elementary civil duty not to violate and abuse others appears to be unrecognized or dishonoured by the significant minority of men in modern societies which is responsible for domestic violence and abuse against women and children. The women's movement, by pressing women's rights to respect and civility in intimate relationships, reasserts and seeks to impose clear and basic moral duties on men. These duties underpin male claims to being members of a community with laws and a peaceful political process. In this sense feminism challenges men to remember the moral conditions of their citizenship. And it challenges the state to use its authority coercively to remind men about these conditions if they happen to forget or ignore them. We will return to some of these issues again in more detail when considering family policy in chapter 5 (also Roche 1988c).

3   *Ecology and citizenship*

If anything, the ecological movement, even more clearly than feminism, is concerned with the politics and morality of duty. Of course it champions rights, and it does so in two distinct registers at that. In the first register ecology champions the rights of the non-human (animals, environments, nature etc.) on behalf of the non-human, rights which are claimed against humans. Nature's rights thus imply (and with ecology's help, *impose*) duties for humans. Ecology thus addresses itself to the often agonizing debates and struggles within and between modern human states and societies, and indeed within each individual, between on the one hand *human* needs, desires and rights and on the other hand duties we impose on ourselves by our recognition, such as it is, of the rights of the *non-human*.

It is certainly possible to dispute whether the rights and duties recognized in this form of ecological analysis are 'genuine', given that they have very different features from conventional moral and citizenship-based rights and duties recognized between people. For instance, 'nature' is not a conscious moral agency or a citizen, and only such entities can be said to understand and possess rights, to choose to claim them, to know when they were satisfied etc. Humans can in principle make no rights claims against nature, nor can we discuss with nature the adequacy of our discharge of our duties to it etc. However such criticisms as these are somewhat less undermining of ecology's moral discourse when its second register is considered.

In its second register ecology champions nature and the environment on behalf of posterity. Thus generations of humans as yet unborn are assumed to have rights to an environment at least as resource-rich and as undegraded and undamaged as the one the present generation inherited. The 'rights of future generations' are thus deemed to impose duties of environmental 'stewardship' on all individuals communities, organizations and nations (e.g. Porritt 1984; Steward in Andrews 1991). Like nature, future generations cannot reciprocate the performance of duties. It is thus not unreasonable to argue that in this way (and of course in many other non-ecological ways) an intergenerational moral relationship or community exists in human affairs. This implies that all explicitly or implicitly purely *intra-*

generational conceptions of social justice and of the proper distribution of ecological and other forms of welfare *must* incorporate an *inter*-generational element which imposes a set of unreciprocated duties on the present generation to provide ecological welfare to future generations.

Whether or not the sphere of civil society and of our social citizenship can be said to include animals – as ecologists, or at least many 'animal rights' supporters might wish to propose – is obviously arguable. However, in its second register ecology challenges the dominant paradigm of social citizenship in a number of ways. First, it asserts the importance of human duties, indeed it asserts their primacy in some respects over human rights. Secondly, it requires us to rethink what we mean by welfare so as to include environmental factors and values. Thirdly it expands the sphere of our relevant civil society and social citizenship in two ways: it expands this sphere beyond the nation state level to the global level and to other ecologically relevant levels from the global to the local; also it expands it beyond the present generation and requires us to consider the inter-generational dimension of our sociality and of our moral and citizenship duties. I will return to consider the implications of these ecological and inter-generational issues in my concluding discussion of the conflicts and contradictions of contemporary social citizenship (ch. 9; also Roche 1988d, 1989).

III

In chapter 1 I presented an account of the main elements of the dominant paradigm of social citizenship. In this chapter we have sketched out some of the ways in which this paradigm can be seen to be limited and to be open to criticism. The paradigm's main assumptions – whether about the welfare state, or the social structural context of the welfare state, or the priority of social rights over duties or the appropriate sphere and moral community for social citizenship – have all been called into serious question in the contemporary period. The dominant paradigm was a creature of its time and the times have changed. New political ideologies have arisen to pose fundamental challenges to its moral basis, while social changes have posed equally fundamental challenges to the credibility of its structural assumptions. In parts II and III we will take a closer look at each of these challenges in turn. But first we need to consider the problem which has dogged the welfare state and the dominant paradigm throughout the postwar period, undermining its most basic claims to effectiveness and success, namely the problem of poverty.

3
The Limits of Social Citizenship: Poverty and the Underclass in the USA

Poverty is not an unambiguous concept and the definition, explanation and solution for it are controversial matters. Nevertheless, whether defined in absolute, relative or subjective terms, or in terms of some mixture of all three criteria, as the rich are wont to observe, the poor it seems are 'always with us'. That is, it is generally agreed that the growth of the welfare state and of the dominant paradigm of social citizenship in Western society has been shadowed both by the persistence of traditional forms of poverty and also by the growth of new forms of poverty.

Poverty is antithetical to full citizenship. As T. H. Marshall noted (quoting the nineteenth-century philanthropist Loch): '"Pauperism . . . is the social enemy of the modern State. The State wants citizens." How true!' (1981, p. 76). Poverty thus represents a strategically important *limit* for the concept of social citizenship. Beyond this limit in some respects people are not full and participating *members* of society (Townsend 1979), and also they are not full *citizens*. Beyond this limit people are politically and civically as well as socially 'excluded', they are 'second-class citizens' or less (Lister 1990b). The persistence and growth of poverty in modern society can be seen as an enduring reminder of the practical limitations and inadequacies of the dominant paradigm.

Orthodox postwar social policy, whether in the form of the British assault on Beveridge's 'giants' in the 1940s or the American 'war on poverty' in the 1960s, can, on this criterion at least, be said to have failed. Therefore, either as a *theoretical* limit case for social citizenship *per se* or as a *practical* limit on the dominant paradigm's effectiveness and credibility, poverty must inevitably be a recurring theme in any discussion of social citizenship. It will be such a theme in this book. Thus, since poverty is at the heart of the great ideological debates within and surrounding the New Right and Neoconservatism, we will consider it in part II. Also, in new post-industrial and post-national forms, poverty is at the heart of the challenges to social citizenship posed by contemporary structural change. So we will consider it again from a different perspective in part III.

To prepare some of the ground for these discussions of poverty and social citizenship it is necessary at this point to outline some of the main aspects of contemporary forms of poverty, particularly the so-called 'new poverty'. Poverty in the industrial capitalist societies of the West has traditionally been associated with unemployment and social class (e.g. Harrington 1963 (USA); Townsend 1979 (UK)). The 'new poverty', in addition to being associated with unemployment and inequalities of class, is also associated with changing family structure and with multiple deprivations connected with inequalities of gender, ethnicity and age. To a greater or lesser extent it has been a growing feature of every major Western society since the 1960s. But it is perhaps seen in its clearest and most extreme form in the most affluent and technologically advanced Western society, namely the USA.

In this chapter, then, I will illustrate the contemporary problem of poverty in Western society by focusing on its various aspects as seen in the case of the USA. I will begin by considering the idea that certain elements of the contemporary poor constitute an 'underclass' (section I below). I will then look at some of the social factors which are typically found in association with poverty and which may point towards possible explanations for it (section II). Poverty and its explanation, are an inherently controversial, divisive and political matters as we will see in the discussions of poverty diagnoses and policies in chapters 6 and 7. So in this chapter I want to emphasize the areas of relative consensus which exist among social scientists and commentators concerning, first, the existence and scale of American poverty and its underclass (section I) and, secondly, the social factors typically associated with them (section II).

I

The underclass

In recent years there has been much concern and debate in the USA (e.g. Auletta 1983; Mead 1986; Wilson 1987, 1989) – and as a result more recently in Britain (e.g. Field 1989; Murray 1989; IEA 1990) – about a contemporary category of people. In this category many of the serious inequalities of modern society seem to have accumulated to an unprecedented degree, generating severe and multiple personal and social problems. This relatively small but socially isolated, alienated and anomic category has come to be referred to as the 'underclass'. Members of the underclass are effectively not so much 'second-class' citizens as 'non-citizens'. They are, depending on your political view, either unwillingly excluded from citizenship (Lister 1990b) or willingly disdainful of it (the Neoconservative view, see part II). Either way they represent a limit beyond which the order of the democratic and welfare state, and of civil society, together with the social citizenship they imply, breaks down in various ways in a disordered and uncivil form of society.

The underclass, even more so than poverty in general, is thus a theoretically strategic 'limit case' for social citizenship which we need to explore briefly here. Its importance for my analysis of social citizenship is even more underlined by the fact that, as we will see in part II, Neoconservatives claim that the welfare state, the main institution of the dominant paradigm, is largely responsible for the growth of the underclass. On this highly controversial view the institutionalization of the dominant paradigm in the postwar welfare state is ironically responsible for the progressive breakdown of the very social citizenship it ostensibly seeks to promote. We must investigate these and other issues of causation and explanation in parts II and III. But first we need to consider the more descriptive problems of defining the underclass and also of establishing something about its scale and nature.

The idea that a distinctive new underclass has come into existence in contemporary America has tended to be promoted by Right political commentators and Neoconservative social analysts. One liberal and Left response has been to regard the term as having no descriptive substance, as being racist (since the American underclass is predominantly Black) and thus as being a term to be abjured and avoided (e.g. Piven and Cloward 1987; MacNicol 1990). Another liberal and Left response is to hold that the underclass is a useful way of referring to the contemporary inner-city Black ghetto and to the distinctive features of the structurally constrained 'culture of poverty' which has apparently come to prevail there (e.g. Wilson 1987). With criminal problems like assault, murder, drug use and drug-dealing, together with the fear and disorder they generate, escalating to unprecedented levels in America's major cities in the 1970s and 1980s, a feeling emerged that new social processes were at work. These feelings were initially checked out in a number of psychological and journalistic studies (e.g. Sheehan 1976; Sharff 1981; Auletta 1983), and they have subsequently been checked out more systematically by other social scientists (e.g. Ricketts and Sawhill 1988; Wilson 1987; Kasarda 1989; Massey 1990). We will take a brief look at some of these accounts.

The journalist Ken Auletta's rich and substantial study *The Underclass* (1983) did much to publicize the problem and to legitimate the use of the term. It was based on a period of ethnographic work with one group of 26 underclass members on a basic skills training course in New York in 1980. Auletta sets out to tell their stories and also the story of their experience of this small instance of public policy at work. He backed this up with: a study of the training agency itself, a national non-profit organization called Manpower Research Demonstration Corporation (MRDC) which works with Black and white, urban and rural poor and unemployed across the USA; interviews with 250 underclass members in most of these locations; reviews of social statistics; and reviews of relevant academic studies and policy options from Left and Neoconservative perspectives. The study as a whole illuminates and illustrates the essential complexity and also the intractability of the problem of the underclass. Auletta concludes that there are no simple causes or cures, and that while 'some members of the underclass need help [others] are beyond help' (ibid., p. 319).

Complexity is built into the problem of the underclass because 'They don't just tend to be poor; to most Americans their behaviour seems aberrant' (ibid., p. xiii). That is they have behavioural problems as well as material ones, behavioural problems which are subject to normative as well as objective description and interpretation. This issue surfaces again in Auletta's definition of the underclass, namely those who 'do not assimilate' to American society, and in his conception of the mixed composition of the underclass:

> they can be grouped into four distinct categories: (a) the *passive poor*, usually long-term welfare recipients; (b) the *hostile* street criminals who terrorize most cities, and who are often school dropouts and drug addicts; (c) the *hustlers*, who like street criminals, may not be poor and who earn their livelihood in an underground economy but who rarely commit violent crimes; (d) the *traumatized* drunks, drifters, homeless shopping-bag ladies and released mental patients who frequently roam or collapse on city streets. (ibid., p. xvi)

He estimates the numbers of the underclass as sizeable, in absolute terms at around nine million people. In spite of the fact that the criminal segments may not actually be poor, Auletta nonetheless sees the underclass as a sub-set of America's poor, of which they form a relatively small proportion (around a third).

Auletta's study has prompted some social scientists to begin to address themselves directly to the quantitative description and theoretical explanation of the underclass. Katz (1986, p. 277) doubts the utility and purpose of Auletta's attempt to collect together the four elements he refers to under the unitary classification 'underclass'. Nevertheless Ricketts and Sawhill (1988) have been able to operationalize and quantify a related behaviourally-based definition. On the basis of an analysis of unpublished 1980 US Census data they have been able to establish 'the reality of the underclass' (ibid., p. 321) as existing in a great number of American cities and urban areas.

They begin by distinguishing the underclass from the poor on behavioural terms.

> Most observers agree that the underclass is characterized by behaviours which are at variance with those of mainstream America (such as joblessness, welfare dependency, unwed parenting, criminal or uncivil behaviour, and dropping out of high school). (ibid., p. 317)

Census data is not ideal and does not allow a picture of criminality, drug abuse and teenage childbearing to be drawn (ibid., p. 321). Nonetheless it does contain indicators for the other main characteristics, and it also allows comparison and differences between underclass areas and poverty areas to be registered. Thus, while they found that areas of 'extreme poverty' (defined as areas in which 40 per cent or more residents are below the official poverty line) overlapped substantially with underclass areas, nonetheless 40 per cent of underclass areas lie outside extreme poverty areas.

Overall, they found 880 American urban areas to be significantly higher than average on underclass measures (ibid., p. 321). These areas are mainly in the older industrial cities of the north-east (e.g. New York, Baltimore, Newark). However, while their findings confirm the existence of the kind of underclass depicted by Auletta, they do not confirm his estimates of its size. On their assessment around 1.5 million people live in underclass areas and are likely to be affected by the behaviour of underclass members. But since an underclass area is defined as one in which only 40 per cent of the people display underclass characteristics, Ricketts and Sawhill estimate that in 1980 the American underclass consisted of around 500,000 people, a tiny fraction of the American population.

This is a very sobering if provisional estimate, which has not yet been confirmed by a range of other studies. Just as with more qualitative (cultural and psychological) aspects of the underclass the quantitative aspects are extremely under-researched. At the very least, American social policy and social science could do with a complementary analysis of US Census data for 1970 and 1990 to establish something about the direction and rate of change of Ricketts and Sawhill's underclass indicators. However, even on the basis of their 1980 findings, it is possible to argue that the *social effect* of the underclass on all sectors of urban populations is much greater than its apparently relatively small numbers would suggest. But it must also be said that if the underclass *is* confirmed to be as small as Ricketts and Sawhill suggest, then Neoconservative social analysts will need to revise their conceptions of the scale of the threat it presents to society at large. For instance, Mead's (1986) influential study of US work policy, welfare and the underclass relied on

Auletta's apparently excessive estimate. Murray's recent accounts (1989, 1990a) of the threat of the rise of an underclass in Britain comparable to that in America coyly refrains from indicating the exact (or even rough) scale of the phenomenon in America.

But Neoconservatism is not the only perspective in which the underclass looms larger than in Ricketts and Sawhill's account. William J. Wilson, in his various accounts and studies (e.g. 1987, 1989) of the American underclass virtually defines it as equivalent to the contemporary inner-city Black ghetto. In *The Truly Disadvantaged* (1987) Wilson defends and elaborates the concept of the underclass as follows:

> The term *ghetto underclass* refers to (the) heterogeneous group of families and individuals who inhabit the cores of the nation's central cities. (These) families . . . have experienced long-term spells of poverty and/or welfare dependency, (and they include) individuals who lack training and skills and have either experienced periods of persistence unemployment or have dropped out of the labour force altogether, and individuals who are frequently involved in street criminal activity . . . [They] are collectively different from and much more isolated than [the groups] that lived in these communities in earlier years. (1987, p. 143)

Along with Kasarda (1989) and others (e.g. Bluestone and Harrison 1982; Harrington 1984; Piven and Cloward 1987; Block 1987a; Massey 1990) Wilson proposes a structuralist approach to explaining the existence and persistence of the American underclass, focusing on economic forces and economic policy failures. This is very much at variance with Neoconservative explanations which tend to emphasize individual or cultural factors. We will consider Neoconservative explanations and assess them against structuralist criticisms in part II (ch. 6 in particular), while in part III (ch. 7 in particular) we will consider the structuralist approach, focusing on de-industrialization and the effects of post-industrial economic change. The potential for debate and disagreement between these two approaches is indicated in Wilson and Wacquant's recent suggestion (1989) as to how the notion of an underclass should be conceptualized: 'If the concept of underclass is used . . . [it] should not be used as a label to designate a new breed of individuals molded by a mythical and all-powerful culture of poverty. [Rather] it must be a structural concept' (1989, p. 25). However, for the moment it is necessary to return from these conceptual and explanatory issues to less controversial territory in order to fill out the empirical picture of underclass poverty in a little more detail. So now we need to consider the following question: with what social factors has underclass poverty, and American poverty more generally, been found to be typically associated in the 1970s and 1980s?

II

Social factors associated with contemporary American poverty

The main factor traditionally associated with poverty in Western society has been unemployment and loss of labour market income. In particular, the social disaster of mass unemployment during the world economic depression in the 1930s provided a major stimulus to the growth of social insurance, social policy and the welfare state in the USA, Britain and elsewhere (e.g. Rimlinger 1971; Katz 1986; Fraser 1984, chs 8, 9). In the contemporary period poverty has clearly come to be associated with a variety of social factors, such as changing family structure, as we will see in (2) below. But its association with unemployment persists, and it is that we must first consider in the US case.

1   Employment, unemployment and poverty

The *basic* causes of unemployment and underemployment are contentious, although whichever line is taken evidently *some* consideration needs to be given both to the underlying state of the economy and to demographic changes. Nevertheless there is general agreement between American Neoconservatives and their critics about some of the main trends and features of employment distribution and its correlation with poverty. As such, unemployment is at least an 'immediate cause' of poverty whatever the deeper causes and/or reasons for the latter may be.

The employment situation is very different as between young males and young females, whether white or Black. Society's patriarchal assumptions about women's responsibilities for children obviously reduce their ability to participate equally in the labour market with males, particularly if they are single mothers. The main focus of politicians' and analysts' attention has tended to be on the employment problems of young males, particularly Blacks, and we will consider this in a moment. However, single mothers have also been a focus of attention since they are one of the major groups vulnerable to poverty and underclass membership. At least half of all American single mothers seek work and are in employment at any given time (Mead 1989). Consistent with longstanding male employment norms and with the increasing participation of women in general in the labour force in recent decades, single mothers show substantial involvement in the labour market. The poverty problems of unemployed single 'welfare mothers' need to be seen against this fact, and we will consider this further below (2).

In the debate about social citizenship, poverty and the underclass there is no disagreement that unemployment and underemployment are principal correlates or 'immediate causes' of poverty. No doubt poverty can coexist with (some kinds of) employment (Murray 1984; Mead 1988a, 1988c, 1988d) and that the 'working poor' are a reality. There is no doubt either that many poor people on welfare benefits are in a poverty trap in which employment would in the short term lower their real income (also see chs 6 and 7 below). Nonetheless, the vast majority of employed people and their families have incomes and standards of living well above the poverty line, while conversely the vast majority of the unemployed are poor. Persistent employment offers the working poor at least the possibility of some accumulation of property, some possibility of making headway themselves and some resources for their children to build on. By comparison, persistent unemployment offers nothing.

The concern in the debate about work and work policy for the employment patterns of *young* males and females reflects the concern that unemployment or underemployment in youth makes persistent employment in later life extremely difficult to achieve and virtually guarantees the persistence of poverty. We will look first at the situation of young Black males and then at the situation of single mothers.

Employment and unemployment statistics are notoriously problematic and contestable. Nevertheless, and with due acknowledgement of the economic successes of employed Blacks and the Black middle class (Wilson 1987; Steele 1990) there is little doubt that there is a serious employment problem among young Black American males (e.g. Levin 1982; Duncan and Hoffman 1984; Freeman and Holzer 1986a, 1986b).

For most young age categories (16–24 years) Black male unemployment rates have been at least double white rates since the mid-1960s, standing at around 35 per cent for Black teenagers (16–19 years) in 1980. These rates are not a wholly reliable guide to the underlying picture of employment and labour force participation. In 1962 59 per cent of all young Black males (16–21 years and out of school) were employed. By 1983 this figure had fallen to only 45 per cent, compared with 73 per cent of equivalent whites (Freeman and Holzer 1986b; Novak 1987b, p. 32). In 1984 around 50 per cent of young Black males (16–24 years) had 'no work experience at all' (ibid., p. 33). This is particularly the case for young males (1) in families on welfare and who live in public housing (Lerman 1986; Freeman and Holzer 1986a; Novak 1987b, p. 34) and (2) who live in poor and underclass areas (Novak 1987b, p. 36; see also Ricketts and Sawhill 1988).

Neoconservative social analysts, aware of charges of using racist stereotyping and claiming to avoid this, have been prominent among those identifying this problem. Left social policy analysts Piven and Cloward (1987) declare themselves bemused by the 'ambiguous' and 'tangled data' (p. 65) and sceptical of all simplistic causal explanations. Nonetheless, they too appear to accept that there is a real social problem to address and explain (also Harrington 1984), while liberal social policy analysts Ellwood and Summers forthrightly declare 'the labour market situation for young blacks is bad and getting worse' (1986, p. 73; also Levin 1982, ch. 3; Freeman and Holzer 1986a, *passim*).

2 Family structure and the 'feminization of poverty'

In general in contemporary societies family structures are becoming diverse and complicated. The traditional image of marriage and of the two-parent two-child 'nuclear' family pattern, largely generated by and functional for industrializing societies, no longer holds true (e.g. Wicks and Kiernan 1990; Roll 1989; Hauser and Fischer 1990). Divorce rates have risen, seemingly inexorably, throughout the postwar period, recently stabilizing at two-thirds of all American first marriages (although marriage remains popular and remarriage rates remain high). Rising divorce rates together with rising unmarried cohabitation and single parenting has helped to produce what the distinguished Neoconservative politician and social commentator Daniel P. Moynihan calls a 'post-marital society' in contemporary America (Moynihan 1989). Single-mother families are a particularly important phenomenon in this scenario.

Single-mother families are produced either by divorce, breakdown in cohabitation in child-rearing couples together with desertion by fathers, or by outside-of-marriage ('illegitimate') births together with desertion by relevant males, particularly the natural father. The 'feminization of poverty' is thus interlinked with what we can refer to as 'the masculinization of parental irresponsibility'. The breakdown of both marriage and cohabitation for both whites and Blacks, but particularly the latter, can be seen in the trends in 'normal'/'traditional' childhoods, i.e. in the percentages of all children in each group who are able to live with both natural parents throughout their childhood (0–17 years). In 1950 81 per cent of white children and 52 per cent of Black children had a 'normal' childhood. By 1980 the respective figures were 30 per cent and 6 per cent. Thus in 1980 each white child could expect to spend a third of his or her childhood in a single-parent family, while the corresponding figure for each Black child was over a half of his or her childhood (Moynihan 1989, p. 22). Moynihan notes that this is 'a huge transformation' which has been produced 'in just one generation' (ibid.).

In addition there are the interlinked problems of out-of-marriage births and births to teenage females. Traditionally, rates for both of these phenomena were relatively low among whites (e.g. 1.6 per cent illegitimate births in 1950) and Blacks (e.g. 20 per cent illegitimacy *c*.1900). However, by the mid-1980s the corresponding rates were about 16 per cent for whites and about 60 per cent for Blacks (Moynihan ibid.). Connected with this there is the explosion in teenage pregnancies, which are predominantly 'illegitimate'. As a proportion of all illegitimate births, they have risen from 15 per cent to 51 per cent in the period 1960–82 (Ladner 1988, p. 299). In 1979 516,000 births, 16 per cent of *all* births (15 per cent of all white births and 27.5 per cent of all Black births) were to teenagers (Auletta 1983, p. 69).

Whatever disagreements there may be over the psychological benefits/disbenefits and morality of these developments, not to mention their causes, the *financial consequences* for women and children are fairly clear and agreed on all sides. The 'feminization of poverty' (Auletta 1983; Besharov and Quinn 1987, pp. 9, 50) is a reality, together with, one might add, the 'juvenilization of poverty'. As far as the latter goes Moynihan points out that 'family structure is the principal correlate of child poverty . . . children in single-parent families are poor and there are more and more of them' (1989, p. 22). For the Left Piven and Cloward concur: 'The growth of families headed by women is a main source of the rapidly rising poverty among women and children. [This] is not in dispute' (1987, p. 62).

An analyst of the Black American family, Joyce Ladner (1988), accepts that the 'increase in female-headed households [is] alarming' (p. 303). This is particularly so, in her view, with respect to that part of the increase due to the increase in Black teenage pregnancies, given the multiple problems these tend to entail for both the mothers and the children involved. In Ladner's view the teenage mothers' 'inability to complete high school, find an adequate job, and find child care encourage long-term welfare dependency' (p. 301). In 1975 over 50 per cent of all Aid to Families with Dependent Children (AFDC) benefits were paid to women who had been or currently were teenage mothers (Auletta 1983, p. 69). Public costs of AFDC and other in-kind benefits to teenage mothers stood at $16 billion in 1985 (Ladner 1988, p. 301).

While other groups of the poor declined or showed small increases in the 1970s, the proportion of single mothers in poverty increased by around 40 per cent (Auletta 1983, ch. 5), composing about 50 per cent of all poor *families* by 1979 (Auletta ibid.; also Murray 1984, pp. 130–1) and 56 per cent by 1985 (Novak 1987b, p. 17). The President's National Advisory Council on Economic Opportunity in 1981 warned:

> All other things being equal, if the proportion of the poor in female-householder families were to continue to increase at the same rate as it did from 1967 to 1978, the poverty population would be composed solely of women and their children before the year 2000. (quoted Auletta 1983, p. 69)

Without prejudicing the subsequent discussion of explanations and policies for these problems in part II, a number of things emerge from this review of the generally agreed facts and problems concerning modern American families, employment and poverty.

(1) First, it is important to note how *interlinked* family structure and employment is. On the one hand, from an objective viewpoint high rates of young Black male unemployment do not provide nurturant conditions for marriage and family formation. Neither are they likely to do so in the perceptions of poor Black females, or in the perceptions of poor Black males. But non-marriage and single parenthood virtually guarantee persistent poverty for the women in this situation, together with very low levels of participation in employment (Duncan et al. 1984). On the other hand, while it remains a matter of speculation what the effects of mothers' and (where appropriate) fathers' long-term or recurrent unemployment is on their children's preparation for and attitudes to work, there is, to say the least, no reason to believe that these effects are positive.

Earlier we noted that most single mothers are employed (53 per cent in 1987, according to Mead 1989), and of these only 10 per cent are in poverty (Mead 1988d). However, the situation with unemployed single mothers is very different: 56 per cent of these are in poverty (Mead 1988d). Single mothers who are dependent on AFDC/welfare tend not to seek employment (e.g. only 5 per cent were in employment in 1987, according to Mead ibid.). There is a patterned connection of income with employment status here which is hard to dispute. It would seem to be the case that (1) the fact that many young single mothers are poor and dependent on welfare is importantly connected with (2) the fact they are often not in regular (or in many cases in any) employment. This patterned connection can be conceded without implying or favouring any particular causal explanation or rationale for this state of affairs.

(2)   Secondly, it is important to note that the trends from the 1960s to the present which we have reviewed can reasonably be said to constitute significant *breakdowns* or transformations of traditional patterns of employment and family in contemporary America. An ethical and voluntaristic way of speaking comes most naturally to Neoconservatives and evidently contains prejudgements about causation. Nevertheless, Novak's view of the situation, particularly in poor and underclass areas, is a sufficiently apt characterization to carry some force. He observes that in such areas 'two pillars of the traditional ethic appear to have broken down: the husband-wife family and regular full-time work' (1987b, p. 37). This 'traditional ethic' with its stress on social obligations constituted the main element of the traditional understanding of social citizenship. As we noted in chapter 1, some aspects of these patterns and obligations were also tacitly assumed and taken for granted by the dominant paradigm of social citizenship, in spite of its explicit emphasis on social rights.

In this chapter we have briefly reviewed some of the generally agreed aspects of contemporary American poverty and its correlates (also see Eberstadt 1988; Handler and Hasenfeld 1990). We are now in a better position to consider the challenge contemporary poverty poses to the dominant paradigm of social citizenship, particularly as interpreted and 'explained' by Right political ideologies. The Right's ideological challenge, its alternative vision of social citizenship and its conception of the social policies necessary to realize this vision are the main concerns of the discussion in part II, to which we now turn.

PART II

The Neoconservative Challenge: Social Duties and Cultural Change

4
Neoconservatism, Citizenship and Welfare

I

Citizenship and the Right: Neoconservatism and the New Right

1   The New Right, Neoconservatism and citizenship

The most important ideological challenge to the dominant paradigm of social citizenship in recent decades has undoubtedly come from the Right. Unlike the critiques and alternatives promoted by the 'new social movements' the Right has been in a position to put its analysis into practice in a number of Western nations in the 1980s through the governments of Reagan, Thatcher and others.

As with any political perspective, the Right exists as an alliance and a debate; that is, it contains within it a range of distinctive viewpoints and also a range of contradictory positions on particular issues. For my purposes in this book, we can identify 'radical' and 'mainstream' Right positions. The former can also be referred to as New Right or 'neo-liberal'; the latter can also be referred to as 'Neoconservative' (which in turn contains centrist 'sceptical liberal' and more radical 'social libertarian' wings). Briefly, the difference between 'radical' and 'mainstream' Right positions hinges on the degree of antagonism they show towards the idea and role of the state and government *vis-à-vis* civil society and the capitalist economy. Broadly

speaking, the radicals are very antagonistic, while the mainstream are more tolerant, and this difference is particularly
marked along the same lines regarding the state's welfare role.

In this and the following chapters I am mainly concerned with
mainstream Right or Neoconservative views. I will outline the
main differences *within* the mainstream in chapters 5 and 6. In
this chapter I will present an initial assessment of the relevance
of the Right to the kind of interests in the analysis of citizenship
in general and social citizenship in particular I am pursuing in
this book.

First, then, the 'radical' Right. The 'radical' (New) Right hold
strong libertarian views on the rights of the individual (e.g.
Nozick 1980), on free market capitalism (e.g. Hayek 1973, 1986;
Friedman 1962, 1980) or on both. Their support for the primacy
of human freedom over all other values leads them to be
profoundly antagonistic to the notion that government and the
state ought to have much of a role in human affairs. In Nozick's
moralistic terms any state beyond the most minimal is morally
illegitimate because it cannot but infringe people's 'natural'
rights (Nozick 1980; Paul 1982). (Oddly by such rights he means
almost exclusively people's *civil* rights to life and property,
rights which of course are not 'natural' but socially constructed;
Roche 1988b). In the more political economic terms of Hayek
and Friedman, a more-than-minimal state threatens modern
society with both 'the road to serfdom' and economic stagnation.

From the point of view of an interest in the theory and
practice of citizenship, radical New Right views are of limited
relevance since these views seem to have no use for and little
understanding of the idea of citizenship. *Social* rights and social
citizenship are, of course, anathema for the likes of Nozick. But
in his and other New Right views *political* rights and the idea of
citizenship in a political community seem to fare little better,
along with the general idea of moral obligation. 'Natural rights'
are apparently 'duty-free' and imply no corresponding 'Natural
duties'. All of this is ironical and self-defeating, since it is only
from political citizenship and within a political community that
the legal framework of the free society the New Right claim to
admire can be built, defended and improved, while the notion
of 'duty-free' 'natural rights' is simply an egoistic delusion.
Extreme New Right perspectives have actually been of little

practical political relevance – even to politicians who admire them – because of their essential unreality and utopianism. Given all this, I intend to concentrate in this and the following chapters on the more *mainstream* Right and Neoconservative positions. They are more relevant to the analysis of social citizenship not least because of their considerable political influence on American, British and some European nations' approaches to social policy since the early 1980s.

As we noted in chapter 2, the mainstream Right (e.g. Levitas 1986; King 1987) and the new social movements (e.g. Scott 1990) all share certain features from the point of view of the analysis of citizenship. In different ways, as far as the *nature* of citizenship goes, each present radical challenges to the dominant paradigm's emphasis on *social rights*. Thus they each require us in different ways to reassess the nature and place of *social duties* in our conception of the nature of citizenship and of the moral community it implies (also Pierson 1991, chs 2, 3). (It is also notable that, like the new social movements, the New Right has a relatively inarticulate and ambivalent *concept* of citizenship, as we shall see.)

As against this similarity, as far as assumptions about the social structural *context* of citizenship go, the mainstream Right, unlike the new social movements, has relatively little new to offer. For instance, it has no challenge comparable in its radicalism to ecology's critiques of (1) the effects of the industrial economic form, and (2) the irrelevance of national territorialism and of isolated nation state power to the scale of modernity's ecological problems (e.g. Porritt 1984). Rather, with some tactical reservations and differences of emphasis, on the whole the mainstream Right tends to share many dominant paradigm assumptions about citizenship's social context. For instance, allowing for rhetorical difference, the capitalism whose virtues it lauds is effectively conceived in national terms (e.g. Gilder 1982; Berger 1987), without taking much account of contemporary structural economic changes. It undoubtedly attacks the welfare state (e.g. Murray 1984), and would like to see it cut back or otherwise transformed. Nonetheless, ultimately it tends to assume the existence and value of a comparable system of welfare pluralism and national functionism to that assumed by the dominant paradigm.

In the mainstream Right's vision, civil society (e.g. common cultural values, capitalism, voluntary action and the family) clearly has much more of a leading role than does government. But even in some of the most extreme *laissez-faire* versions, government is tacitly recognized to have at least important regulatory roles. In any case the nation state and the various infrastructures it provides for national markets and a national civil society are all taken for granted in most versions of New Right and Neoconservative political and social analysis.

So Right perspectives are important in the challenges they present to the dominant paradigm assumptions about the *nature* of citizenship, social rights and the welfare state. But they tend to be less challenging on wider structural and *contextual* issues. With this in mind we can next consider the main positions within the mainstream Right, or Neoconservatism; in particular their critiques of the American welfare state will be considered in section II below. We will then be in a better position to consider their various diagnoses and policy solutions for the 'limit case' of social citizenship, namely poverty.

2   Neoconservatism and citizenship

What I am calling the 'mainstream' Right position is probably best represented by American Neoconservatism (Roche 1990b, 1992a). This position has been promoted in a number of in-fluential writings by leading American sociologists and social policy analysts associated with academic journals such as *The Public Interest* and privately funded think-tanks such as the American Enterprise Institute (Ehrenreich 1987). Their principal concern is with the reform of social policy and of the American welfare state (such as it is) in terms of various values of 'civil society', particularly individual liberty and autonomy, family and capitalism. Unlike the radical New Right, few of them are willing to press their critique of the welfare state to the point of wishing to see it abolished in all of its aspects. On the contrary, most of them concede an important role for government, whether at the local or national level, and for public expenditure in the welfare field.

American political sociologist Seymour M. Lipset attributes

the term 'Neoconservatism' to the Left social policy analyst Michael Harrington (1963, 1984) and considers that it refers to 'a loose network of a few individuals and journals' (quoted Walker 1986). Other commentators, noting its political influence in the 1980s, see it as more organized and conspiratorial (Ehrenreich 1987). However, as far as the major writers go, 'Neoconservatism' is evidently a fairly loose and flexible label for a range of views containing, as we will see in chapters 5 and 6, considerable differences of emphasis and even contradictions.

Neoconservatives range from 'sceptical liberals' on the more collectivist 'left' flank of the position, to 'social libertarians' on the more individualist and market-oriented 'right' flank. Many notable Neoconservatives (e.g. the sociologists Daniel Bell and Nathan Glazer, and the policy analyst Charles Murray), are people who had held 'dominant paradigm'-type views about American social policy in the 1960s, the 'Great Society' period of major anti-poverty and compensatory education programmes. Over the 1970s they lost the faith because of what they saw as the failure of welfare policy, thereafter coming to very different conclusions about the courses and solutions of poverty and other social problems. Daniel Bell, Nathan Glazer, the influential Democratic senator Daniel Moynihan and others tend to take a 'sceptical liberal' position. They are cautious about the purposes and limits of government action and spending but willing to argue for it where needed and where effective, while Charles Murray, along with the sociologist and policy analyst George Gilder and other notable writers, takes a more clearly 'social libertarian' line. They are basically opposed to much state welfare spending. But they are also aware of the social and cultural conditions necessary for both the effective operation of the market and for social order. In addition, they are aware of the more-than-minimal and residual relevance of government to the provision and support of those conditions. This distinguishes them from extreme quasi-anarchist libertarians of the Nozick type.

Intellectual movements need various fora for debate, particularly journals. An important forum for Neoconservatives' views and debates has been the journal *The Public Interest* founded by Daniel Bell and edited by Nathan Glazer and Irving Kristol. Such movements also need publicity and political influence, and with the advent of the Reagan presidency they got both. Gilder attracted some attention early on with his book *Wealth and Poverty* (1982), a vigorous defence of capitalism's wealth-creating character. In this work he also criticized the role of welfare policy as both a drag on capitalism and a failure as an anti-poverty instrument. Subsequently Murray attracted even more attention with a similar message in his book *Losing Ground* (1984). This provided an apparently thoroughgoing assessment of the effectiveness of American social policy in the period 1950–80, against a review of time-series data on poverty, employment, incomes, education and family structure. The study is actually less convincing than it at first appears, since Murray notably disregards data which he seems to be aware would disturb his picture, such as that indicating the success of social policy in respect of the elderly. Overall, he concluded that social policy and state social spending were failing to solve the problems they were addressing, that they were often doing more harm than good and that they needed rolling back. We will consider this analysis further in section II below.

More recently Neoconservatives have focused particularly on work policy and family policy. Following President Reagan's unsuccessful attempts to mandate more coercive forms of 'workfare' policy in 1984–5, Lawrence Mead published his major review of the development of American work and welfare policy since the 1960s. Its title and theme bluntly challenged the American 'liberal' version of the dominant paradigm of social citizenship: *Beyond Entitlement: the Social Obligations of Citizenship* (1986). The following year, with President Reagan announcing his intention to 'finally break the poverty trap' (Novak 1987b, p. 1), and Senator Moynihan and others promoting new Family Support legislation (Moynihan 1989), Michael Novak edited an influential report on family policy by a large group of Neoconservatives entitled *The New Consensus on Family and Welfare* (1987). We will consider these and other contributions to the debate on work and family policy and the social obligations of citizenship in the following chapter.

These and other significant studies (e.g. Gilbert 1983; Butler and Kondratas 1987; Glazer 1988) are some of the major contributions of the Neoconservative movement to debates on American social policy in the 1980s. The debate has been joined by a number of notable Left analysts critical of Neoconservatism (e.g. Harrington 1984; Piven and Cloward 1987; Block 1987b; Wilson 1987). It is also worth noting that American Neoconservatives have had some influence outside their country, notably in Britain in British New Right and Thatcher government circles in the 1980s. For instance, Gilder has links with the British New Right think-tank, the Institute of Economic Affairs, who helped him prepare the British edition of *Wealth and Poverty*. Murray has been interviewed at length by the British social work journal *Community Care* and has published an account of what he sees as the development of a British 'underclass' in the *Sunday Times* (Philpott 1988; Murray 1989). He has also contributed to another British New Right think-tank, the Centre for Policy Studies, which organized a conference for ministers and senior Conservative Party figures on 'The crime culture' in May 1990 (James 1990). In addition, American Neoconservative work policy and family policy approaches have been influential for a number of years on British government and Tory Party views (e.g. Heseltine 1989, also Segalman and Marsland 1989; Flynn 1989), increasingly so in recent years. We now need to consider the mainstream New Right or Neoconservative critique of American social policy, beginning with a brief overview of the American welfare state and American approaches to social citizenship.

II

American social citizenship and the Neoconservative critique

1   Social citizenship and the American welfare state

In the dominant paradigm of modern social citizenship the appropriate institutional context of citizenship is understood to be a welfare state operating within a welfare pluralism. This pluralism is produced and sustained by the state, culture (e.g. family) and capitalist economy operating as a relatively integrated 'national functional' system. Obviously various distinctive versions of this paradigm are possible; we briefly considered

British Left collectivist and liberal versions in chapter 1. In addition, each advanced Western nation has evidently developed a distinctive pattern of welfare state institutions, with distinctive legitimations and with distinctive philosophies underpinning them. Nonetheless, the main types of underlying philosophy, such as British welfare statism, European social democracy and American (social) 'liberalism' have a lot in common, as do the various welfare institutions they legitimize. National functionalism and state welfare can be sought for and achieved in different ways, but from the point of view of my argument in this book they are best understood as variations on the common themes of the dominant paradigm.

Having said all of that, it nonetheless remains true that the USA has many unique features of history and geography, of economic and political power and position, which set it aside from other Western nations. In a recent analysis of this American 'exceptionalism' Daniel Bell (1989) draws attention to America's unique mix of attitudes to the state and civil society and to the general relevance for late twentieth-century Western societies of America's strong 'civil society' traditions. Consistent with this, American welfare state institutions, and also popular attitudes both to these institutions and to social citizenship, have some distinctive features which should be noted.

Equal citizenship in America has largely been fought for in political-military (Revolution, Civil War) and politico-civil (Black and other civil rights) arenas and struggles. Equal citizenship is understood to be inconsistent with involuntary poverty, and state interventions to tackle such poverty have received popular support. But equal citizenship is deemed to be consistent with the considerable economic inequalities and status differences generated by American capitalism. The American Dream became a reality for generations of immigrant poor. The promise of American capitalism (of economic success, social mobility and personal freedom – in a word welfare), in return for hard work, was largely kept.

Any state welfare commitment which developed in this context was always likely to be seen as a relatively residual system, within an explicit welfare pluralism. It was to be seen essentially as a safety net, backing up the operations of labour

market, voluntary action and the family. And it was strongly
limited both by capitalist interests and popular interests, particularly at state and local level, in controlling the powers and
tax-take of central government. Thus in America conceptions of
citizenship have tended to remain centred on political and civil
rights. The legitimacy of *social* rights has tended to be grounded
in their residual character (as rights to assistance in times of
involuntary poverty) rather than in any more ambitious understanding (as in Europe) of their potentially egalitarian role. Such
residual social rights do not provide a very clear or developed
basis for a strong and popular conception of 'social citizenship'.

Nonetheless, such a conception of social citizenship does exist
in modern America, but it is founded on notions of *duty* rather
than *rights*. American individualism stresses individual responsibility (personal duties of self-care, self-control and self-
development; duties of accountability to others for personal
actions etc.) and the social obligations of membership (i.e. the
obligations traditionally required by membership in the social
institutions which were understood to foster and finance individualism, namely the family and the labour market). As
Mead puts it, 'American equality requires equal obligations as
well as rights' (1986, p. 238). In Britain and Europe the notion
of social citizenship has meant more to the political Left and
liberal centre because of the assumed egalitatian implications of
strong notions of social rights. Thus America is something of an
exception in this respect, as in others. While there is some
recognition of the strategic political importance of the concept
of social citizenship on the American Left (e.g. Walzer 1985;
Ehrenreich 1987), the main advocates and users of the notion
have been Neoconservatives (e.g. Mead 1986; Novak 1987b).
What is involved in the duty-based notion of social citizenship
was clearly expressed by Mead.

> The following seem to be the main social obligations of adults in
> the United States today:
>
> Work in available jobs for heads of families, unless aged or
> disabled, and for other adult members of families that are needy.
>
> Contributing all that one can to the support of one's family (but
> public assistance seems acceptable if parents work and cannot
> earn enough for support).

Fluency and literacy in English, whatever one's native tongue.

Learning enough in school to be employable.

Law-abidingness, meaning both obedience to law and a more generalised respect for the rights of others.

Work for the employable is the clearest social obligation. (1986, pp. 242–3)

Mead is aware that these sorts of duties might be said to be 'private' rather than 'public' matters of the kind normally associated with citizenship. Nonetheless, in his view they *are* informal social duties of citizenship because 'Americans seem to regard them as mandatory.' Finally, his view of their place in American society is worth noting: 'The role of the social obligations is to balance the array of social rights guaranteed by government' (ibid., p. 246). This indicates one of the main lines of the Neoconservative critique of the American welfare state. It concerns the effects of the development of this 'array of social rights' (i.e. the welfare state) on the 'balance' between rights and obligations, that is on the character of contemporary American social citizenship. But first let us briefly consider what this array of rights is and what it amounts to.

In his history of American welfare Michael Katz (1986) gives an account of the long and fraught process, running 'from the poorhouse to the present' involved in the building of what he designates as America's 'semi-welfare state'. That is, as a system, the American welfare state is relatively structurally 'incomplete' when compared with many Western European welfare states. The 'incompleteness' is clear enough in areas such as health services, child benefits and services and, in general, in the universality of social rights and the national character of the organization and funding of welfare services in Europe as compared with the USA (e.g. Friedmann et al. 1987).

The American welfare state is a patchwork of insurance payment, cash assistance and in-kind benefits organized and financed at a number of levels (mainly organized at state and local level and financed at federal level) (Leiby 1978; Weir et al. 1988; Magill 1989; Handler and Hasenfeld 1990). It involves a very large scale of public expenditure. According to one authority in 1980 this amounted to about $500 billion (including education). This represented around a fifth of US GNP and over half of all federal expenditure (Morris 1987). It is essentially a two-tier system. The upper tier is based on contributory and insurance principles; it provides unemployment, work injury and total disability cover for those of working age and generates pensions and health care (Medicare) for retired ex-contributors. The lower tier is based on public assistance or poor-relief principles, that is on relief of the needs of those with no or low income, principally the elderly, the totally disabled and single-parent families. People in these categories can receive both cash assistance (through two programmes, Supplemental Security Income (SSI) and Aid to Families with Dependent Children (AFDC)) and also in-kind benefits (such food stamps and medical and housing assistance).

Although the overall scale of the system is large, it should be noted that the upper tier consumes by far the greatest share of funding. For instance, one assessment of total expenditure on the elderly in 1980 suggests that people in the upper tier received $178 billion while people in the lower tier received $13.7 billion, the comparable figures for the totally disabled being $20 billion as against $12 billion (Ellwood and Summers 1986). Cash assistance for poor single-parent families through AFDC (a target of much criticism by Neoconservatives, as we shall see), came to $12.5 billion or under 0.5 per cent of GNP in 1980 (ibid.).

The two tiers are further distinguished by the differing incentives they provide for achieving or increasing earned income. The insurance-based upper tier rewards such efforts with increased benefits, while the poor-relief lower tier operates a 'poverty trap' mechanism of reducing benefits for every increase in income above a given level. Finally, those in the insurance tier benefit from the 'fiscal and occupational welfare states' to which Titmuss first drew attention in Britain (chapter 1 above) and by which governments among other things provide tax concessions to private occupational health and welfare schemes. Robert Morris suggests that these benefits 'now contribute more to our social support system than does government', that they 'tend to go to the highest paid workers in a few major industries', and that they tend to 'unbalance the safety net system' of the American welfare state (Morris 1987, p. 88).

This system has been growing and taking shape for more than 50 years, beginning with 'Progressivism' and President Roosevelt's New Deal policies in the 1930s (e.g. Leiby 1978, chs 12–14; Anderson 1978; Piven and Cloward 1971, 1987; Garfinkel and McLanahan 1986, ch. 4; Weir et al. 1988; Handler and Hasenfeld 1990 chs 2, 3). These poor relief and public works policies were designed to counter the poverty and destitution produced by unemployment in the Great Depression and they included the introduction of social insurance and also of AFDC (initially intended only for widows). This system was expanded massively a generation later in President Johnson's Great Society policies in the 1960s. These were designed in response to Black demands and rebellion to win the 'war on poverty'.

Growth continued until the early 1980s and President Reagan's 'war on welfare' (Bremner 1986; Katz 1986; Carballo and Bane 1984; Garfinkel and MacLanahan 1986, ch. 5; Block 1987b; Hasenfeld and Hoefer 1989; Handler and Hasenfeld 1990 chs 4, 5). Reagan's policies succeeded in cutting AFDC, disability programmes and other such bottom tier relief in the early 1980s. But during the 1980s the trend for overall social expenditure nonetheless continued to rise in Reagan's America, as indeed it did in Thatcher's Britain (Brindle 1990c; Pierson 1991, p. 173). In the case of the USA this was because of the expansion of the upper tier of the system, namely because of increases in tax-subsidized and transfer payment-subsidized social insurance programmes (Morris 1987, p. 86; Magill 1989, table 3, p. 357).

2   The Neoconservative critique of the American welfare state

What do mainstream Right or Neoconservative social analysts and commentators make of America's 'semi-welfare' state? For Neoconservatives the American welfare state is a problem for three distinctive sorts of reasons. They claim, first, that it is positively *dysfunctional in economic terms* (i.e. it acts as a drag on the capitalist economy and this reduces the welfare generated by labour and consumer markets); second, that it has had only limited *welfare effects* (i.e. that it fails to reduce poverty); and, third, that it is positively *dysfunctional in welfare terms* (i.e. it actually contributes to poverty and social problems, and in particular that it tends to cause the growth of an 'underclass').

Well into the Reagan presidency Charles Murray (1984) published his widely read and penetrating Neoconservative critique of American social policy. This presented an articulate rationale for the kind of welfare expenditure cuts Reagan had attempted in the first years of his first term (1980–82). But it also appeared to provide an intellectual licence for a further more thoroughgoing assault on the welfare system during his second presidency. Murray took the extreme or radical 'welfare dysfunction' view and we will discuss this view later.

But first it is important to note the essential ambivalence of most Neoconservatives towards state welfare. This holds for supporters of the 'economic dysfunctions' and 'limited welfare effects' views (and also as we will see later, even for the 'welfare dysfunctions' views). Their ambivalence can be related to their diversity of views about social citizenship. We will now briefly consider this ambivalence in supporters of the 'economic dysfunctions' and 'limited welfare effects' views (1) and (2) below), and also what this tells us about moderate Neoconservative views of social citizenship ((3) below). We can then turn to consider the more extreme position of 'welfare dysfunction' exemplified by Murray's critique in a little more detail ((4) below).

i 'Economic dysfunctions' Since a good deal of my discussion in chapter 5 but also in part III concerns the relation between welfare and capitalism I will reserve more detailed comment on the economic dysfunctions thesis until then. However, in brief, the thesis holds that welfare-state spending raises taxation and inflation while reducing investment, work incentives, entrepreneurial incentives and economic growth. Nonetheless, it should be noted that as strong a supporter of this thesis as George Gilder gives capitalism whatever credit there is to be had for the welfare state, seeing it as 'the burly offspring of an essentially capitalist idea' (Gilder 1982, p. 114), namely the idea of insurance. He sees 'an important role in principle for state welfare' in what he calls 'the capitalist welfare state' (ibid., p. 111). And although this role is only beneficial, up to a point (which in his view most current welfare states have transgressed, ibid., pp. xxii, 115), nonetheless his position is that 'All civilized societies offer welfare programs as a safety net' (ibid., p. 24). However, somewhat inconsistently with his critique of the welfare state and for reasons to be explored in the next chapter, Gilder also advocates the introduction of a universal non-means-tested system of child or family allowances in the USA (ibid., p. 24). One commentator, noting the inconsistency, has observed that ironically this 'would represent the greatest expansion of the American welfare state since Medicare' (Carlson 1987, p. 35), one of the major measures of the much criticized Great Society era.

ii 'Limited welfare effects' Most Neoconservatives seem reluctant to take the view that the welfare state *overall* is a failure. Rather they tend to see it as having produced successes as well as failures, and as having intrinsic *limits* within which it performs satisfactorily and outside which it does not.

An acknowledged welfare success is with policy for the elderly (Novak 1987b; Moynihan 1989). Thus Daniel Moynihan claims 'The social-welfare system enacted in this century has all but eliminated poverty among the aged' (1989, p. 22). Another success is the reduction in long-term infant mortality (Novak 1987b, pp. 6–7), while, as we saw in chapter 3, the main failures have been with the growth of poverty among single mothers and children, black single mothers in particular, and among black youth. Moynihan argues that the single-mothers problem is a relatively new 'post-industrial society' problem. He believes that it is unresponsive to a welfare-state policy based on industrial society assumptions about family. In the face of the combination of familial and drug problems Moynihan acknowledges, 'I do not know what to do' (1989, p. 26). Echoing Nathan Glazer (1988, 1990), he notes that there are limits to what it is possible to expect state social policy to achieve. Irving Kristol argues in a similar vein:

'The basic achievements of the New Deal plus a few of the achievements of the Great Society will endure. [Thus] most

Americans support a welfare safety net. [But] There are a lot of people who are simply self-destructive. . . . I don't know what to do about them. Nor does anyone else.' (quoted Scott, 1987b)

Glazer rejects the idea that the welfare state has been a total failure: 'There are certain aspects which are universally accepted and unshaken' (quoted Scott, 1987b). In his view, the accession of Ronald Reagan to the presidency represented the 'victory of a conservatism that accepted the lineaments of the welfare state' (1988, p. 57). In particular what we earlier saw as the upper (contributory) tier of the American system, (and what Glazer 1988 calls Welfare I) 'still expands and is sacrosanct' (1988, p. 170). Evidently the reverse is true for the bottom poor-relief residual tier ('Welfare II') 'which is in increasing disrepute' (ibid., p. 170). In general his view is that 'There is no escape in a modern developed nation from the major social programs that were developed under Franklin D. Roosevelt and expanded in the years since then – social security, unemployment insurance, some form of health insurance, which will undoubtedly be expanded to cover populations not yet covered' (ibid., p. 58). (This is particularly so for 'The low-income working poor without job-related benefit' (ibid., p. 50; also his 1982).) In Glazer's view the role of the state in welfare is 'crucial' (ibid., p. 139), but there are essential *limits* to this role and it must be developed in partnership with the various non-state welfare sectors (also his 1990; and Gilbert 1983, ch. 7).

iii Moderate Neoconservatism and social citizenship Moderate Neoconservatives evidently experience considerable ambivalence about the American welfare state's effectiveness and also about what to do about those areas where it has apparently failed. What implications does this have for Neoconservatives' views of social citizenship? Clearly they concede and even endorse citizens' social rights and the principle of substantial assistance by government in a range of areas. But, reflecting the two distinct tiers of the welfare system, moderate Neoconservatives reserve their endorsement for the upper tier. This is because it appears to require a recognition and exercise of personal responsibility and also of an obligation to contribute in order to justify one's own and one's family's current or subsequent welfare benefits. It embodies a principle of 'just deserts'.

This is in line with the picture of American 'social obligations of citizenship' drawn by Mead and which we noted earlier (see also Morris 1987). One of the problems with the bottom tier of the system for Neoconservatives is that it appears to concede social rights exclusively on the basis of need, with no reference to personal responsibility, citizens' social obligations or the principle of 'just deserts'. The bottom tier has also been ineffective and unable even to slow the growth of some forms of poverty, while in addition to that there is the suspicion by radical Neoconservatives that the bottom tier's failures are *caused* by itself, that is caused by its effect of undermining of the social obligations of citizenship. It is to this welfare dysfunction critique that we now turn.

iv Radical Neoconservatism, 'welfare dysfunctions' and 'welfare classes' Murray's (1984) Neoconservative critique of American social policy from 1950 to 1980 gave voice and intellectual support to a number of beliefs long and widely held on the Right of American politics. The main belief was that the growth of the welfare state has *caused* a growth of poverty and in particular that it has caused the growth of crime, social disorganization and a dependent 'underclass' in the black ghettos of America's major cities. This had been articulated earlier by the radical Neoconservative sociologist George Gilder (1982) but Murray made the case more systematically.

A related belief was that, in spite of its alleged ineffectiveness, economic costs and the social costs of the damage it was doing, the welfare state had become a self-perpetuating and self-aggrandizing institution. It had become the vehicle and instrument of a new class of welfare bureaucrats and professionals, academics and politicians, with a vested interest in a 'big state' and little interest in capitalism, impervious to criticism and unaware of, or indifferent to, the real consequences of their activities. This sort of view had first been developed by sociologists in the 1970s looking at changes in modern social structure. Indeed a leading sociologist, Daniel Bell, later to become identified with Neoconservatism, had proposed that such a new knowledge and service class could be expected to develop as modern industrial societies moved towards a 'post-industrial' form in his classic study of 'post-industrial society' in 1973. However, the nature, role and prospects of such a class seemed to Bell to be more benign and generally positive in the early 1970s than they were to appear, later in the 1980s, to Neoconservative sociologists like Peter and Brigitte Berger (1983, ch. 2), and policy analysts like Murray (1984, ch. 3). For Murray this 'intelligentsia' (ibid., p. 42) created the egalitarian 'elite wisdom' of the Great Society social policies of the 1960s. His argument is that one such welfare state-dependent social class, located both in the middle and at the top of American society, unwittingly helped to create another such dependent class, the underclass located firmly at the bottom of that society (Ehrenreich 1987).

We have already noted the essentially two-tiered structure of America's welfare state and the differences of scale between the tiers. We have also already noted the ambivalent assessment of the system by moderate Neoconservatives, with most of them strongly supporting the larger upper tier. This helps to explain a deceptive character to Murray's account and critique. He presents himself as addressing the welfare system as a whole. It is a whole system whose massive expansion is allegedly planned and administered by the liberal intelligentsia from the 1960s through to the 1980s.

As Murray points out, from 1950 to 1980 public spending on what he chooses to call 'the core programs' of federal social welfare expenditure (measured in constant dollars) increased massively, for example by factors of 6 in health services, 13 in public assistance (AFDC etc.), 24 in education, 27 in social insurance and 129 in housing. It is against the peaks and troughs in time-series data about these sorts of expenditures that Murray plots movements in other social problem indicators (such as poverty, crime, school drop-out rates, unemployment and family structure; see ch. 3 above). Correlations between movements of the former and the latter data over time allow him to infer a causal relation between the two sets of factors they measure. The upshot of these analyses is certainly that social problems have increased in spite of massive welfare spending increases. Murray argues that alternative causes, 'The easy hypotheses – the economy, changes in demographics, the effects of Vietnam or Watergate or racism – fail as explanations' (ibid., p. 9). He therefore feels justified in proposing increased state welfare spending as the prime cause of the increases in social problems. We will consider alternative explanations later (e.g. ch. 7 below). But first we can note some weaknesses in his general picture and his policy conclusions.

In spite of his expansive conception of social policy Murray makes it clear that he is nonetheless not going to discuss the elderly in his book, only those of working age and their children: 'Social policy for the elderly is a completely different topic, demanding a full treatment of its own' (ibid., p. 59). There is a good reason for this. As noted earlier, other Neoconservatives concede that social policy to abolish poverty among the elderly is a relative success story. It does not fit Murray's model of 'losing ground' and state culpability, so he simply leaves it out. This is in spite of the fact that it is by far the single biggest sector in American social policy and social spending.

Once again, bearing in mind the scope of Murray's original conception of social policy his conclusions are interesting. His most radical proposal is aimed at tackling the problem of welfare dependency, poverty and the underclass. It is one of a number of 'thought experiments' he undertakes in the book and one he recognizes to be politically unrealistic.

> Our final and most ambitious thought experiment consists of scrapping the entire federal welfare and income-support structure for working-aged persons, including AFDC, Medicare, Food Stamps, Unemployment Insurance, Workers Compensation, subsidized housing, disability insurance, and the rest. It would leave the working-aged person with no recourse whatsoever except the jobmarket, family members, friends, and public or private locally funded services. It is the Alexandrian solution: cut the knot for there is no way to untie it. (ibid., pp. 227–8)

This would effectively take out the bottom tier, together with a significant part of the upper tier of the America welfare system, and it would undoubtedly save a lot of tax-payers' money (also Rothbard 1982). Yet Murray has nothing to say about the major and successful spending sector of support for the elderly and makes no proposal to cut it, while he proposes no cuts at all in the massive spending sector of education, merely proposing an organizational change towards a voucher system. Finally Murray has nothing to say about the massive and relatively invisible fiscal and occupational welfare states (see chs 1 and 2 above). His 'radicalism' then is in considerable measure mere rhetoric. The state-financed welfare/educational systems which he takes for granted and would protect remain vastly expensive in absolute terms and their costs are continually growing.

To tolerate or protect educational, pensions and other public spending areas as he does is certainly not to align himself with the Nozickean *laissez-faire* New Right, to say the least. To do so is, on the contrary, to implicitly condone high and rising levels of state social expenditure, irrespective of whatever savings might be made as a result of 'scrapping the *entire* federal welfare and income-support' programmes he selects. The welfare state might be rolled back to a certain extent, but only to grow again, and to 'lose more ground'! On the other hand, what positive approach is he recommending to American citizens to tackle the problems of poverty and the underclass? Along with other apparently 'radical' Neoconservatives it would appear that ultimately Murray has little else to offer but literally the rhetoric of moral reform, in particular the clarion call back to the traditional work ethic and family ethic, the rhetoric of social citizenship *as* social obligation. We now need to explore some of the most important aspects of Neoconservatism's rhetoric of moral reform and its diagnoses and cures for contemporary poverty and the underclass in greater detail, first in relation to the problems of the modern family (ch. 5) and secondly in relation to the problem of unemployment (ch. 6).

5
Reforming Social Citizenship I: Neoconservatism and Family Policy in the USA

In chapter 3 we reviewed some of the long-term trends in American family structure and family problems. The general picture is clear enough: divorce, illegitimate birth and single-parent families are all growing long-term and they tend to be strongly associated with poverty. The same sort of trends are evident in most other advanced Western societies, (e.g. Roll 1989 and Room et al. 1989 on Europe; Wicks and Kiernan 1990 on Britain). While there is little disagreement about such facts, and that they effectively amount to a 'breakdown' of the 'traditional' family pattern, assessments of this situation differ greatly. So on the one hand many feminists and Leftists welcome the apparent reduction in male influence over women and the achievement of greater female independence that this breakdown implies and they tend to favour policies to cope with its costs. On the other hand New Rightists and Neoconservatives, adopting what we can call a pro-family or 'familist' approach, lament and criticize the breakdown and look for policies to halt and reverse it (Roche 1990b). In this chapter we will explore Neoconservatives' diagnoses of the *causes* of the breakdown of the family (section II below), together with their proposed policy *cures* for the problem and its associated problems of poverty and second-class citizenship (III below).

However, to set the scene for this, it is first necessary to outline some of the main features of Neoconservatism's assumptions about the general relationship between family and citizenship. In modern society these particularly relate to the role of the traditional nuclear family as a social basis for modern democratic citizenship.

I

Family, democracy and citizenship: Neoconservative perspectives

From the ancient Greeks to the present the relation between the social institutions and values of family on the one hand and of the state and politics on the other has often been seen as an uneasy, ambiguous and potentially conflictual one. In the *Republic* Plato did not trust the family to rear good rulers in the ideal state. By 'nationalizing' and communalizing the rearing of his Guardians and Philosopher Rulers he sought to eradicate the political and cultural influence of family on the polity. In *Antigone* Sophocles dramatizes the perennial potential for conflict between state and family loyalties and duties. He rightly shows us the potential sexual politics of this conflict (in the form of patriarchal power versus matriarchal morality). But the conflict also registers the perennial problems of excluding familial influence (given its association with favouritism, nepotism and corruption) from the spheres of law, politics and the state.

In the modern period – and particularly in the Western nations with their capitalist economies and ostensibly liberal democratic polities – the relationship between the familial and the political has been seen in terms of the relation between the 'private' and 'public' dimensions of social life. Thus family is seen as 'the private sphere' *par excellence* in which privacy, private space and time, private property and private personal relations are valued above all else, while politics is seen as concerned with public affairs which occur in a 'public sphere' distinct from the private sphere. But this distinction is simplistic. Law has always penetrated and helped constitute the private sphere, and the development of the welfare state has taken this 'structural politicization' of the private sphere (Roche 1987) to a qualitatively new level in the mid- and late twentieth century. Consequent on this, since the 1970s in particular, the private, the personal and the familial have become actively politicized arenas of debate and conflict. Some of the main elements in this politicization of the familial have been the feminist critique of patriarchy, and also Neoconservative pro-familism. These movements have joined issue in numerous moral and political controversies around such problems as abortion, child abuse, parental rights and so on.

Contemporary familism comes in various political and analytical hues from Neoconservative versions (below), to sociological versions (e.g. O'Neill 1987; Roche 1988a) and interestingly to feminist versions (e.g. Elshtain 1981; Roche 1988c). Most familism tends to take the line that the distinctiveness of the familial private sphere must be defended against both structural politicization by the welfare state and also active politicization by feminism and other political movements. This may appear to be an anti-political stance but Neoconservative theorists see it very differently. They see themselves as defending not only the key institution of 'civil society', but also the fundamental social institution on which a democratic state and political order depends. Paradoxically, then, although familism's attempt to defend the family from politics (and, let it be added, from many other social and cultural forces it deems to be negative) may appear to be anti-political its deeper purpose is, it is argued, very political. Family must be conserved and defended against the political in order to make the political possible. This kind of view can be seen in two of the most notable Neoconservative familist discussions, Brigitte and Peter Bergers' *The War over the Family* (1983) and Michael Novak's *The New Consensus on Family and Welfare* (1987).

For Novak 'The family is the matrix within which the citizen is well-formed or misshapen. No institution is so important, yet so easily overlooked' (1987b, p. 16); 'The family is the main incubator of the habits of free citizens' (ibid., p. xvi). Novak's conception of the American citizenship which good families foster is one that emphasizes personal responsibility and social obligations rather than rights: 'The free society must by its very nature regard each citizen as responsible, self-reliant, and self-governing . . . Only citizens able to govern themselves can fulfil the social duties inherent in a self-governing republic' (ibid., p. 4). Similarly, the Bergers point out that the idea of democracy assumes that humans in principle have an ontological potential for freedom as well as having some kind of moral right to it; the real institutions of democracy in any nation require that this potential be developed practically and in concrete individuals (1983, p. 170). Various social systems have been tried throughout history and in the twentieth century. In the Bergers' view experience categorically shows that only *one* system is capable in practice of producing *en masse* the 'self-reliant and independent-minded individuals' (ibid., p. 170) who value individual responsibility which the idea of democracy abstractly implies and which the institutions of democracy concretely require (ibid., p. 175).

This system is that of nuclear family, or as they refer to it the 'bourgeois family'. In their view this system has now become as much a characteristic of the working class as of the bourgeois class (ibid., pp. 126, 157). Thus it has the status of a common ideal for society as a whole, however much concrete family patterns may diverge from the ideal (ibid., p. 185). They emphasise that: 'The family, and specifically the bourgeois family, is the necessary social context for the emergence of the autonomous individuals who are the empirical foundation of political democracy' (ibid., p. 172). They reject the Marxist-derived critique of familial private property as an environment generating possessive individualist attitudes. From an onto-logical and psychological point of view children need to know what things and places 'belong' to them in order to define their own identities, to be secure and to be in a position to com-prehend what 'sharing' and acting 'socially' and altruistically is all about (ibid., p. 175). They also reject (ibid., p. 173) neo-Marxist-derived critiques of the repressive character of families and their alleged responsibility, on the one hand, for modernity's 'authoritarian personalities' (Critical Theory perspectives e.g. Adorno 1950) and on the other hand, for the disordered selves also characteristic of modern capitalist society (Anti-Psychiatry perspectives, e.g. Cooper 1967). By contrast the Bergers provocatively claim that it is precisely the communal and permissive child-rearing implied and advocated by these critiques of familism which can be empirically shown to be the principal sources of authoritarianism and personality problems in modern society.

The Bergers argue that democracy depends on a number of social conditions, among them the existence and reproduction of self-reliant and responsible individuals; a certain degree of moral consensus about the society's basic values (ibid., pp. 175–6); the existence of elements of continuity and havens of personal stability in a changing social order (ibid., p. 177); and social institutions which bridge the cultural pluralism democracy encourages (ibid., pp. 184–5). In their view the traditional family structure and ideal is the major, and in some instances the only, social institution which has all of these characteristics and effects. They conclude: 'Historically, the bourgeois family preceded what we know as democracy . . . (It could) survive under non-democratic or even totalitarian polities . . . (But) we doubt whether democracy could survive the bourgeois family' (ibid., p. 178). Indeed the Bergers give the bourgeois family credit for supporting much more than democracy. They see it as the primary humanizing, socializing and morality-engendering agency in modern society, a foundation of modern civility and civilization. It is in their view inextricably involved in the long process of modernization. It has been a 'motor of modernisation' (ibid., p. 105) generative of much of modernity's rationalization and individualization processes. Because of its prominent role and basic functions for democracy and modernity they believe that 'the future of modernity is very much linked to the future of the family' (ibid., p. 99).

What does this familism imply for the Neoconservative conception of citizenship in general and social citizenship in particular? It implies that the private sphere of the family is *not* best construed – as it tends to be from most other political perspectives – as a quasi-public arena in which citizens equipped with civil and political rights exchange and conflict with each other, mobilizing state authority and resources where possible to do so. Rather, the family *incubates* citizen potential; it incubates people capable of becoming citizens and of acting like this in the public sphere. On this view, then, the public sphere, with its relatively formal citizenship is better left outside the family door (albeit to the limited extent that it can be in the modern world of intrusive forms of law and state authority; e.g. Habermas 1987 on 'juridification' and 'colonization'; Donzelot 1980).

On the other hand *within* the private sphere of family life family members have commonly understood traditional rights and obligations in respect of each other. These can be understood as informal forms of social citizenship. The Neoconservative conception of the family's relationship to citizenship, then, involves the following ideas. First, it involves distinguishing between informal social citizenship and (relatively) formalized civil/political citizenship. Secondly, it involves understanding social citizenship as the project which cultivates the familial sphere and which helps to defend it against the incursions and demands of civil/political citizenship, politics and the state. Thirdly, it involves understanding the exercise of social citizenship in the family as one of the main prerequisites for civil/political citizenship. So while social citizenship may appear to be a- or anti-political its deeper nature and purpose in modern society in relation to democracy gives it a definite, if somewhat paradoxical, political character. This exercise of social citizenship in its turn constitutes the point and purpose for the mobilization of citizens in the public realm and for political action to create pro-family state policies (III below).

Neoconservative familism, with its committed defence of and elaborate rationales for the role of the family in modern society, has emerged to counter two sorts of contemporary challenge to that role. On the one hand, at the level of ideology and politics, the 1970s saw the rise of the women's movement and of the feminist critique of familism. On the other hand, as we have seen at the level of social structure, or institutionalized patterns of behaviour, social trends began to indicate significant long-term problems with the family, amounting in many eyes to a crisis and 'breakdown' of Western society's family system. Neoconservatism's policy cures for these problems (particularly for the structural problems) derive from their diagnosis of the causes of this breakdown. It is to this diagnosis that we now turn.

II

The 'breakdown' of the family: the Neoconservative diagnosis

The 'breakdown' of the family is both a general phenomenon in American society and also appears in a concentrated form among the poor and the underclass. As we saw in chapter 3, family structure is a principal correlate or 'immediate cause' of poverty. Neoconservative approaches to explaining any behaviour, from non-work to non-marriage, tend to refer in the first instance to individual agency and individuals' decisions and psychological conditions. But, as with the problem of the breakdown of the work ethic (ch. 6 below), they are prepared to refer to *general cultural trends*, particularly to changes and (arguably) crises and breakdowns in modern collective morality. In addition of course, as we saw earlier (ch. 4), they also tend to regard the growth and influence of the state, particularly the welfare state, with considerable suspicion. They see it as having a causal influence both on general social morality (and thus indirectly on the family) and also (directly) on the family structures and values of the poor and welfare-dependent. We will look at Neoconservative accounts of the family breakdown problem firstly at the general societal level (1 below) and secondly at the level of the poor and the underclass (2 below).

1   Family breakdown and society in general

The notion of the 'breakdown' of the dominant family pattern and traditions in Western society can be conceived in two distinct ways, namely the 'loss of functions' thesis and the 'breakdown of core functions' thesis. The former has been much discussed and debated in sociology and social history and addresses the family's adaptation to the growth of *industrial* society; the latter is the focal concern for the current debate between Neoconservative familists and their opponents, and addresses the family's adaptation to the growth of *post-industrial* society. The 'breakdown of the family' in terms of the 'loss of social functions thesis' can be summarized as follows. With the rise of capitalist industrialization and then the growth of the welfare (and educational) state the family progressively lost the status it had had in pre-industrial society as an economic production unit, as an educational unit and, to a certain extent, as a welfare-providing unit. In the course of the process of modernization family structure became distinctly nuclear, specialized and functional for the needs of industrial capitalist society. It became specialized in the core personal functions of procreation, early child-rearing, the satisfaction of sexual and companionship needs, being a 'haven in a heartless world' and so on.

The 'breakdown of the family' seen from the point of view of the 'breakdown of core functions' thesis takes the story one step further. Reviewing the history of the modern family, the social historian Edward Shorter (1977) sees the emergence of the 'post-modern' family. This concept relates to the same sort of issues as those addressed by the moderate Neoconservative Daniel Moynihan (1989) with his concept of the 'post-marital' family pattern emerging in 'post-industrial' society. This involves the problem of the breakdown of the core personal functions in which the family has arguably come to specialize in the industrial era. In Western societies the family's procreation role is reducing (as birth rates slide to below replacement rate for the current population); its early child-rearing role is reducing as women continue to press into the labour market; and its various psychological and sexual roles are evidently reducing, as indicated by rising rates of divorce and single-headed family formation.

The main Neoconservative account of the 'breakdown of core functions' thesis is that of the Bergers (1983) and it runs as follows. In the view of the Bergers contemporary developments are inexplicable outside of an historical and sociological perspective on the whole process of modernization. As we saw earlier, they see family structure as being a relatively autonomous and 'active' (1983, p. 106) causal factor in capitalist and industrial modernization. They depict it variously as being a 'carrier' and 'motor' of modernization (ibid., p. 105) and as being 'both an agent and a conduit of modernisation' (ibid., p. 116). They also believe that the 'loss of functions' thesis has been exaggerated (ibid., p. 143); that is that family structure and functions were nuclear prior to industrialization and the core personal functions remain highly significant for modernity (ibid., chs 7 and 8). Nonetheless, these functions are threatened and need defending against the further current and future developments of the process of modernization. The Bergers observe: 'The family appears as the victim of the very forces that it gave (and still gives) birth to' (ibid., p. 107).

According to the Bergers' analysis, modernization at the level of collective consciousness and culture consists of the two processes of rationalization (e.g. secularization, bureaucratization, scientization etc.) and individualization (presenting abstract and socially decontextualized identities to people etc.). Modernity is threatened by two 'disintegrative developments' which arise from the modernization process itself and from responses to it, and which have been articulated culturally and politically by sections of the middle class (ibid., p. 126). These developments, which the Bergers call 'hyper-modernization' and 'counter-modernization', involve an attack on and an undermining of the common (and otherwise in their view reasonable and defensible) belief in the legitimacy of the family and the functionality of its role for modern individuals and societies. If they remain uncontested they threaten modern society with 'decadence'. Decadence is defined not as a disease of the social organism but as a situation of inauthenticity and nihilism. This is a situation of collective hypocrisy in which members of a society hypocritically claim to believe in values (here family ideals) which they know no longer have any actual influence on their behaviour (ibid., p. 131).

'Hyper-modernization' involves 'the radicalisation of modern themes to the point where the earlier fabric of bourgeois society can no longer hold them' (ibid., p. 118). Rationalization and individualization have each been subject to this process of intensification and exaggeration, particularly so in ways which impose on the institution of the family. Rationalism (i.e. the rise of science and a secular humanist culture) had already undermined the religious rationale and legitimation for the marriage, and the family. The Bergers argue that 'hyper-rationalization' has gone much further than this. In the twentieth century it has extended the scientific and technological attitude and approaches into the such personal spheres as sexuality, consciousness, the body, personal relations and the family through disciplines and 'sciences' such as psychology. This tends to discredit traditional beliefs and common sense simultaneously, substituting for them a new kind of quasi-scientific 'common sense' and popularizing it particularly among the 'educated' middle class (ibid., pp. 118–20). 'Hyper-individualism', which is exemplified in movements such as feminism and psychotherapy, involves an increasing emphasis on the isolated individual and his or her projects of self-attainment over and against all other collective entities such as the family. The family is thus coming to be treated as merely one among many social instruments at the disposal of egocentric individuals and disposable by them in the course of their pursuits of their lifelong self-attainment projects (ibid., pp. 120–2).

'Counter-modernization' consists of resistances to rationalization and to individualism. These involve counter-cultural movements attacking core institutions and processes of modernity which embody these values (such as the institutions of science, technology, bureaucracy and the bourgeois family). Thus counter-cultures attack the family for institutionalizing 'false values, especially a false rationality repressive of authentic emotions and a false individualism prohibiting true community' (ibid., p. 123). The Bergers suggest that nineteenth-century populism, Marxism, bohemianism and the 1960s counter-culture and commune movements are examples of some of the main counter-modern movements which have contained distinctive anti-familial aspects. As with the other hypermodern developments, these have had mainly a middle-class constituency (see also Bruce-Briggs 1979 and Gouldner 1979). They have thus undermined the legitimacy of the bourgeois family within the very class which originally generated it. As Neoconservatives and sociologists the Bergers imply that these cultural and political developments have virtually amounted to a form of 'class treachery'. Furthermore, their effect has been to promote permissiveness, moral relativism and the breakdown of morality, in a word 'decadence', in contemporary American society (also Lasch 1980). With this as the general context we can now consider Neoconservative familists' explanations of the more specific problem of the breakdown of the family among the poor and the underclass in particular.

2 Family breakdown among the poor and the underclass

i The 'welfare trap' 'Family structure is the principal correlate of child poverty' (Moynihan 1989, p. 2). As we saw in chapter 3, poverty has become 'feminized' in America, leading a trend which is occurring widely in Western society (e.g. Brown 1989 and Wicks and Kiernan 1990 on Britain; Room et al., 1989 and Roll 1989 on Europe; also ch. 8 below). Divorce, 'illegitimate' births and teenage pregnancies leading to single-parent (i.e. largely single-mother) families are all part of this pattern. The rates for most of these indicators of 'family structure breakdown' tend to be far higher among the American underclass than among the general population (ch. 3, pp. 65–7; Besharov and Quinn 1987, pp. 50–2; also Murray 1989 and 1990a on Britain).

Neoconservatives have tended to cite two sorts of causes for this. On the one hand, as a background factor there is the 'decadence' and 'permissiveness' of contemporary culture, particularly as regards the regulating of sexual relationships and the control of sexual hedonism (see 1 above). On the other hand, the closer and more important factor stimulating family structure breakdown can be argued to be the existence and growth of the welfare state, and of the social rights of citizenship, particularly the massive extension of AFDC since the 1960s; that is, the cause is the extension of the social rights of citizenship and their effects on the social duties of citizenship.

The existence and growth of a large-scale non-contributory welfare benefits system is argued to undermine marriage and the family in poor and underclass communities in a number of ways. Charles Murray (as we have seen in chapter 3) and George Gilder have been among the leading Neoconservative proponents of this explanation. Their various interpretations of this explanation in the debate with liberal and Left defenders of the welfare system have emphasized (1) its 'incentive' and 'enabling' effects, (2) its 'trapping' effects and (3) its 'deregulation' effects on sex roles and sexual identity. We can take these in turn.

(1) The 'incentive' and 'enablement' effects of welfare on family structure and poverty have been argued notably by Murray (1984, 1986, 1989) and also by Gilder (1986). Incentive and enablement arguments are respectively more and less sophisticated conceptions of the effect of welfare benefits on poor people (mainly teenage girls and women) who are assumed to be relatively economically rational agents. AFDC rules in

most states in effect confine eligibility to single mothers and reduce or remove it from married couples and from households where a partner or young adult offspring work (or, more importantly, this is how clients *perceive* AFDC eligibility). This system, then, effectively operates a set of 'perverse incentives' (Murray 1984; Gilder 1986), or at least a set of facilitators and enablements (Murray 1986, 1989) which 'reward' single-headed family formation. Since single-headed family formation is one of the prime conditions for continued poverty and welfare dependency, the welfare system is the cause of problems it was intended to cure.

The system's incentives and enablements are argued to engage most directly with girls and women, while its deregulatory effects are argued to be felt as much, if not more, by males, as we will see in a moment. Thus teenage girls in poor communities are alleged to be given an incentive to get pregnant in order to get on welfare. It is worth noting that it is not just Neoconservative sociologists who hold this view; the poor themselves seem to do so also. An *L.A. Times* opinion survey in 1985 found that 70 per cent of the poor women interviewed agreed that it is 'often' or 'almost always' true that 'poor young women have babies so they can collect welfare' (cited Novak 1987b, p. 15). On this view, single mothers are encouraged to remain single in order to remain eligible for benefit, while women in less than satisfactory marriages and partnerships are encouraged to divorce or break up the partnership in order to gain the independent and relatively secure income provided by the welfare system. Overall, the welfare state, whatever its goals, appears to have constructed a system of 'rewards' for behaviour that the wider culture claims to regard as problematic and negative in all sorts of ways (from the moral to the social and economic), together with a system of 'penalties' for behaviour (like marriage, self-reliance etc.) which it claims to regard as positive and valuable.

However, not the least of the problems with the 'incentive' argument is that it is evidently over-simplistic. It has been shown that AFDC cash incentives are in reality no incentive or reward. They are meagre at best, and in any case they declined substantially in real terms (30 per cent, Ellwood and Summers 1986, p. 68) over the course of the 1970s, thereby reducing their appeal as incentives. Yet the numbers on welfare rolls did not decline and single-parenting continued to increase. In addition there is significant underclaiming of available benefits, which casts a shadow over the picture of them as offering strong incentives (Hill 1988). Also the variation of benefit levels between states does not appear to be correlated with rates of 'illegitimacy' and of children in single-parent families. Given this, Ellwood and Summer argue that 'AFDC has far less to do with changes in family structure than has been alleged' (1986, p. 70; also Piven and Cloward 1987, pp. 52–62).

In response to this line of criticism Murray (1986) has conceded that it is too simplistic to argue that welfare achieves its effects on poor women by *motivating* them, for instance to produce illegitimate children. He comprehensively rejects Ellwood and Summer's measurements of the real value of welfare income and of its relationship with illegitimacy rates; thus he rejects the basis of their argument. Nonetheless, he believes that welfare has its effects on poor young women by *enabling* (rather than motivating) them to produce 'illegitimate' children. He assumes that poor young women 'naturally' like babies and would wish to bear and care for them (1989). The issue is not a motivational one, but rather a matter of the strength of obstacles and costs weighing against what is 'natural' and independently motivated action. Murray assumes that, from the young woman's point of view, the relevance of welfare is not to the question 'why?', but rather to the question 'why not?'

The disorganization and poverty of the underclass community in his view have already removed obstacles such as 'the moral imperative of marriage' (1986, p. 4) and the deterrence of the 'stigma' of 'illegitimate' pregnancy. Parents and schools in poor areas have become unable, as well as unwilling, to support this moral imperative with rewards and sanctions (ibid., p. 10). The remaining obstacles, namely of hunger, destitution and insecurity, are removed by the welfare system. Whether or not it offers a positive incentive, welfare provides an income which is both secure and also perceived to be 'enough' to be able to survive adequately (e.g. about 65 per cent of local median household income; Murray, ibid., p. 5)

(2)   What evidence is there which could throw some light on the Neoconservatives' claims about the welfare system's alleged

causal role in supporting family-based poverty? Social researchers on this topic have tended to be unimpressed with a straightforward causal ('incentives') argument, while the 'enablement' approach is complex and has yet to be explored. Nonetheless, questions have been asked about whether the system operates to get its clients off its books and out of poverty, or whether – once clients are on its books – the system unwittingly has the effect of trapping them there. Independent evidence in support of the existence of one form or another of incentive/enablement and trapping effects has been produced in recent years by a number of liberally inclined social scientists such as Garfinkel, McLanahan, Ellwood, Summers, Besharov, Quinn, Bane, Ladner, Duncan and Coe (see Bibliography) and others. Garfinkel and McLanahan's study (1986, chs 1–3, *passim*) is probably the most comprehensive and authoritative in this field. However, for the purposes of my discussion in this section we can take a brief look at some more recent studies, including Garfinkel and McLanahan's own contribution to the contemporary debate about the underclass.

Besharov and Quinn (1987) point out that most of the women who go on AFDC at any given time do so for a relatively short period of time (i.e. under two years). However, most of the *expenditure* goes to women who are on welfare long-term (e.g. seven or more years). Nearly 25 per cent of AFDC recipients stay dependent on welfare for 10 years or more (op. cit., p. 54; also Bane and Ellwood 1986). Ellwood and Summers (1986) believe that this group are not 'trapped by welfare per se' and that their situation is explained by difficulties in finding work or marriage because of their children, and also because of male desertion (op. cit., p. 72). Nonetheless 'this dependent group is a legitimate source of concern' (ibid., p. 72). What are the main characteristics of this group? And, if AFDC does not *motivate* or enable their dependence, are Ellwood and Summers nevertheless right to claim that it does not *trap* them?

Besharov and Quinn's (1987) analysis of the characteristics of AFDC users suggests that the principal difference between the long- and short-term users is whether or not they have ever been married. Divorcees tend to move off welfare much more rapidly than 'never-marrieds' on welfare, either through gaining employment or through remarriage. On past evidence of women who are 'never-married' when they began to receive AFDC, (many of whom are teenagers), 40 per cent will stay on welfare for 10 or more years (ibid., p. 54). Besharov and Quinn conclude that:

> Divorce and out-of-wedlock births . . . are the root causes of the 'feminization' of poverty. But much more than a divorce an out-of-wedlock birth to a young mother is a direct path to long-term poverty and welfare dependence. Whatever the moral implications of our high illegitimacy rate, its economic consequences are a matter of urgent concern. (ibid., p. 55)

The possibility that AFDC use may be something of a trap for the single mothers, particularly the 'never-marrieds', who use it is also indicated in McLanahan and Garfinkel's (1989) analysis. They suggest that the main problems of poor single mothers revolve around their tendency to be unmarried, unemployed (having 'a weak attachment to the labour force', ibid., pp. 94–5; also discussion of Mead, ch. 6 below), and socially isolated (ibid., p. 96; also Wilson 1987, 1989). They conclude that: 'AFDC and other means-tested welfare programmes undermine the labour force attachment of poor single mothers by promoting female headship and reducing the likelihood of marriage. Also AFDC promotes social isolation by encouraging nonemployment at a time when married mothers are entering the labour force in increasing numbers' (ibid., p. 101). They also point out the 'poverty trap' and employment disincentive effects of the 'high taxation' involved in a system which reduces real income (i.e. welfare income, health care and other benefits) to effectively negate the value of any gain in cash income from employment.

An additional problem for defenders of the American welfare system as it currently stands is that the system's dependency or trapping effects can be shown to be significantly *inter-generational*. 'Cycles of deprivation and disadvantage' (no less, of course, than cycles of advantage among rich elites, the middle class and the affluent working class) are a stubborn reality in contemporary capitalist societies. Besharov and Quinn observe that in poor female-headed families, particularly those beginning with an out-of-marriage birth and headed for long-term welfare dependency, 'the plight of the children is distressing' (1987, p. 55). McLanahan and Garfinkel indicate their likely future in their observation that 60 per cent of the daughters of welfare mothers after they came of age (at 16 years) will themselves receive at least one year's benefit, while 40 per cent of *this* group are likely to go on to become long-term welfare-dependent (McLanahan and Garfinkel 1989, p. 98; also Garfinkel and McLanahan 1986 and Ladner 1988). McLanahan and Garfinkel conclude that a small group of mainly Black single mothers in northern urban ghettos is 'reproducing itself', and that 'too heavy a reliance upon welfare can facilitate the growth of an underclass' (1989, p. 104). We will return to this issue in (3) below.

On all of these counts then the welfare system contains some trapping effects and long-term dependency risks for poor single mothers and their children who get involved with it. However it should be noted that, unlike Murray and the Neoconservatives, McLanahan and Garfinkel and other such commentators believe that these effects can only be cured by reforming and expanding the welfare system, not by abolishing it or cutting it (e.g. Garfinkel and McLanahan 1986, ch. 6). We will return to these policy issues later (section III below).

(3) Besides the various trapping effects considered so far, Neoconservatives argue that in addition the welfare state promotes family structure breakdown and thus poverty among the poor and the underclass by assisting with what we can call the 'deregulation' of sexuality. Other 'permissive' and 'decadent' forces in the wider culture and society are deemed to be responsible for promoting this (see discussion of Bergers above). Deregulation involves a loosening of social and interpersonal controls over sexual and related impulsive, hedonistic and aggressive behaviour, and the setting adrift of sexual roles and of human sexual identities. Human sexual self-control and self-definition as masculine or feminine is evidently inextricably bound up with people's upbringing in, experiences of, attitudes to and commitments to family.

The Neoconservative general view of the relationship between sexual regulation and the family is expressed eloquently and controversially by Gilder (1986) and also by the Bergers (1983). It consists in a forthright endorsement of the traditional sexual division of labour within and outside the family, with women seen as essentially mothers and 'homemakers' and men as 'breadwinners' and fathers. On this view such marriage and family roles and responsibilities are necessary for the security and socialization of human infants and children (Berger and Berger op. cit., ch. 7). This is one of the great 'civilizing' tasks of the family. But the other great civilizing task is equally important. As Gilder expresses it, it is 'the taming of the barbarian' (1986, ch. 4), namely the regulation of the otherwise anti-social and destructive forces of males' natural aggression and their sexual hedonism and promiscuity. 'It is the sexual constitution not the legal one, that is decisive' here in bringing males to the 'duties and disciplines of citizenship' (op. cit., p. 39). This occurs primarily through the commitments and sacrifices involved in the institution of the family, namely love, monogamy and fatherhood, and the discipline of playing the 'breadwinner' role. It also occurs through the controlled aggression and energy required by the (traditionally) mainly male world of work in which the bread is won.

Ironically for apparent spokesmen for the traditional patriarchal order, Neoconservative familists like Gilder and the Bergers tend to wax lyrical about the moral superiority of women and the primacy of matriarchy, and tend to idealize motherhood. Thus Gilder holds that 'woman's morality is the ultimate basis of all morality' (1986, p. 169) and that they are morally superior to men (ibid., p. 176); 'The maternal role [is] paramount' (ibid., p. 169) and 'Women, uniquely [are] in charge of the central activities of human life.' 'The woman's place is in the home, and she does best when she can get the man there too, inducing him to submit most human activity to the domestic values of civilization. Thus in a sense she also brings the home into society' (ibid., p. 177). In Gilder's view such maternal and familial regulation, the basis of civilization in all societies, is breaking down in the modern American ghetto. Ghetto and underclass males tend to be 'untamed' or unregulated by any serious and long-term commitments to conventional social roles, particularly the roles involved in marriage, breadwinning, fatherhood and being an employee. Children grow up in fatherless families, and, given the ghetto environment, this experience is particularly problematic for boys and teenage males. Lacking a mature familial male role model, they seek their masculinity in the predatory sexuality, hedonism and aggression of the immature young male peer group and its street culture. This in turn has proved disastrous for Black ghetto communities. Although they form a small proportion of the overall American population they contribute around 50 per cent of all American drug addicts, prisoners and violent criminals (Gilder op. cit., p. 79). As communities they are terrorized and victimized by the rootless and predatory males they have produced but have been unable adequately to socialize or control.

At first glance it may not be obvious why this disaster has got anything to do with the welfare system. Elements of the ghetto problem were identified a generation ago by the Moynihan Report (1965). Its critique of the female-dominated or female-headed structure of Black ghetto families and the 'tangle of pathologies' associated with them was produced just *before* the welfare system entered its major expansionary phase. In any case the welfare system engages mainly poor women and barely touches ghetto males (Gilder op. cit., p. 89). Yet from his interviews with ghetto males Gilder reports that they felt as trapped by welfare as did the women of their community. First, they often use the resources, (housing etc.) provided for welfare mothers, albeit on a transient basis, and they are thus indirectly dependent on welfare along with the women. Secondly, the woman's welfare income represents a strong disincentive to males to seek work and play a breadwinner role, at least in the legal economy. Gilder notes: 'In virtually no state could a typical ghetto man easily earn enough to compete with the benefit package available to a mother of small children' (1986, p. 91). He argues that this has two results. First, the males withdraw from the fields of competition (marriage and employment) in which it is most likely that they will 'lose' and thus lose self-esteem. Thus many tend to drift towards very intermittent and casual employment and towards the underground economy (hustling), and significant proportions drift into crime or into demoralization and parasitism and into drink or drug addictions. Secondly, women withdraw from the males, at least in the sense of seeing them as potentially 'marriageable', and either delay marriage or rule it out altogether. They thereby substantially increase the risk that they themselves will become long-term welfare-dependent.

This sort of picture of the destructive processes at work in the ghetto underclass is evidently not a mere figment of the imagination of white Neoconservative moralists like Gilder and J. Q. Wilson (1985) or of social observers like Auletta (1983). We have already reviewed the social science evidence on single mothers and on the women's side of the story. In addition, Black American sociologists have recently begun to confirm aspects of the male side of the story. In spite of the fact that in the mid-1960s Civil Rights leaders Bayard Rustin and Martin Luther King sympathized with the Moynihan Report's picture of 'the tangled pathology of the black ghetto family', the (usually white) liberals and Left took it upon themselves to charge it with 'racism' (see Rainwater and Yancey 1967).

The result of this was virtually to proscribe serious study of the negative aspects of Black family structure for a decade or more (Wilson 1987, ch. 1). But a largely male-inspired and organized social disaster – featuring hopelessly high rates of drug addiction and of violent crime, particularly of remorse-less violence against strangers – has been unfolding and building in the Black ghetto since the 1960s. It has both saddened and bemused liberal and Left veterans of the 'war against poverty' of that era. Charles Silberman observes: 'The new criminals have been so brutalized in their own upbringing that they seem incapable of viewing their victims as fellow human beings' (quoted Harrington 1984, p. 184). Michael Harrington notes that the 'aimless brutality' of young Black male crime is 'something new and inexplicable' (op. cit., p. 185). His observation was made prior to the recent advent of 'wilding' (wild street violence by young gangs and friendship groups on innocent passers-by), which merely amplifies his point.

Black sociologists, while stressing the structural inequalities and sources underlying them, nonetheless have begun to piece together a picture of the ghetto underclass which recognizes the breakdown of the family and of the 'sexual constitution'. They blame this 'deregulation' on social isolation and dislocation caused by structural racial and class inequalities and economic forces rather than on personal character or the welfare state. There are clearly important differences between their analyses and those of the Neoconservatives. Nonetheless, with all due account taken of the political and analytical differences, it is worth noting that in one version or another, the long-buried 1960s themes of the 'culture of poverty' (e.g. Leacock 1971) 'cycles of disadvantage and deprivation' and the 'transmission of poverty' are again becoming common currency in the debate and diagnosis of ghetto and underclass problems (Wilson 1987, 1989, pp. 185–6). Before we turn to family policy (II below) we should briefly consider this revival of the 'culture of poverty' theme.

Wilson (1989) considers behaviour such as 'overt emphasis on sexuality, idleness and public drinking' to be frequently occurring 'ghetto-specific practices'. They do not 'take on a life of their own', need not be internalized and are susceptible to reductions in structural inequality. Nonetheless, they are readily transmitted 'by precept, as in role-modelling' (1989, p. 186). Similarly, Elijah Anderson (1989) studying the sex codes of Black inner-city youth confirms the problem young males have in facing up to the roles of dependable husband and breadwinner. Unlike Gilder, he blames it on the poor job prospects available to ghetto males rather than the welfare system. Nonetheless, the results, and their knock-on consequences, are comparable. That is, deprived of the familial and employment avenues to gain, prove and test their masculine identity (and, on Gilder's analysis, to regulate it) young Black males pursue the street culture of the peer group.

The peer group's norms and rites of passage require the young male to prove his manhood both by having casual sex with as many young women as possible and, also, where possible, by getting them pregnant, giving them 'his baby'. The peer group does not associate manhood with taking responsibility for these children and playing a father role to them. The evidence on the growth of 'illegitimate' teenage pregnancies and on male desertion of families testifies to the strength of the peer group and the failure of the regulation of male sexuality and identity from all other sources. On the other hand, although it is a slowly declining influence, Testa et al. (1989) in their study of Chicago poverty data show the continuing relationship between Black male employment status and marriage. They find that 'Employed men are more likely than jobless men to marry after the conception of their first child' (op. cit., p. 90). John McAdoo (1988) finds that *employed* black males make effective fathers. Testa et al. show that the restricted pool of marriage-able (i.e. employed) males in the ghetto limits women's willing-ness to enter marriage, while on the other hand as regards women with poor 'economic prospects' – in which we must surely include long-term welfare-dependent women – they imply that these limit the pool of women considered to be marriage-able by males (ibid., p. 91). Evidently *both* the economic context (*pace* Neoconservatism) *and also* the welfare system, whether directly or indirectly (*pace* liberalism and the Left), have a part to play in explaining the deregulation of sexuality and the breakdown of the family in the ghetto.

These, then, are some of major family problems facing contemporary America together with various diagnoses. What is to be done about them? Neoconservatives and others advo-cate the development of 'family policy'. We now need to take a closer look at what this might refer to, the directions in which Neoconservatives believe it ought to be developed and what it means for their conception of social citizenship.

III

Family policy and family duties: the Neoconservative cure

1   Background

i   The political debate   In chapter 1 we saw that in the early postwar period (1950s and 1960s), the heyday of the dominant paradigm of social citizenship, it was assumed that in order to develop a 'social policy' the only really relevant vehicle and instrument to concentrate on was the welfare state. The family, the main non-state welfare institution, was largely taken for granted and given a relatively residual and marginal status in social policy. However, in the last two decades in Western societies a highly charged politics of welfare and the family has emerged. The background for this (as we have indicated in chapters 2 and 4 and in earlier sections of this chapter) has been the development of various profound structural crises, limita-tions and breakdowns both in the welfare state and in the traditional family system. At the ideological and political level the women's movement has emerged to challenge the patriarchal assumptions of both the welfare state (e.g. Wilson 1977; Pascal 1983) and the family (e.g. Barrett and McIntosh 1982); the New Right and Neoconservatism have emerged to defend the family and capitalism against the welfare state (see ch. 4); and the Left, particularly in Britain, has struggled to organize a relevant and persuasive defence of the welfare state against the Right's familists and marketeers (e.g. Plant et al. 1980; Goodin et al. 1987; Walzer 1985; Jordan 1987; Wicks 1987).

The upshot of all this is that during the 1970s and, particularly, the 1980s, the massive actual and potential welfare role of the family has begun to be better understood across the political spectrum. In addition, the possibilities for defending and building on it in pursuing social policy goals and objectives, rather than ignoring it or working against it, are also coming to be better understood. The notion that 'family policy' should be developed, while of particular concern to the Right, has received considerable cross-party political and governmental interest in the USA and Britain in recent years. But so far all of this interest has produced relatively little in the way of tangible results, as we will see later. In the present section we are concerned particularly with the policy principles and proposals for a family policy developed by American Neoconservatism in recent years. These derive from Neoconservatism's analyses of the nature and causes of the family problems of contemporary society both in general and among the poor in particular, which were reviewed in section I above.

In the recent period the idea of 'family policy' has begun to be seen as having a comparable importance for contemporary social policy as the idea of 'the welfare state' has long had for 'dominant paradigm' social policy. However, the political discourse of social policy and social citizenship has continued to be that of *rights* – i.e. new forms and aspects of citizens' formal rights such as all citizens' welfare rights; Black and ethnic minority civil and social rights; women's civil and social rights; the rights of children, youth and the elderly, and so on. The New Right and Neoconservatism have also used the language of citizens' rights in their attempts to defend family institutions and values as they see them. In particular they have supported the notion that *parents* have basic rights both to exercise an important influence over their children in areas such as education, welfare and control and to) to negotiate (and to resist where relevant) the influence of the state over their children in these and other respects. Their view of *children's* rights is less clear. They seem to assert, against feminism, that children have rights to traditional mothering. But how children's rights to state protection against bad and abusive parenting (or even simply low-quality and unlucky parenting) are to be reconciled with the priority given to parents' rights is not clear. However, the main language Neoconservatism has used to defend the family and promote family policy is that of *citizens' informal social duties*, rather than rights, as we will see in subsection 2 below.

The potential scope of 'family policy' and of the family politics connected with developing it is vast, given men's, women's and children's needs and rights as citizens, and given also the range of laws and state policies which infringe on them as family members and which affect their capacity to perform their duties to each other. In principle it is possible for governments to try to gain a picture of the likely effects of legislation on the family by building in 'family impact' monitoring and assessments into its implementation and administration (2 below). But this is easier said than done, even for a single piece of legislation, while the ambition of practically achieving such monitoring for the whole legal and administrative machinery of the modern state, even of its welfare state sector, is a daunting prospect. Family *policy* may present itself in nationally co-ordinated and comprehensive terms at governmental level. But family *politics*, whether at grassroots or national level, is much more like a fragmented sphere filled with a multitude of single-issue and special-interest campaigns and lobbies, from abortion to homosexual parenting. Little sustained sense of the common familial ground between them seems to emerge from all of this. However, this common ground is perhaps most tangibly present in situations of divorce and single-parenting where the traditional-model family has either broken down or never taken shape. Here the division of labour around parental child-care duties needs to be (re)negotiated between separated parents and/or between them and the state.

Many of the important elements of family policy in modern

society develop in the context of the state's stance towards single-parenting, particularly (1) towards single-parenting's division of parental responsibilities and its support needs 'after the fact' but also (2) (where appropriate and possible) in terms of its prevention in the interests of the children involved. The main line of Neoconservative interest in family policy, supports (1) assessment of the impact of legislation on families; (2) the development of policies to encourage marriage, promote parental rights and to prevent family breakdown and single-parenting; and (3) the development of policies for single-mothering which both coerce the absent father to perform some parental duties and which also support the mother in her performance of these duties. It is over this latter policy line, and in particular, over the relevance of work policy to family policy that the Neoconservative position has recently begun to fall apart. We will come to this important internal debate within Neoconservatism in chapter 6. First we need to briefly consider the development of American family policy (section 2 below). We can then turn to some leading Neoconservative versions of what a genuinely pro-family policy should look like.

ii The family policy context After decades of talk about family policy, many authorities concur that as a matter of fact by the 1980s America had actually failed to develop much that could be said to amount to such a thing. For instance, Kagan et al. ask 'Does the United States have a family policy?' (1987, p. 415). After reviewing relevant policy and analysis they are drawn to the conclusion that 'there is no coherent American family policy' (ibid., p. 419). Ellwood and Summers, in their notable contribution to the debate on welfare dependency, state 'We know of no serious policy that encourages family formation' (1986, p. 73). However, political interest in it continues un-abated, indeed has been growing in recent years. For instance, over 70 bills concerned with aspects of child care were brought to Congress in 1987 (Brown 1989, p. 70) and there have been a number of important new policy initiatives in recent years which we will come to in a moment.

Political interest in the American family and its welfare has a long history stretching back to the eighteenth century (Bane 1978; Masnick and Bane 1980; Garfinkel and McLanahan 1986, ch. 4; Handler and Hasenfeld 1990, chs 2, 3). In the modern era Roosevelt's creation of AFDC in 1935 during the New Deal was a milestone, and concern for the family has been a recurrent theme in most postwar presidencies. The 1960s were notable years for family policy and much of the current debate in the 1980s and 1990s contains echoes of their concerns. In 1962 President Kennedy declared that public policy 'must contribute to the attack on dependency . . . family breakdown and il-legitimacy' (quoted Novak 1987b, p. 73). In 1965 the Moynihan Report advocated that federal policies should 'be designed to . . . (enhance) the stability and resources of the Negro American family' in order to enable Black Americans to share equally in 'the responsibilities and rewards of citizenship' (Rainwater and Yancy 1967, p. 94). In the same year President Johnson declared, 'The family is the cornerstone of our society,' and, 'The breakdown of the Negro family structure' was an important problem to which 'Welfare and social programs better designed to hold families together are part of the answer' (ibid., pp. 130–1).

In 1973 Walter Mondale influenced the Senate to take up the idea of family impact assessments. Jimmy Carter, as presidential candidate in 1976, committed himself to implementing this and to the 'design (of) programs and policies that support families' (quoted Kagan 1987, p. 415). However, a heated debate be-tween liberals and conservatives ensued in the late 1970s around the morality of tolerating divers family structures and of involv-ing the state in the family at all. This effectively stymied any progress in family policy other than at the level of analysis (e.g. the Keniston Report 1977).

President Reagan showed a strong interest in promoting a conservative version of family policy throughout his presidency (e.g. Garfinkel and McLanahan 1986, ch. 5). In 1987 he in-troduced an Executive Order (12606) requiring 'family impact assessments' to be made in 'The formulation and implemen-tation of policies' by the federal government. The main assess-ment criteria are the effect of policies on the following issues: 'the stability of the family' and 'the marital commitment'; 'the authority and rights of parents'; the ability of the family to 'perform its functions'; 'disposable family income'; the public image of 'the status of the family'; and young people's understandings of their behaviour, their personal responsibility and the norms of society. The Reagan administration provided an umbrella for a certain degree of consensus to begin to emerge between liberals and Neoconservatives on family policy. This has been manifested in, among other things, the report of Michael Novak's working seminar on family and welfare (Novak 1987b) and a number of other influential reports on this subject from a range of political perspectives (Novak 1987b, pp. 74–83; also Gilbert 1983, ch. 5). In addition, the Family Security Act, inspired by Daniel Moynihan (Moynihan 1989) among others, was enacted in 1988.

We can now take a brief look at the Neoconservative familist principles and policy proposals to be found in some of these and other statements. They derive from the Neoconservative diagnosis of the long decline of the family in American society in general, but particularly among the poor which we reviewed earlier, and they are intended to halt this decline.

2 Neoconservative family policy analysis and proposals

The Neoconservative conception of social citizenship emphasizes the duties rather than the rights associated with it, and this is particularly so in the field of family policy. Neoconservatives see citizens' family duties as including those of husbands and wives, of parents and young children, and of mature children and old parents to respect and care for each other, ideally for life. Thus parents' *rights*, for instance, are understood to be *the rights to assume profound responsibilities and duties*. From this perspective the Neoconservative version of state family policy consists of *enabling* parents, for instance, to perform their duties to their children. Thus on the one hand an active family policy would aim to clear away accumulated governmental, bureaucratic and other obstacles and interferences to parents' performing their duties. On the other hand ideally it would also aim to provide effective support (income and services) to parents and family carers in the performance of their duties, as and when they needed and requested it. In this section we will first illustrate Neoconservative 'family policy' thinking from the two important accounts by the Bergers (1983) and Novak et al. (1987b) ((1)

below), and then consider the influence of these and related ideas on the actual development of contemporary American family policy ((2) below).

i   Neoconservative family policy proposals: Bergers and Novak
The Bergers acknowledge that there are no panaceas for the intractable problems of the family in modern society (1983, p. 195). They restrict themselves to outlining six general principles on which a pro-family policy should be based (ibid., pp. 204–14).

The primacy of the family and of familial core of children must be recognized by society in public policy.

The private sphere must be respected and restored by the state (e.g. toleration of sexual preferences, the state to keep out of divorces and not house divorced families etc.).

The plurality of family forms should be respected, in spite of the cultural importance of the bourgeois family form.

In their view any family is likely to be a better carer than the state, and the state should provide child and carer allowances to help families perform this function.

Families need to be empowered *vis-à-vis* professionals in state welfare, health and education services (the voucher concept should be considered for many areas in addition to education).

Parental rights and authority need to be restored.

In general, policy needs to support communities, together with the role of 'mediating structures' and institutions such as churches, voluntary associations etc. In the Bergers' view this set of principles is most likely to 'capture the middle ground' and to provide for some consensus in the 'war over the family'.

Novak's (1987b) collaborators in his working seminar on the family and welfare included various notable Neoconservatives such as Murray, Mead, Kondratas and many others. As with the Bergers, Novak and his group also point to the emergence of a considerable potential for consensus over family and welfare policy in the late 1980s as compared with the division and controversy over it in Jimmy Carter's presidency a decade earlier.

The new mood is characterized by the tacit acceptance, even among old liberals, of moderate Neoconservative assumptions, and a trust (as against the early 'cuts' years of the Reagan presidency) in the seriousness, even compassion, of Neoconservative concerns for the poor and welfare-dependent.

Novak and his colleagues begin from such assumptions as the following. Economic growth is a necessary but not sufficient condition of resolving poverty. But experience has shown that there are no quick policy fixes available and that change will take time. The blanket category of 'the poor' must be disaggregated for analytical and policy purposes into its very different elements which present very different needs and problems. The American poor are different in the communities they live in (only 6 per cent live in high-poverty ghettos), their age and health status (20 per cent are old and disabled), whether or not they live in families (35–40 per cent consist of women and children in single-mother families) and so on. Lack of personal responsibility and commitment to family life is a basic problem for some of the hard-core poor and welfare-dependent (the underclass). Their problems will not necessarily be tackled simply by increasing social expenditure. Rather, it is a problem of values and behaviour, and public policy needs to address it as such. Thus, among other things policy needs to co-ordinate, and to provide material resource and moral support for whatever there is in the institutional and cultural environments of poor people and their communities which works to support the values and practices of family life and of personal responsibility. Welfare and family policy 'must insist upon personal responsibility and social obligation' (Novak 1987b, p. 18).

Novak and his colleagues, in developing their policy proposals from these Neoconservative assumptions, took account of a number of other current diagnoses and policy prescriptions. Although these came from a variety of perspectives they also seemed explicitly or implicitly to share some of these assumptions and to point in parallel policy directions. Reports by Governor Bruce Babbitt, by Governor Mario Cuomo and by the main welfare professionals' associations (the American Public Welfare Association (APWA)) produced in 1986 concurred on the following sorts of policy proposals. Tax relief on low income should be increased and made variable by family size. Publicly funded health-care provision should be extended and increased. AFDC and other welfare programmes should include more males and two-parent families, and they should be improved. Welfare system services to children and families (e.g. counselling, training, nutrition, health benefits, child care etc.) should be greatly expanded. Action should be taken to tighten up on support payments to families from absent parents and services. Welfare system interventions should be aimed at clients' self-sufficiency and discharge, and they should be incapable of being used for long-term dependency. Finally, work and training should be enforced through workfare programmes (ibid., pp. 74–82).

Novak and his group for their part make policy recommendations very much along these sorts of lines. Their aim is to address directly the various behavioural problems and dependencies involved in underclass poverty, rather than merely trusting to economic growth and increased employment opportunities to solve the problem. They, along with Babbitt, Cuomo and APWA, support tax reliefs on earned income for the working poor and a welfare system designed to be transitional and to counter the current systems' dependency-enabling and trapping effects. They stress the vital role in poor communities of 'intermediate' institutions such as churches, charities and business philanthropy and initiatives. The rights of people in poor communities must be supported and empowered. Rights to defence against the terrorism of crime and parents' rights to choice and participation in their children's education and to demand high standards from it are particularly important. But above all else the family (and the social obligations of citizenship involved in marriage and parenthood) must be strongly supported by all non-state and state agencies involved in welfare and family policy.

As we have seen in this chapter, this 'social duties' agenda has three main features. First, Novak and other Neoconservatives' defence of parents' *rights* means supporting the imposition of *duties*, since parental rights logically and practically imply parents' self-imposition of duties. Secondly, Novak and his group are emphatic that males have duties to support the children they father. These duties stand independently of whether or not the father's relationship with the mother breaks down and they split up or divorce. In paticular, among the poor, 'fathers of out-of-wedlock children receiving AFDC should be identified by mandatory paternity findings; all fathers should be held to child-support obligations, and efforts should be made to collect from them' (ibid., p. 102). Finally, it is a family duty that parents should work to keep their children, and single parents should not be exempt from that duty. So parents in receipt of welfare should be required to prepare for, seek and gain employment. Since the vast bulk of single-parenting is single-mothering, effectively Novak and his group strongly recommend that ultimately all single mothers on welfare should be put on workfare programmes. School-age teenage mothers are exempted from this, but they should be required to complete high school and get initial work training as a condition of their receipt of benefit.

Novak and his group propose that:

> It is essential that all able recipients should be enrolled in work, duration-limited education, or short-term training programs in return for collecting welfare benefits . . . Those involved in work programs, whether staff or participants, should be expected to regard every job, even part time and at a minimum wage, as an obligation to society, as important to future work experience and as an occasion of self-development. (ibid., p. 112)

However, in spite of its consensualist intentions, this sort of strong support for workfare as a key element in family policy is in fact highly controversial to other pro-family Neoconservatives, as we will see later (ch. 6, section III). First, it should be noted that some elements of this agenda are beginning to be realized in contemporary American policy-making.

ii Contemporary American family policy developments Two policy initiatives in particular are worth noting in this context: the Family Support Act 1988 and the Wisconsin state Child Support system developed since the mid-1980s.

(a) Daniel Moynihan, one of the architects of the Family Support Act 1988, describes it as 'the first redefinition of the purposes and expectations of the welfare system since the system began in 1935' and as a 'toughminded approach to post-industrial social issues' (Moynihan 1989, pp. 26, 27). The Act is in fact a moderate step in the direction of a supportive version of workfare and of an ethos and dynamic in the welfare system towards bringing home to welfare clients the social obligations of citizens to work (for a critique see Handler and Hasenfeld 1990, pp. 209–15). It aims: 'To assure that needy families with children obtain the education, training and employment that will help them to avoid long term welfare dependency.' (quoted Brown 1989, p. 72).

Currently there are vast differences between, on the one hand, those enrolled on welfare and, on the other, those nominally enrolled on work programmes, and also between the latter and the minority of this group who actually actively participate in the work programmes. The Act aims to raise the active participation rate of employable welfare recipients in work programmes to 22 per cent by the mid-1990s. It extends welfare benefits coverage to unemployed fathers on the condition that they perform at least 16 hours per week in government jobs. It also extends the eligibility of welfare mothers for workfare by reducing the age of their children below which mothers are exempt from work requirements (from six years to three years old; Mead 1989, pp. 167–8). One section of the Act proposes the development of a new Job Opportunities and Basic Skills (JOBS) programme providing customized services to assess welfare clients' needs for educational, child-care and support services along with their work skills and experience. Child care is guaranteed during training and for a year after the client begins in employment. Furthermore, earned income is given greater tax relief than previously (Brown 1989, p. 73).

(b)   Earlier we noted the concern of Novak and his group for a tough public policy stance on the enforcement, particularly on deserting fathers, of parental duties to children. This is consistent with Congressional legislation of 1984 which requires states to hold back the cost of support payments from the wages of absent parents (effectively, absent fathers) if they have defaulted for up to a month. This legislation also required states to set up agencies to specify standards for the performance of this social obligation of citizenship (Brown 1989, p. 71; also see Handler and Hasenfeld 1990, pp. 221–4).

The best known and apparently most effective state Child Support agency developed under this legislation is that of Wisconsin (Garfinkel and McLanahan 1986, chs 5, 6). The Wisconsin approach has been used as a model for the implementation of a similar system at national level in Australia (Brown 1989, p. 48) and for the planning of new family policy initiatives in Britain (such as the Child Support Bill 1991 (e.g. Brindle 1990a)). Irwin Garfinkel, its designer, proposes that its 'philosophical premise is that parents are responsible for supporting their children and government is responsible for seeing that the children receive a sufficient amount of support' (quoted Brindle 1990a; Garfinkel and McLanahan 1986).

The Wisconsin strategy has four elements. First, in cases of out-of-wedlock births (20 per cent of all births in Wisconsin in 1987 and 50 per cent in the main urban centre Milwaukee) where paternity is uncertain, the district attorney is mandated to establish paternity using compulsory blood and DNA tests on relevant named males to do so. Mothers are compelled to name the father or possible fathers, or face loss of their AFDC benefit. Secondly, once paternity has been established, the mother is compelled to seek child support from the father who is then legally liable for it. The court sets the support level according to a standardized table (i.e. 17 per cent of father's gross income for one child, 25 per cent for two etc.) without reference to the size of either the mother's or father's income. Thirdly, the father's employer deducts the support payment from his salary, forwarding it to the Child Support Agency which then either passes it on in total to the mother, or, if she is on welfare, passes on a standard payment (Garfinkel and McLanahan 1986; Brindle 1990a).

This is the extent of the system so far. However, Garfinkel envisages the development of a fourth stage to complete the Wisconsin strategy, namely the establishment of a child support 'income' for every child of an absent parent guaranteed by the state in case of fathers' failure to pay. The system so far has substantially increased the amount the state collects from fathers (from $43 million in 1982 to $221 million in 1989) and has thereby saved some public expenditure. But since the fathers of welfare mothers' children have little income, child support from this source is unlikely to reduce welfare mothers' dependency on AFDC. In the context of the enforcement of parental duties it is also worth noting that in 1988 Wisconsin introduced 'learnfare' as part of its welfare system; that is, parents on welfare must ensure that their children aged between 13 and 19 years (for whom they receive AFDC benefit) attend school until they graduate, or suffer loss of benefit. This system does not save public money and was not intended to do so. However, it has had some success in improving school attendance rates. In a report on the programme social researcher Tom Corbett observes that learnfare is an expression of enduring concepts such as civic virtue, self-reliance and personal responsibility (quoted Brindle 1990b; also Handler and Hasenfeld 1990, pp. 224–8), all concepts which are, as we have seen, central to the Neoconservative conception of citizenship.

IV

It is arguable whether such a thing as a coherent national family policy exists in most of the advanced Western societies. Certainly the existence of such a thing in contemporary America has been doubted (as we noted earlier also Kagan et al. 1987, p. 415; Ellwood and Summers 1980). Nonetheless, the vigorous debate about the various versions of and rationales for such a possible national family policy indicates its growing political importance. In this chapter we have seen something of the common concern that both Neoconservatives and liberals have to develop a pro-family policy. Each side in American politics has framed that response in terms of social citizenship, whether emphasizing familial duties or rights or both.

As we have seen, Neoconservatism in particular has addressed itself to three orders of problem: first, the breakdown of the 'traditional' family structure and familial ethic; secondly, the limit case of non-citizenship in the form of the poverty/underclass problem associated with family breakdown and assumed to be in part caused by it; and thirdly, the general cultural crisis (of intra-generational socialization and inter-generational cultural transmission etc.) with which family breakdown is also understood to be associated. Later we will assess the value of Neoconservatism's attempt to reform social citizenship in moral terms by rehabilitating the 'family ethic'. But first, in chapter 6, we must examine the other main school of Neoconservative social analysis, namely that concerned with the attempt to reform social citizenship by rehabilitating the other great secular social ethic of modern societies, namely the 'work ethic'. We will then be in a better position to review Neoconservatism's overall conception of modern citizenship and of the need for it to undergo a moral reformation.

6
Reforming Social Citizenship II: Neoconservatism and Work Policy in the USA

In chapter 1 we saw that the dominant paradigm of social citizenship, at least in its British Beveridge version, appeared to grant citizens (or at least male citizens) new informal *social rights to employment* (conditional on the structural potential for full employment and the state's political will to make it a priority in economic policy).

Of course, if *work rights* was the 'figure' then, in the language of chapter 1 this stood out by virtue of a 'ground' which it overshadowed and marginalized but which it nonetheless depended upon. This 'ground' consisted in a set of beliefs about the moral and sociological importance of *work duties*. These included patriarchal beliefs about women's household, child-rearing and elderly relative carework duties and beliefs about parental carework duties regarding children's health, schooling and law-abidingness. They also included assumptions such as those of Marshall, noted in chapter 1, regarding the trade-off for organized labour between work and welfare rights on the one hand and 'industrial discipline' on the other. Finally, they also explicitly assumed either employment (notionally to fund unemployment insurance) or a willingness to work if in receipt of unemployment benefit (demonstrated by checks on claimants' 'availability for work', 'willingness to accept suitable employment' etc.).

Nonetheless, within the dominant paradigm, work rights have tended to receive the spotlight, whether in national economic policy or in everyday perceptions of social citizenship and of the relevance of the welfare state for ordinary citizens. However, two factors have conspired to challenge this work-rights emphasis since the mid-1970s and to turn the political spotlight on its background assumptions about work duties. One factor concerns the nature and direction of contemporary economic change; we will postpone detailed discussion of this until chapter 7. The other arises from the general Neoconservative ideological challenge to welfare rights we have been considering so far. As in the sphere of the family, the Neoconservative challenge to the dominant paradigm in the sphere of work takes the form of asserting the priority of duties over rights, and we will deal with this argument in this chapter. However in doing so, and particularly in evaluating the Neoconservative challenge, I will draw on some of the arguments about structural change which are to be developed later (e.g. ch. 7 below). So it is necessary here to anticipate the later discussion in order, briefly, to indicate some of the main effects of structural change which are relevant to a consideration of Neoconservative arguments, effects on contemporary attitudes to work and unemployment in particular.

Arguably, contemporary economic change since the mid-1970s has helped to cause a growth of structural unemployment and/or underemployment (via a dual labour market, flexibilization of labour and other processes to be considered later). For the moment we need to note some of the effects which might reasonably be attributed to them. This has tended to foster a general political and cultural environment in Western societies since the mid-1970s in which both the ordinary citizen's social right to work (the right to a job) and also the citizen's social duty to work (the duty to get a job) were simultaneously undermined. It is true that during this period the cultural status of much employment and of many workers' psychological commitment to it (as measured by overtime, productivity etc.) may have increased. But this is compatible with a general undermining of the work ethic as such. The cash nexus has tended to replace the work ethic, and the extrinsic rewards of income for consumption have replaced the intrinsic moral and other rewards of the job itself and/or employment *per se* (e.g. Westergaard and Resler 1976; Rose 1985).

This general structural undermining of work rights and duties, together with its generally anomic implications and effects, left its mark most clearly and deeply among members of the poor and the underclass who were most affected by the growth of unemployment/underemployment. On the one hand this development arguably undermined a key dimension of their informal 'civil society'-based social rights (to a job with a 'living wage') for which formal state-based welfare rights were and are financially and psychologically relatively poor compensation. On the other hand their objective dependency on welfare state support arguably generated a dependency attitude and culture which undermined their commitment to the work ethic and to the social duty to seek and hold employment. Liberals and the Left stress the former aspect of the problem, and tend either to ignore, reject or underplay the latter aspect, and the New Right and Neoconservatives stress the latter aspects and tend to ignore reject or underplay the former aspect.

In this chapter we will confine our attention to the Neoconservative side of the argument, particularly as regards work problems among the American poor and underclass. We will give the liberal/Left side of the argument more attention in the discussion of structural change in chapter 7.

In chapter 3 the problem of unemployment/underemployment in contemporary America was briefly outlined, together with its generally agreed association with poverty and underclass membership. For Neoconservatives these trends indicate a 'breakdown of the work ethic', and in this chapter we will consider their diagnosis of the causes of this problem and their policy cures for it. The main Neoconservative diagnosis of the breakdown of the work ethic among the American poor is that of Lawrence Mead (e.g. 1986) and in section I below I give an account and critique of his emphasis on the psychological and cultural attitudes and processes (or 'internal barriers') which he argues inhibits underclass members from gaining employment. Mead is also one of the main spokesmen for the Neoconservative policy cure for such unemployment, namely 'workfare'. This policy aims to motivate the poor to seek and gain employment by making the servicing of their social right of citizenship to welfare conditional upon their performance of the citizen's social duty to work. In section II I develop a critique of Mead and others which focuses on the risks of (1) overambition, (2) incoherence and (3) depoliticization involved in the workfare policy.

Finally, in section III I provide an overall assessment of the Neoconservative challenge. Its project of attempted 'moral reformation' challenges the dominant paradigm's approach to social policy on both the work and family policy fronts. But my analysis suggests that the Neoconservative project is badly flawed on a number of counts. First, it mistakenly underplays or ignores structural explanations for the underclass. Secondly, it fails to come to terms with the amoral and anomic character of capitalism and thus with the fact that its commitment to capitalism undermines its appeal to citizenship 'ethics'. Thirdly, Neoconservatives criticize the dominant paradigm for promoting too much of a duty-free concept of social rights and apparently failing to understand the moral and political logic that 'rights imply duties'. But, conversely, Neoconservatism can itself be criticized for an equally one-dimensional view of this same logic and for failing to see that 'duties imply rights'. Finally, Neoconservatives are in any case profoundly split on *which* duties of social citizenship they wish to see modern society recalled to. Traditional conceptions of family duties cannot easily be reconciled with work duty in modern society, and contemporary American Neoconservatism is rife with contradictions and divisions on this issue.

I

The 'breakdown' of the work ethic: the Neoconservative diagnosis

The main American Neoconservative analyses of work and work policy in recent years have been produced by Lawrence Mead (1986, 1988a–d, 1989). Since he has also been the clearest and most important Neoconservative proponent of the relevance of a 'social-obligations-of-citizenship' approach to social policy in general and to work policy in particular, I will focus on his diagnoses and prescriptions here.

In his major study of American work and welfare policy,

Beyond Entitlement (1986) Mead acknowledges that the problems of 'breakdown' trends and problems outlined earlier (ch. 3
above) in traditional American family and employment patterns
are general phenomena, not restricted to the poor, with complex
causes (1986, pp. 25, 82). The welfare state, as Murray (1984)
argued, may have contributed to them. But Bell, in *The Cultural
Contradictions of Capitalism* (1976) had earlier pointed to the
problem of reconciling contemporary capitalism's need for mass
consumption (and thus for self-indulgent hedonism, a new
'consumer ethic'), with its traditional need for a 'work ethic'.
Echoing this, Mead entertains the thought that 'Perhaps capitalism, by its very success, undercuts the social discipline it
depends on' (1986, p. 41; also Ehrenreich 1987). Thus he
acknowledges that 'the American workforce may be less skilled
and motivated than it once was' (ibid., p. 2), while the long-
term rise of such problems as crime, low educational achievement, family breakup and to a lesser extent unemployment
suggest that a breakdown of psychological and sociological
'functioning' is widespread. Thus Mead asserts that 'functioning
is an issue for American society as a whole' (ibid., p. 25).
Nonetheless, his main concern is with the minority of Americans
who are poor and, using Auletta's study as a guide, with the
smaller minority who compose the welfare-dependent and the
underclass (ch. 3 above). It is in these groups that what Mead
refers to as socially significant 'functional' or 'competence' problems, and what others refer to as 'behavioural' problems, can be
said to be concentrated.

For Mead the basic 'functional' problems are unemployment,
underemployment and welfare dependency. According to his
diagnosis they are mainly 'voluntary' and are caused by an
inability or unwillingness on the part of the individuals involved
to recognize and understand that citizenship carries social
obligations as well as welfare rights. His prescription is for the
state to pursue an interventionist, expansive and above all
authoritative 'workfare' policy. Welfare benefits for the able-
bodied working-age unemployed should be made conditional on
their efforts to find and hold employment; the work ethic, or the
citizens' social duty to work, should be enforced.

Mead believes that 'Much of the remaining poverty in the
United States is due to high unemployment and nonwork among

the poor. If low-income men and welfare mothers worked regularly, the underclass would be well on its way to dissolution' (op. cit., p. 70). Mead's assumptions about what it is that best explains non-work is straightforward and voluntaristic: 'Much of measured unemployment is voluntary in the strict sense that many job seekers, both on and off welfare, refuse to take some available jobs' (1988b, p. 265). Thus the 'enforcement theory' implicit in workfare policy rests on an assumption that 'jobless-ness reflects choice more than necessity' (ibid.).

What does it mean to say that 'non-work' is 'voluntary'? According to Mead's analysis, it means that on the one hand liberal and Left explanations of non-work as 'involuntary', that is as responses to perceivedly insurmountable structural 'barriers' to employment, are inadequate. On the other hand, as against Murray's explanation, it does not imply that joblessness is an entirely rational choice explicable in terms of the 'logic of the situation'.

For Murray the welfare state unwittingly produces a situation of perverse incentives to remain unemployed, influencing the choices of those who are assumed to be job-seeking. Mead's picture of underclass members' choice and agency is very differ-ent from this. Basically he accepts a 'culture of poverty' view which accepts human choice and agency but which sees them as containing aspects of ambivalence, non-rationality and lack of competence. We will take a brief look at these negative and positive arguments in turn.

1 'External barriers' to employment: economy and society

Mead (1986, 1989 etc.) considers a number of 'external' barriers in the economic and social context of employment which are commonly claimed to explain non-work among the poor and the underclass. The main economic factors cited tend to be (1) the structural unemployment in northern industrial cities and regions, the 'rust belt', caused by de-industrialization in the 1980s. Associated with this are (2) the 'spatial mismatch' and (3) the 'skills mismatch' between the unskilled inner-city poor and the new sources of employment in the high technology post-industrial economy (located either in the suburbs, or in the south and west 'sunbelt', or in foreign economies, particularly Third World nations). We will need to consider these factors again later in the context of a general review of post-industrial change (ch. 7). For the moment, however, we will focus on Mead's views of their relevance.

Mead does not accept that these factors present the barriers that they are claimed to. Unlike the 1930s, periods of recession in the 1970s and 1980s have not actually reduced total employment in the American economy. On the contrary, he points out that 'total employment rose 35 per cent between 1970 and 1985' (1989, p. 158). In addition, overall unemployment rates in the late 1980s have been low, indicating a tight labour market (ibid.; 1988a, p. 45; also his 'job optimist' view 1988d, pp. 43–5).

Mead argues that skills and spatial mismatches are not insuperable barriers to achieving *some* kind of employment, as indicated for instance by the scale of immigration in recent American history (1988d; 1988a, p. 45). Immigrants evidently overcome severe 'spatial mismatch' problems and typically do not have the education and skills required by a high technology economy. Nonetheless, their economic achievements indicate the existence of a plentiful supply of unskilled jobs. They also indicate to some extent another theme of Mead's that the level of employer demand for labour is not an independent variable *vis-à-vis* labour supply. That is, labour demand is strongly influenced by characteristics of the labour supply, having to do with positive work attitudes and motivation as much as with skill levels (1988d, pp. 48–9, 53–54). These are some of the implications of his observation that 'Millions of immigrants, legal and illegal, have flooded in to the country to do jobs for which, apparently, citizens are unavailable' (1989, p. 158). In addition, Mead notes research on the poor and the underclass which indicates that on the one hand many unskilled (and 'not very good') jobs are available in the ghetto (since most unemployment and employment experience there is highly transitory and subject to a rapid turnover). On the other hand, as far as the jobs available only in the suburbs or at a distance go, the commuting problem is not among the most important reasons for the inner-city unemployed not getting them (Mead 1989, pp. 160–1; Freeman and Holzer 1986a, ch. 4).

'Barriers' to employment which have been claimed to exist in the *social* context of the poor and the underclass include above all else, of course, racial discrimination, but also the 'poverty trap' and disincentive effects of welfare, and the lack of child-care facilities for single mothers on welfare in particular. Along with Murray (1984, ch. 6) and other Neoconservatives Mead is strongly inclined to discount the role of racial discrimination. Since the Civil Rights movement a Black middle class has evidently emerged (Wilson 1987; Steele 1990), and working-class Blacks who have committed themselves to active and persistent participation in the labour market and to long-term employment have seen the income gap between themselves and comparable whites continue to narrow (Mead 1989, p. 161). He acknowledges evidence of some employer discrimination against unskilled Black men and youths perceived to be 'uncooperative' in favour of white and Black women, but he regards this as defensible in moral and economic terms and does not concede it as evidence of racial discrimination *per se*. He discounts the disincentive effect of welfare, implying that virtually any employment would almost certainly raise welfare mothers' cash incomes above welfare benefit levels, and he could find no evidence to defend the claim that child-care support represents a problem. His interpretation of the evidence he considered is that it shows that 'most working mothers, rich and poor, manage to arrange child care fairly easily' (ibid.).

Finally, the idea that non-work is voluntary rather than a product of barriers and structural constraints seems to be implied in the views of the poor themselves about the job situation they face. Only 16 per cent of non-working adult poor Blacks believe that inability to find a job of some kind is the main reason for their non-work, while 71 per cent of non-working inner-city Black youth believe that a job at the minimum wage is 'fairly easy to get' (ibid.).

If employment is one of the major social obligations of citizenship, and if the barriers to getting a job are not only not insuperable but, arguably, barely constitute barriers at all, then according to the Neoconservative view what induces citizens to opt voluntarily for non-work?

2   'Internal barriers' to employment: culture and psychology

Mead considers three main sorts of 'internal barriers' to employment and predispositions to non-work in the minds and attitudes
of the poor and the underclass: economic, political and cultural/
psychological. First, then, there is the notion that the choice of
non-work and welfare dependency is a product of a rational
economic calculation. Mead argues that this view fails because
people have stayed on welfare even though available employment is more profitable than welfare and even when real benefits fell both absolutely and relative to employment income
throughout the 1970s (Mead 1988c, p. 64; also 1986, p. 78).
But it mainly fails because, as instanced in behaviours such as
illegitimacy and crime, 'the mentality of most long-term poor
people today is decidedly *non*-economic' (1988c, p. 65), impulsive and short-termist. In Mead's view, if the poor were
rational economic calculators 'they would seldom be poor in the
first place' (ibid., p. 65).

Secondly, there is the notion that 'nonwork is political'. Mead
acknowledges that effectively the only employment available for
poor unskilled Blacks is 'dead-end', 'dirty' and degrading low-
paid menial work. Accepting this kind of work can be plausibly
presented as acquiescing in a form of 'racial subjugation' and a
'denial of rights'. In this situation then, 'nonwork is analogous to
a strike for better wages and working conditions' (1988c, p. 65;
also 1989, p. 161). Indeed frustration with such work was found
to be one of the causes of the urban riots of the 1960s (1986,
p. 78). Mead appears to concede some limited force to this
analysis, particularly as far as many young Black ghetto males
go with their 'uncooperative' attitudes to employers etc. Nonetheless, it does not square with other studies of the poor, particularly of the welfare mothers he is most concerned with,
which find them to be deferential rather than rebellious. Nor
does it square with studies of workfare clients who do not
experience the enforcement of work obligations as punitive,
unjust or even negative. In any case, individual and often
secretive non-work hardly qualifies as 'political' action to the
extent that such action is by definition 'proud, open and collective in nature' (Mead 1988c, p. 65).

Finally, there is the notion that non-work and welfare dependency derives from the kind of psychology or mentality fostered by a 'culture of poverty' (Mead 1986, p. 79; 1988c, pp. 65–6; 1989, pp. 161–2). In Mead's view this is 'the most persuasive interpretation of nonworking psychology especially for welfare mothers' (1989, p. 162; for comments on Mead's view see Wilson 1989). In Mead's interpretation the culture of poverty is 'pathological' in that it influences the poor to act against their own ideals and good intentions, not to mention their own self-interests; in a word it influences the poor to act against themselves. 'Parents want their children to avoid trouble but lose control of them to a street life of hustling and crime. Children want to succeed but lack the discipline to get through school. Girls want to marry and escape poverty but succumb to pregnancy and welfare' (1988c, p. 65). Thus the poor say that they desire to work. But because of their expectations and ideals they make the implementation of that desire conditional on the availability of good-quality jobs (relatively high incomes, good prospects for promotion etc.). Thus in Mead's view non-work among the poor is not in the main a problem of the low *quantity* of jobs available but rather a problem of their *quality* both as perceived by the poor and objectively (Mead 1988d).

The vicious circles possible here are evident. Intermittent and perhaps 'uncooperative' commitment to low-quality employment, indeed abstention from it altogether in many cases, allows no significant work record to be accumulated. This in turn badly disadvantages people in the labour market, disqualifying them from good-quality employment and rendering the aspiration for it increasingly unrealistic wishful thinking. Persistent refusal of work perceived to be demeaning and failure to achieve good-quality employment in turn undermines self-esteem, self-confidence and motivation producing further failure and discouragement, and so on.

Mead believes that in the culture of poverty poor people develop an 'irresolute mentality': 'They *want* to work but feel they *cannot*' (1988c, p. 66; 1989, p. 162). At the heart of the culture is an attitude of fatalism and defeatism or at least a belief in its own people's 'inefficacy'. The latter belief holds that forces and agents beyond the control of the culture and its members are responsible for whatever successes and failures its members experience. In its turn 'inefficacy seems to be the result primarily of weak socialization . . . erratic parenting (and failure) to internalize goals such as work and self-reliance with enough force to feel them as obligations' (1988c, p. 66).

Mead clearly makes a case for the 'culture of poverty' as a provisional candidate explanation, given both the weaknesses he claims to discern in competing explanations and also its fit with the relevant statistical and survey data he presents. Nevertheless, this case is less than convincing as we will see later in assessing Neoconservatism (section III below).

From Mead's Neoconservative perspective, then, the 'culture of poverty' encourages 'voluntary nonwork' and the 'breakdown of the work ethic'. This breakdown can be interpreted as a failure to honour the ethic, and it thus serves to promote a breakdown of one of the major forms taken by social citizenship and its obligations. This diagnosis of the cause and nature of the problem carries obvious implications as to the most appropriate and effective policy cure which we must now consider.

II

Workfare and work duties: the Neoconservative cure

'Workfare' refers to the social policy of making welfare benefits for able-bodied working-age people conditional upon employment or employment-related activities such as vocational training or job-search programmes etc. In this system welfare benefit is effectively a loan to be paid off by work. The policy is capable of a range of interpretations and applications from a liberal/Left 'supportive version' (as in Sweden (Burton 1987); as in some US states, e.g. California (Kirp 1986); and as advocated by some American commentators (e.g. Kaus 1986)) to a Neoconservative 'authoritative' version (e.g. Mead 1986, 1988b; and some US states, e.g. West Virginia). Considerable interest has developed in it in America in the 1980s both among the public at large (Butler and Kondratas 1987, p. 144; also Reischauer 1989), among liberal social policy analysts (e.g. Walzer 1985; Levin 1982; Garfinkel and McLanahan 1986; Handler and Hasenfeld

1990), but particularly among New Right and Neoconservative politicians and social analysts. Nonetheless, it remains the case that no unequivocal compulsory national workfare policy has been implemented in the USA (Burghes 1987).

An attempt to produce a national mandatory workfare policy by the Reagan presidency in the mid-1980s (GAO 1984, 1985) was defeated by Congress in favour of a permissive and 'supportive' framework for job training (JOBS 1988). Thus what American policy experience there is to draw on exists either in an equivocal form at the national level (i.e. in work-test and work-incentive aspects of programmes intended to implement *welfare* policies (Mead 1986)) or in a variegated and patchy form at the individual state level. Assessments of the effects various states' forms of workfare policy have on poverty, welfare dependency and employment are also equivocal (Gueron 1986; GAO 1984, 1985; Mead 1988b, 1989, pp. 164–6), and few effects are agreed. It would appear that in practice workfare policies do not seem to save much public expenditure, rather the reverse, and that they appear on the whole to be regarded positively by (the minority of) welfare claimants who have experienced them over the years.

There are, then, at least three main themes, or hubs around which the arguments about workfare policy swing and collide: (1) governmental level (federal or state?); (2) programme aims and organization ('authoritative' or 'supportive'?); and (3) effects (big or small? positive or negative?). These themes, of course provide focal points for arguments between the Left, liberals and the Right, or between Republicans and Democrats. But more important from the point of view of this discussion is the fact that they also provide focal points for divisions and contradictions *within* Neoconservatism and within its conception of social citizenship. A review of the full range of arguments about workfare would be out of place here. Instead I will consider the three themes of workfare policy debate mainly in so far as they illustrate 'internal' divisions and contradictions in the Neoconservative perspective. Such 'internal' problems serve to undermine both the strength of Neoconservatism's challenge to the dominant paradigm of social citizenship and also the credibility of one of the alternative approaches to social policy it implies.

1   Workfare and governmental level/scale

Neoconservatives evidently differ among themselves about whether the scale of central government in general and of the welfare state in particular, is or is not an issue of major concern. As we have seen, in an ideal world Charles Murray (1984) would happily eradicate the bulk of the bottom-tier non-contributory welfare benefits system. He trusts that forcing able-bodied working-age adults to sink or swim in the labour market would solve the 'voluntary nonwork' and work ethic/work discipline problems described by himself (1984, ch. 5), by Mead (above) and by others. Whether this would be economically effective is questionable. Even if it were economically effective, whether such an a-political and politically de-contextualized process of learning to swim in a labour market would improve people's understanding of their role and responsibilities as citizens *per se* is even more questionable. Murray represents the New Right libertarian anti-statist flank of Neoconservatism. So the versions of social and political community (and thus citizenship) he is most positive about – to the extent that he is positive about *any* besides markets – tend to be *local* communities (i.e. neighbourhoods and, at a stretch, cities and local states). This sort of willingness to favour the local/state governmental level and its form of citizenship over the national level and its form of citizenship is evident also in other Neoconservative social policy analysts some of whose views we will illustrate in a moment.

On his side of the argument, as the leading Neoconservative proponent of workfare, Mead is clearly committed to a scheme at national level embodying the dominant mood of the American public and being expressed in terms of the language and social responsibilities of *national* American citizenship. It should address the functioning and competence problems which Mead believes are ignored in the perspectives of anti-statists like Murray (Mead 1986, p. 86). As against both New Right libertarians and the liberal welfare establishment, government policy needs to make its presence felt and be authoritative and not permissive or *laissez-faire* ('The welfare state must finally *be* a state' Mead op. cit., p. 29). Against the New Right in particular, Mead points out that it is the (permissive and non-authoritative) *nature* of government in the welfare state and not its *scale* which is the main problem leading to the perpetuation of poverty, non-work and 'lack of functioning' (op. cit., p. 14 etc.). Finally, Mead is clear that a national workfare policy would be expansive and expensive. First, it needs substantial public expenditure on child-care support services to an expanded group of welfare mothers involved in it (1988c, p. 67; 1989, p. 161). Secondly, it implies an expansion of 'welfare to cover more low-skilled fathers so that more of them could be reached by workfare programs' (1989, p. 168). Thirdly, *if* it were successful in raising the participation of the poor and underclass in low-pay, low-status, low-quality jobs, the case for the state to intervene in the labour market to improve the quality of such jobs (since this is a 'political' matter) would be strengthened (e.g. 1989, pp. 167, 169).

Two important sets of criticisms of workfare policy by Neo-conservatives have been produced by Gilder (1987) and Butler and Kondratas (1987), and we will explore these further in section III. But part of their critique strikes at the 'scale of government' issue. Thus they believe that a national workfare policy would encourage the growth of the central state and the welfare state in terms both of expense and power. This belief seems to be justified whether national workfare policy was developed by conservatives (like Mead as we have seen) or by liberals. Noting the emergence of liberal and Left support for 'supportive' workfare, Butler and Kondratas comment 'Dreams of a beneficent all-powerful welfare state die hard' (1987, p. 149). As against a national workfare policy as the main anti-poverty policy, they emphasize the importance of local community and individual state-level self-help initiatives by Blacks in ghetto areas and in general the importance of the state role as against the federal government role in anti-poverty policies. (For a response to this by Mead see his 1988a.) In similar spirit Gilder argues that a national workfare scheme would 'vastly expand the US welfare state' (1987, p. 20) and even that it would 'subvert the foundations of capitalism' (p. 21). In a veiled reference to Mead among others he rejects his fellow Neo-conservatives' 'unthinking rush to a "workfare" state' (p. 20).

2   *Workfare aims and organization*

We have noted that over the years different American states have developed different interpretations of workfare policy. The older 'authoritative' versions emphasize the sanctions or 'sticks' of withdrawal of benefit in the event of clients' non-compliance with work-search programmes and requirements. The newer 'supportive' versions (the 'newstyle workfare' of California, Massachusetts etc.) emphasize the 'carrots' of child-care services for welfare mothers, transport allowances, work-preparation programmes, job-search clubs, personal counselling services etc., intended to attract and encourage rather than coerce clients' participation. The older authoritative versions ambitiously aimed to get welfare recipients off the welfare rolls and into long-term employment, and to do so in order to reduce public spending as much as to bring their citizenship duties home to them. However, the problems of poverty and the underclass have proved to be both expensive to address and also too intractable and complex to be very amenable to single-factor diagnoses and quick-fix cures (Gueron 1986; GAO 1984, 1985; Wiseman 1987a, 1987b; Handler and Hasenfeld 1990, chs 4–6).

The newer supportive versions of workfare are perhaps less ambitious about what counts as success. Besides the aim of promoting clients' long-term employment (and given the difficulty of achieving this) such programmes also set themselves aims of an adult education or even adult resocialization kind; that is, they encourage clients to be less passive and fatalistic, to take a confident and participative approach to employment opportunities and to the workfare process (work preparation, job search, counselling etc.). They aim to develop in their clients a better understanding of the practical implications of society's expectations of its adult members (e.g. expectations that people should be as proactive and self-reliant as possible, that they should act in a responsible and reciprocal way with others, with organizations and with the state etc.). This is the ethos of the Californian and Massachusetts versions of workfare (Kirp 1986) and also of the employment opportunity provisions (JOBS) of the Family Security Act 1988 (Moynihan 1989; Brown 1989).

In either or both of these forms there are some inherent

problems in principle for workfare policy and for the Neo-conservative defence of it which we can briefly note here. These problems can be expressed in an emphatic way by saying that the policy risks being judged as (1) over-ambitious, (2) incoherent and (3) depoliticizing.

i The risk of over-ambition Mead acknowledges in his diagnosis of the causes of non-work that there are several candidate explanations referring to structural factors and barriers to employment. He succeeds in challenging some of the claims of these candidates. But he does not attempt to demonstrate the utter irrelevance of these factors, nor could he succeed were he to try. Non-work by the poor and the underclass on this account remains a phenomenon with many conditions and causes. 'Voluntary non-work' is a behaviour produced by people in a variety of life situations, whether by single mothers on welfare or by young males who may be involved in street crime, and so on. On this account as well it remains a phenomenon intelligible in terms of a number of possible motives and reasons (all of which Mead chooses to refer to using indiscriminate and undefined terms such as 'dysfunction', 'incompetence' or similar words). Apparently this essentially complex phenomenon which is the product of a mixture of causes and reasons can be changed by a single line of policy, workfare, which attempts to do no more than to enforce the duty to work. But complex problems surely need complex solutions.

In this situation, moderate and defensible claims for workfare might see it as one policy in the battery of policies that it is necessary to develop in order to address various dimensions of the complex problems of 'voluntary non-work' among the poor and the underclass. Other Neoconservatives recognize this complexity. Thus Glazer (1988) advocates a range of welfare, education, training and health-care reforms to tackle the problem, while even Murray (1984), often assumed to be a one-note welfare abolitionist, actually has other notes in his repertoire, including reform of the public education system. It is in this spirit that Wiseman argues 'We should not expect workfare to be the final solution to any welfare problem because the scope of workfare programs is too narrow. [They] operate only *within* the welfare system' (1987a, p. 47). In his view the more important and influential policy fields (education, health etc.) lie outside this system. Being over-ambitious about workfare or 'dropping everything else for workfare' in Wiseman's view 'is wholly unjustified'. Rather the question to ask welfare politicians is not whether or not they have a workfare policy but 'What *else* are you doing?' (p. 47).

ii   The risk of incoherence   The version of workfare policy Mead presented in *Beyond Entitlement* was clearly an 'authoritative' and 'tough-minded' one. It aimed at solving the 'functioning' and 'competence' problems of the underclass by enforcing the citizens' obligation to work. But there is a problem here. Such enforcement of obligation is likely to work best with those who already understand what the obligation is, who have decided not to honour it, who need to be authoritiatively reminded about it and who are likely to change their behaviour because of such an authoritative reminder. But Mead's target group, the underclass, are people with 'functional' and 'competence' problems (1986) who have been socialized in a culture of poverty (1989). Thus they can hardly be assumed to understand adequately the citizen's duty to work (to seek and hold employment). This lack of understanding is evident in Mead's own observations about the unrealistic expectations the underclass have about appropriate employment and their disconnection of aspiration to work from actual behaviour, non-work, as we saw earlier.

For Mead the underclass do not have a pre-understanding of the duty to work and are not conventionally rational. They need a kind of 'public education' (1989) about the citizen's duty to work, which virtually amounts to a resocialization. But if all this is true then pursuing workfare policy as an 'authoritative reminder' is likely to be a waste of time and money. According to Mead's own analysis there is no good reason to expect it to be effective. If underclass problems are problems of ignorance, incompetence and poor socialization, then they need to be tackled by programmes which have an educational and resocializing character, in other words programmes of the 'supportive' kind which have developed as 'newstyle workfare'. It is well known to be difficult to design coherent policies and programmes combining   punitive/disciplinary   and   therapeutic/educational aims in many fields, from penal policy to educational policy. Either one aim or the other tends to come to dominate the policy ethos, or operational 'philosophy' (i.e. the professional expertise, routine practices and self-understanding), of policy-makers, programme managers and front-line officials. This problem of incoherence is an evident risk in the contemporary development of alternative versions of workfare in American social policy.

Mead argues that his review of the nationwide work-require-ment (WIN) element of AFDC (delivered through various state programmes) shows that programmes using most authority (sanctioning non-compliance by summons, hearings, grant re-duction etc.) have most effect in raising work effort and work placement among welfare clients (1988b). But on the other hand he also accepts the findings of other authoritative assessments of workfare such as that of Gueron (1986, for MRDC, see ch. 3, p. 58 above) which show that:

> Successful workfare programs encourage intensive interaction between clients and staff and among the clients themselves . . . Recipients are not coerced; they are expected to participate . . . Relationships are the main lever . . . The work obligation is levied more through these interchanges than impersonal bureau-cratic requirements . . . Programs that rely heavily on legal coercion are much less able to motivate and thus much less successful. (1989, p. 166)

Whether it is indeed possible to retain the degree of authori-tativeness and obligation Mead requires from work-enforcement policy through such informal and essentially 'supportive' pro-cesses remains to be seen. The professional and practical press-ures and contradictions facing the staff in such programmes are evident. So too is the problem of the status and perception of participation in the new supportive personal services available on workfare programmes. Is this part of the work that poor citizens are expected/required to perform to fulfil their social obligations, or does it represent an extension of their social rights? There are clearly great possibilities for confusion and incoherence on all fronts – whether it be participant experience, policy development or academic assessment – in the current state of play of American workfare policy.

iii   The risk of depoliticization   Workfare policy, on the Neo-conservative interpretation, attempts to underpin politically and to institutionalize a connection which is assumed to hold for society in general between the political status of citizenship and the economic status of employment, namely that it is a citizens' social duty to seek and hold employment. The risks of in-stitutionally *segregating the social dimension of citizenship* from its core 'civil' and 'political' dimensions is an important problem. It affects both the dominant paradigm (and its use of the welfare state to supply 'social' rights, as we suggested in chapters 1 and 2), and also Neoconservatism (and its attempts to use the welfare state to enforce 'social' duties through workfare). One of the problems about welfare dependency from the point of view of my analysis is that it undermines citizenship in the sense of encouraging the experience of claiming 'social rights' to become disconnected from – indeed to overshadow – claimants' under-standings of their broader (civil/political) citizen status with its (civil/political) rights, powers and responsibilities. But workfare is no cure for *this* aspect of the problem of welfare dependency.

Workfare programmes *may* (at a stretch) be capable of being interpreted, as Mead suggests, as 'form(s) of public education' (1989, p. 166). And they may or (as in the case of merely authoritative versions) they may not address the humanity and personality of the client. But they evidently do not attempt to address themselves to clients in their full status as citizens. For instance, they do not present themselves as programmes of adult *political and legal* education addressed at clients' understanding of the relationship in their society between the state, law and the economy, between citizenship, law and employment etc. No employer, particularly those offering low-quality employment, makes any attempt to address these sorts of issues in their personnel training programmes (to the extent that they have such things), let alone in the mere experience of the employ-ment they offer. In my view it is fanciful, not to say intellectually irresponsible, for Mead and this school of Neoconservative social analysis to imply that employment *per se* constitutes any kind of a serious education for, or even address to, citizenship *per se*.

Mead's views about the relationship of workfare to the political aspects of employment and unemployment are worth noting in this context. First, as we have seen he dismisses the notion that non-work among poor and underclass Black males might be a form of political protest against the low quantity and quality of jobs available to them. This does not fit his conception either of politics or of the underclass as dysfunctional and relatively non-rational. Secondly, he acknowledges that the quality of employment is essentially a *political* matter (susceptible to change by government policies on minimum income, health and safety regulation, health cover for workers etc.). Thirdly, he implies that the poor and society at large ought not to engage in the politics of employment quality with a view to improving it *until* authoritative workfare policies have had their intended effect of coercing the underclass into the only kind of employment available to them, namely 'dirty' low-quality employment: 'the problem of economic participation . . . must be solved *before* (my italics, MR) issues of equity can even get on the (political) agenda . . . New economic claims can be made only by citizens in full standing, who in this culture must have a work history' (1989, p. 169). The depoliticizing tenor of this is clear enough. Honouring the social obligations of citizenship is apparently distinct not only from the other dimensions of citizenship but it is also the *prerequisite* for being admitted to them. The social duties of citizenship are *pre*-political and those who fail to honour them can hardly be considered to be citizens at all. Workfare policy thus can hardly be conceptualized (ironically, as the authoritative version sometimes implies) as an exercise of reminding citizens of duties they have allowed to lapse. Rather it is more of an exercise in the 'pre-political' constitution of the very opposibility of citizenship for people who are assumed to be effectively non-citizens.

Even as a reminding exercise for genuine citizens, workfare policy can be presented in terms which attempt to depoliticize it. Thus Mead often compares the work ethic and citizens' obligations to work with citizens' duties to pay taxes. By analogy, the state has a right to enforce the former just as it has the latter. With this analogy, Mead is implying that both sorts of duties are uncontroversial and politically innocuous, that they are a-political or pre-political conditions for politics and citizenship. But on closer inspection the analogy in fact suggests the very opposite of what Mead intends. Tax duties are highly political matters subject to the citizens' perceptions of what is fair and unfair, and subject also to their political powers to make and remake tax law through the democratic process. Popular resentment against poll taxes as inherently unjust initiated the Peasants' Revolt in fourteenth-century Britain and more recently has helped to bring down Margaret Thatcher, the longest-serving prime minister in modern British history. Indeed Mead seems to have overlooked the degree to which the American nation state and its citizenship derives historically from the politics of opposition to perceivedly unjust British colonial taxation. If tax duties are supposed to be an analogy for work duties it is clear that they are honoured by a *politicized* citizenry exercising the *political* judgement that they are tolerably just. The tax duty analogy thus suggests the very opposite of the depoliticized conception of social citizenship Mead would like us to see in it.

Finally, it is worth noting that the tax obligation analogy opens up a Pandora's box of more general problems for the Neoconservative theory of social citizenship. It enables major and (for Mead's position) embarrassing questions to be raised about the anomic character of the contemporary capitalist order in general, whether in America, or in other nations, or throughout the minimally morally and legally regulated global economy.

Individual and corporate tax evasion and tax avoidance are themselves important industries in modern capitalism. We need to develop a *rounded* conception of the problem of the breakdown of social citizenship obligations and of the politics needed to reaffirm and enforce such obligations. Such a conception would address itself to the problems of ensuring that affluent individuals and powerful national and multinational corporations as well as the poor and the underclass recognized their social obligations (to pay taxes, to obey the law, to work etc.). To focus exclusively upon the latter and to turn a blind eye to the former reveals a clear bias in Neoconservatism's social analysis, social philosophy and social policy. We will return later to some of these issues, particularly those of corporate citizenship and social obligations at national and global levels (ch. 9).

3   Workfare effects

In the course of the discussion of American workfare policy in this section some of the main points about its effects have already been indicated. Although a few substantial assessments exist (e.g. Gueron 1986; GAO 1984, 1985; Mead 1986) it is not easy to establish a clear picture of workfare's effects. This is partly because of the variegated nature of work-enforcement programmes at state level. It is also partly because of an elastic understanding of their aims and thus of what would *count* as a relevant 'effect' (Wiseman 1987a). As we noted earlier, 'authoritative' programmes aim mainly at client employment, and perhaps also at public spending reduction. More 'supportive' programmes, while aiming at employment, aim also at client attitude and behaviour change and at their participation in new service provision. Such programmes tolerate where necessary a growth of public spending to achieve these aims.

There *is* a strong Neoconservative interest in and support for workfare policy, in part claiming to articulate American public opinion on work and welfare issues. Nonetheless, Neoconservatism is fundamentally divided on the value of the possible effects of workfare in principle, because of the importance of familism to Neoconservatism, which we explored in chapter 5. Thus a clear Neoconservative familist *critique* of workfare exists. This holds that one of workfare's main likely effects is to *obstruct* citizens in the performance of their social duties, specifically their family duties to care for children.

We will consider this important fissure and contradiction in Neoconservatism's conception of social citizenship later (section III (4) below). But first we need to consider the Neoconservative challenge to the dominant paradigm in the two key areas of work and the family in more general terms.

III

The Neoconservative challenge: an assessment

1 Neoconservatism and social citizenship: strengths and weaknesses

Over the course of the last three chapters we have explored many of the most important aspects of Neoconservatism's challenge to the dominant paradigm's assumptions about social citizenship. Earlier (chapter 2) we suggested that any substantial paradigm of citizenship in general, and social citizenship in particular, must imply three sorts of conception: of social citizenship's *nature* (as an intersubjective and moral 'world'); of its social structural *context*; and of its '*historicality*' (that is the change in citizenship's nature and context over time). In each of these terms Neoconservatism poses a clear and politically powerful challenge to the dominant paradigm.

First, Neoconservatism opposes a duties-based conception of the nature of citizenship and its world to the orthodoxy's rights-based version. Secondly, it proposes a positive conception of modern capitalism and its markets as a uniquely powerful and historically irreplaceable economic system for supporting personal freedom and mass prosperity, and as the main element in the 'welfare pluralism' which has come to prevail in the West in the mid- and late twentieth century. It opposes this to the orthodoxy's overestimation of the importance of government, taxation and public spending for citizen's welfare; its overestimation of the role and potential of the welfare state; and its various negative attitudes to the social fact of the inherent structural plurality of welfare in modern society and capitalism's role in this, attitudes which range from complacency, to studied ignorance, to antagonism. Finally, as regards assumptions about social change, Neoconservatism argues for the long-term regressive effects of the growth of the welfare state, and proposes a vision of modernity's general cultural crisis and need for moral reform. It opposes this to the dominant paradigm's assumptions about the positive character of the growth of the welfare state and modernity's long-term socially *progressive* character.

To make the nature of this challenge clearer and to provide some basis for assessing it we have focused on its handling of the limit case of social citizenship, namely poverty, and in particular the contemporary problem of the underclass. We saw that Gilder, Mead, Novak and others have proposed interesting and noteworthy, if controversial, explanations – both of an individualistic/voluntaristic type and also of a 'culture of poverty' type – for the existence and reproduction of underclass poverty. In general, the Neoconservative challenge has made a strong case for putting the following notions back on to the academic, ideological/political and social policy agendas: (1) the importance of capitalism for welfare, and also of welfare pluralism, (2) the importance of social duties and responsibilities for a defensible conception of social citizenship, and (3) the prob- lematic character of contemporary trends and social changes for the future of social citizenship. However, clearly there are weaknesses in the Neoconservative approach which we need to briefly consider in this concluding section. These concern its explanation of the underclass (2 below), its conception of the general relevance of capitalism for citizenship (3 below) and the coherence of its conceptions of duty and of social policy (4 below).

2   The problem of the underclass

Neoconservatism's revival of the 'culture of poverty' and associ- ated 'cycle of deprivation' theses in the moralistic terms in which they present them tends to present a relatively simplistic and one-dimensional (i.e. individualistic/agent-centred) view of what is inevitably in reality a complex two-dimensional (i.e. agent- structured) social phenomenon. Ironically, like the dominant paradigm, they evidently underplay the importance of major long-term socio-economic changes such as those involved in residential location and the demand for labour. These sorts of factors have been emphasized in recent studies of the underclass by liberal and Left social analysts such as Wilson (1987, 1989), Kasarda (1989), Harrington (1984), Bluestone and Harrison (1982), Block (1987b) and others. In their view the contem- porary ghetto underclass has been formed mainly by two sets of economic forces, namely *uneven economic growth* and *de- industrialization*, largely beyond the control of underclass members. In the first place, Wilson (1987) argues that general economic growth, together with the expansion of the welfare state, from the 1960s to the 1980s benefited middle-class and skilled working-class sections of inner-city ghetto communities, who then tended to move out to live in the suburbs. But they had been the mainstays of the basic social institutions (i.e. churches, schools, shops, recreational organizations, etc.) of the ghetto communities, which functioned to cushion people in periods of economic difficulty and generally to promote social order and organization. With their removal the residual community in the ghettos became a socially isolated concentration of the most disadvantaged, hopelessly vulnerable to the effects of negative economic forces.

In the second place (as Bluestone and Harrison 1982, Wilson 1987, Kasarda 1989 and others argue, and as we will explore in more detail in chapter 7), a process of de-industrialization has occurred, in the same period. This has involved structural shifts in contemporary capitalism towards high-skill services, and spatially towards the suburbs, the 'sunbelt' cities or the Third World, which have conspired to reduce employment opportunities in the ghetto and to keep unemployment high and rising. Neoconservatives' dismissal of these factors is unconvincing, as we have seen in our discussion of Mead's views in this chapter. High unemployment in its turn can be argued to produce a breakdown of family structure, an increase in welfare dependency and both directly and indirectly an increase in poverty and crime.

The 'culture of poverty' and the 'cycle of deprivation' theses (e.g. Leacock 1971) were controversial in their heyday of the 1960s. And, couched in Neoconservative terms, they remain largely speculative and controversial when applied to the contemporary underclass phenomenon. There is precious little evidence in the form of new detailed and systematic studies in the ethnography, psychology or social history of contemporary ghetto life to support them directly. Nonetheless, some evidence for a *structurally* interpreted version of these theses is beginning to emerge. Thus Wilson and Wacquant 1989, Anderson 1989 and others have provided interesting insights into the cultural processes through which the structural problems of uneven economic growth and de-industrialization are lived through in residualized ghetto communities. Their accounts of the social isolation of ghetto residents and of the effect of the absence of 'legitimate' role models on young males indicate the need to relate structure to situation and agency in research in this area. A more sociologically rounded picture and understanding of the life of the poor in contemporary America than that provided by Neoconservatism is clearly needed. This is not only for reasons of sociological accuracy but also, and more importantly, to provide a better basis than appears to exist currently for policy formation and political action.

Overall, Neoconservatism is to a considerable extent ambiguous and incoherent in its conception of the poor and underclass citizen as simultaneously capable of moral reform by authoritarian reminders about duty *and* socially incompetent and psychologically incapable of rational self-control and thus of consistent moral action. Also, finally, Neoconservatism is limited by its simultaneous trust and belief in both the economic power and potential of an (ideally) minimally morally and legally regulàted capitalism and yet also the moral power and potential of traditional duties to reform social citizenship and to tackle poverty and underclass problems. Each of these sets of contradictory beliefs clearly underestimate the importance of the structural context of contemporary social citizenship and contemporary poverty (see also Handler and Hasenfeld 1990). We now need to consider the latter set concerning Neoconservatism's belief in the relevance of capitalism for citizenship.

3   Citizenship and capitalism

Overall, probably the major underlying weakness in the Neoconservative challenge to the dominant paradigm has been its inability to connect together systematically its two main values. On the one hand, it supports 'morality', and 'traditional', patriarchal, familistic and 'work ethic' morality in particular; on the other, it supports capitalism as an economic system, which is arguably inherently anti-traditional (Weber 1970; Marx and Engels 1969, e.g. p. 52) and (*pace* Hayek 1973 and Popper 1966), amoral or even anomic (Durkheim 1964; Merton 1968). This problem has been recognized by Neoconservatives (e.g. Berger and Berger 1983; Bell 1976 and ch. 5 above). It is particularly clear as the dynamics of contemporary capitalism have begun to undermine each of the two main traditional ethics. On the one hand, it is tending to undermine patriarchal familism by demanding full and unrestricted access to the adult labour supply without initial reference to economically arbitrary 'social' categories such as gender; On the other, it is tending to undermine the work ethic by stimulating hedonistic consumerism and by promoting the status and value of identities and lifestyles built around leisure and consumption rather than work and production (e.g. Baudrillard 1988; Offe 1985b).

One of the consequences of these developments for Right-wing politics has been the growth of a number of serious splits and divisions. New Right libertarianism seems to be prepared to follow the market to whatever anti-communal, anti-social and amoral territory it leads, because of the priority it accords to atomistic individualism and market choice. But, as we have seen, by contrast with this, Neoconservatism wishes to reassert the collective and authoritative aspect of traditional social ethics associated with earlier stages in the development of capitalist civilization. These two positions look set to become even more incompatible than they already are, given the contemporary trajectory of capitalist change. However, another consequence of these changes has been a split *within* Neoconservatism between those who seem to recognize the problem of capitalism's anomic character and those who do not seem to do so. The former emphasize the need to focus the moral reform of citizenship on the traditional family ethic. This ethic appears to operate in a sphere which is (again, apparently) outside the market and economic relations.

We have reviewed the main characteristics, and some of the intrinsic strengths and weaknesses, of this position in chapter 5. But the point we now need to consider is that this position, which (at least implicitly) recognizes capitalism's anomic character has become somewhat detached from and conflictual with the position we have reviewed earlier in this chapter which supports the traditional work ethic.

It is worth making a number of points about this 'ethic'. First, the 'work ethic' is an 'ethic' requiring people to (attempt to) sell their labour in the market for whatever price and under whatever conditions, good or bad, 'just' or 'unjust', the market will provide. In addition, this is not an 'ethic' connected with the various ethics of care and altruism present in most world religions and in modern humanism; that is, it does not oblige people to engage in work for which there is no market and hence no market price, and which has traditionally been performed mainly by women, such as housework, child-care work and care of the elderly. Secondly, as we have noted, the market's effects on the 'work ethic' are highly problematic and include importantly what Bell (1976) refers to as 'the cultural contradictions of capitalism' which pit the 'ethic' of consumerism against the 'ethic' of employment (also Habermas 1975; Offe 1985b). Nonetheless, 'work-ethic Neoconservativism' throws in its lot with what amounts to an idealized, unrealistic and essentially morally limited conception of capitalism's allegedly beneficial effects on morality. Finally, by endorsing the ethical value of participation in the labour market 'work-ethic Neoconservatism' runs into conflict with 'familist Neoconservatism'.

The Neoconservative paradigm of social citizenship, as we have seen in chapters 4, 5 and 6, is afflicted with a number of major weaknesses, not the least of which is this final problem of the lack of a coherent conception of social ethics. To conclude our consideration of the Neoconservative paradigm and its ideological challenge to the dominant paradigm we can briefly illustrate this important problem of its ideological incoherence. Following this, in part III, we will turn to the challenges posed to the dominant paradigm by contemporary structural social change.

4 Neoconservatism, work and family: problems of duty and policy

One of Neoconservatism's main arguments against the dominant paradigm is that the latter's overemphasis on rights obscures the extent to which (social) 'rights imply duties'. But if this is the case, then logically the same applies in reverse to the Neoconservatives' attempt to overemphasize duties as against rights. As they have discovered from their exposure to the responsibilities of government in America and Britain in the 1980s, 'duties imply rights' in social policy, and they do so in practice as well as in principle. The overemphasis on duties in the rationales and conceptual frameworks that Neoconservatives provide for new policy proposals too often obscures the real situation. The reality is both that they have often been involved in the concession and creation of new rights, and also that this has often been a necessary step, a direct consequence of their attempt to make the 'call to duty' effective in practice.

This is clear in the cases of work and family policy we have discussed. For instance, the duty of single mothers to work cannot be enforced unless their rights to child-care services are extended. Or again, the duty of deserting fathers to support their children cannot be enforced without giving new rights to deserted mothers to the man's income. Or again, the duty of parents to take responsibility for their children's education cannot be significantly encouraged without reorganizing the educational system to provide new forms of empowerment and rights to parents, and so on. So this is one line of inconsistency and of potential incoherence and conflict within the Neoconservative position.

A second and equally problematic source of incoherence and conflict lies in the relationship that we may assume exists between *different social duties*. In particular what is the relation between the duty to work and family duty? Neoconservatives have recently taken very different views about this and we need to consider these a little further.

The main proponents of work duties and workfare in America have been Neoconservatives like Lawrence Mead. However, as we noted earlier, besides the 'authoritative' forms of workfare which Mead and others support there are also 'supportive' forms of the kind built into Moynihan's Family Security Act which are acceptable to liberals. In addition, support for the moral value of work and for the importance of the work ethic – whether sociologically, or psychologically, or both – runs across the political spectrum both in theory and in practice. In practice, until recently, Social Democratic Sweden operated a tougher workfare policy for young adults (18–20 years) than does Conservative Britain (Burton 1987; Harper 1990b). In theory, liberal and Left American writers have supported the principle of workfare. Thus political theorist Michael Walzer (1985) argues for the legitimacy of work duties in a just society, while political commentators Nicholas Lemann (1986) and Mickey Kaus (1986) argue respectively for a universal national-service type programme of public-sector work for youth and a 'work ethic state' involving guaranteed government jobs. One flank of American Neoconservatism is intensely suspicious of central state power and tolerant of government only at state level or below, the more local the better. On this flank scepticism about workfare runs deep. As they see it, if the price for honouring and enforcing work duty is the growth of governmental power, and if this in turn carries with it the potential for authoritarianism and for loss of individual liberty, then this policy looks too expensive (Butler and Kondratas 1987, pp. 146–8).

Butler and Kondratas, in developing their 'conservative strategy for welfare reform', argue that, in addition to its potential for authoritarianism, workfare may not save money either: 'not much hard data exist about the cost-effectiveness of workfare (financially) . . . or about its impact on caseload reduction. So conservatives are talking through their hats when they claim that workfare makes people independent and cuts costs immediately' (1987, p. 15). They agree with conservative workfare supporters that 'good welfare policy must involve reciprocal obligations . . . (But) work requirements will not provide a panacea for dependency. [They] are only a small part of the picture' (ibid., p. 145). Moreover, welfare policy needs to encourage the two-parent family, but the attempt to make single-mother families self-sufficient by means of workfare 'is not necessarily a sound long-term policy. Why? Because [workfare] policies do not improve work incentives or opportunities for absent fathers; their effect is to transform mothers into primary earners' (ibid., pp. 145–6).

George Gilder (1986) criticizes workfare for this effect on family in characteristically more colourful style. As we saw earlier, he believes that welfare deregulates sexuality in the ghetto and destroys 'the sexual constitution'. Elsewhere the latter sustains civility and civilization by domesticating and taming males' barbaric natures with the bonds of marriage, monogamy, fatherhood and breadwinning. Taking his stance on the 1965 Moynihan Report's implied solution to the 'tangle of pathology' of the Black ghetto family, Gilder believes that policy should aim 'to restore work and family as instruments of male socialization among the poor' (1986, p. 195). However, by developing the welfare system which followed the Moynihan Report Gilder believes that the US Congress effectively 'deprived the Black family of fathers' (ibid., p. 94). In this context contemporary Congressional interest in workfare indicates that, according to Gilder, 'Congress [wants] now to take away the mothers as well' (ibid., p. 95).

Gilder (1987) has expanded on this theme in his response to fellow conservatives Novak et al. (1987b) and the strong endorsement they give (in the report we considered in chapter 5), to workfare as an essential element in a pro-family social policy. He regards their 'New Consensus' as in reality 'a profoundly antifamily report' which 'joins the unthinking rush to a "workfare state"' (1987, p. 20). He derides their 'tough talk of "responsibility", "obligation" and "duty" as just so much conservative patina on the hard metal of [an expansion of the American welfare state through] government jobs and day-care entitlements' (ibid., p. 20). He is scathing about the notion that enforcement of workfare for single mothers and of child support for absent fathers is likely to do anything but make the problems of the ghetto families and the ghetto underclass worse than they already are.

In his view these problems are not material but moral. Materially the American 'poor' can appear reasonably prosperous both in absolute terms (cf. Eberstadt 1988 on America's 'prosperous pauperism') and also relative to other international standards of living. For instance, according to Gilder, among the American poor there is 40 per cent home ownership; 80 per cent ownership of telephones and colour TVs; widespread car ownership; life expectancy at birth of 70 years; access to health care; access to unreported income which allows their expenditure to exceed their reported income by three times; twice the housing space possessed by the average Japanese etc. 'Their problem is not [material] poverty but a collapse of family discipline and sexual morality . . . [leading to] a stagnant community divided between the dependent and the predatory' (ibid., p. 23). On the women's side, 'female-headed families are . . . a disaster . . . because they are totally incapable of taming teenage boys' (ibid., p. 25), while getting more women into employment 'will only accelerate family decay' (ibid., p. 21). This is because it will give women even more of an economic edge than they already have over their potential husbands with their insecure identities as potential family 'breadwinners'. Women tend to be more successful than men in getting whatever new jobs local economies generate, particularly in poor areas. In the light of this, Gilder believes, 'Female domination of work among the poor is the problem, not the solution' that workfare seems to imply (ibid., p. 21).

On the males' side, they are directly responsible for the problem of 'hard-core poverty'. 'The problem . . . lies with violent and disruptive men and boys, not with unemployed women' (ibid.). Developing child-support agencies, paternity tests, automatic deductions of support from wages and so on for absent underclass fathers is likely to be a waste of time and counterproductive; 'Once the father has left the battle has been lost' (ibid., p. 24). Enforcement of paternal duties 'would ensure that these men (and boys) would stay completely out of work-fare and all other reported employment' (ibid., pp. 23–4). In his view, 'Governments . . . cannot replace families' and they should not try 'to substitute state power for the fabric of family responsibility' (ibid., p. 24) by means of workfare and the enforcement of paternal duties.

Gilder holds that the situation of the ghetto family and under-class is bad and getting worse, and the state should avoid doing anything like workfare and paternity enforcement which is likely to add to the problem. Nonetheless, he thinks that the state can do something useful for poor families by enacting what he calls 'the essential profamily policy'. Ironically (and paradoxically for a Neoconservative) this turns out to be a major new extension of social rights, namely a system of substantial and universal child allowances along lines developed in France and other countries. By supplementing, rather than displacing, poor males' low employment earnings this would help support their breadwinner role and also help 'keep mothers in the home, rather than pursuing menial work that hardly pays for day care' (ibid., p. 24). Needless to say, Gilder's proposed expansion of the welfare state has, to say the least, not been welcomed by some fellow Neoconservatives (e.g. Novak 1987a; Carlson 1987).

In the absence of some such policy, Gilder sees 'the central cities of our nation move increasingly toward a police state for the young men and a child-care state for the women and the children . . . [And yet] as darkness falls, conservatives and liberals get together and whistle workfare' (ibid., p. 25; also Murray 1988a). Novak's 'New Consensus' may hold between (some) Neoconservatives and liberals over workfare. (It is only fair to note that Mead's persistent critiques (e.g. 1988a, 1988b, 1989) of liberal 'supportive' versions of workfare makes that claim sound hollow.) But ironically the message about consensus does not seem to have got through to all wings of American Neoconservatism. The state of affairs between 'familists' like

Gilder and 'workfarists' like Novak and Mead looks more like disarray than consensus. Like the problem of the underclass which inspired it, there is little reason to expect that this division will be bridged, and every reason to expect that it will get worse, as we move through the 1990s.

PART III

The Challenge of Modernity: Social Rights and Political Economic Change

Social citizenship in modern Western society involves rights and duties regarding work at its very heart. Max Weber (1970) and, since him, many others have showed that from the eras of pre-industrial capitalism and early industrial capitalism (eras in which a new market in 'free' labour was created), the West inherited a distinctive 'work ethic' and a conception of the duty to work. This was taken for granted in the postwar period of the construction of modern 'welfare states' and 'welfare capitalism'. In the era of the dominant paradigm these work-duty assumptions were overlaid and overshadowed by the apparent power of the new Keynesian techniques for managing national capitalist economies and their labour markets to deliver 'full employment', and thus to deliver the *de facto* right to work (at least to male 'breadwinners'). In the modern West work in the form of labour market employment is important both for intrinsic 'moral' (including psychological and cultural) reasons, and also for the instrumental reason that it generates income for consumption and thus for survival and welfare. Thus the duty and right to work are intimately connected, instrumentally as well as 'morally', with duties and rights regarding income, and, through income, welfare.

In part II we considered Neoconservative social thinking and social policy. From this point of view, cultural and political changes in modernity (particularly in family structure but also involving capitalist consumerism and the development of income rights in the welfare state) have tended to undermine the work ethic. This in turn has therefore tended to undermine the early capitalist duty on individuals to generate welfare for themselves and their dependants from income derived from the sale of their labour in the labour market. From this point of view, then, the dominant paradigm's provision of work and income rights through national Keynesian and welfare state policies has tended to undermine the work- and income-generating duties which the paradigm itself, and these policies, tacitly presuppose. The Neoconservative case may be badly flawed, as I suggested in chapter 6, but the dominant paradigm evidently remains in great difficulties in Western societies in the early 1990s. And it is not in these difficulties merely because it has been politically, administratively and financially attacked by Right-wing governments in the 1980s.

The radical *laissez-faire* New Right thrust of the Right's attack in the early 1980s has in many respects been seen to fail. In the late 1980s and early 1990s, it has begun to recede and to be replaced in Right politics by Neoconservative approaches. But the problems of the dominant paradigm remain, and they go deeper than the ebb and flow of politics and ideology.

As one commentator notes, 'By the mid 1980s there were two points on which there was widespread agreement across the political spectrum. The first was that the labour market was in a mess, the second that the social security system was in a mess. There was of course rather less consensus on what should be done about either' (Standing 1986, p. 134; also see Offe 1984, 1985b). In part III we will consider some of the arguments that the dominant paradigm's problems are not just ideological but also structural, and connected with sea-changes in the political economy of late twentieth-century Western capitalism.

These are evidently very large and speculative themes. It would be misleading if I claimed to be attempting to do more here than merely introduce them to the contemporary sociology of and policy debate about social citizenship for some preliminary consideration. Warnings about the possible delusions involved in 'grand theory' (e.g. Mills 1970) and recommendations of the need to search for 'middle-range' social theories (e.g. Merton 1968, ch. 2; Marshall 1963, chs 1, 2) have a long and justified standing in postwar sociology. Nonetheless, in periods of major social change such as the present, whatever the inevitable limitations of the exercise, there is no alternative but to make some attempt to grasp the larger picture and to 'see the wood rather than the trees'. The main parts of the larger picture which impinge on social citizenship relate to two changes in the nature of the contemporary Western capitalism evident since the mid-1970s. On the one hand, it is arguable that a shift from an 'industrial' to a 'post-industrial' pattern of economic and social institutions is under way, while, on the other hand, and connected with it, arguably a 'post-national' shift is also under way, away from the national political form and level of organization of the economy to global (and also local) forms and levels. Social citizenship is being (and needs to be) rethought in many ways in relation to these long-term and irreversible processes of structural change.

For the purposes of my discussion here I will consider these two processes of change relatively independently, making some connections as necessary. But in reality of course they are intimately interconnected and, together, they are beginning to change the social order on which the dominant paradigm rests. In general terms they are tending to undermine its operational assumptions about the nature of the labour market and social security systems, and thus about the nature of work and income rights. In more particular terms they arguably tend to generate new and intractable forms of familiar and long-standing limits to modern social citizenship; that is, there are emerging new forms of the 'second-class citizenship' and 'exclusion' from full citizenship involved in being poor and being consigned to 'underclass' and other marginalized social categories and statuses. And this is happening as a particular result of the general impact of post-industrial and post-national processes on unemployment, national labour markets and national welfare systems. These general and particular issues, whatever they also imply for the duties side of social citizenship, certainly require that dominant paradigm social rights be rethought in principle and reconstructed in practice.

In chapters 7 and 8, then, we will consider general issues about, respectively, post-industrial and post-national changes in Western societies. These changes will be illustrated by drawing in chapter 7 on British but also particularly on American data and analyses of post-industrial change, and, in chapter 8, on the key contemporary case of post-national development, namely the construction of the European Community (EC). In each case we will need to consider the problem of new forms of poverty and the possibility for developing new social rights to work and income. In particular, the post-industrial problems of income and thus *income rights* will be emphasized in chapter 7, while post-national problems of work and thus *work rights* will be emphasized in chapter 8.

Finally, in chapter 9 we will review some of the general implications of the ideological and structural challenges to the dominant paradigm for the way we think about citizenship (and for social research into it). The modern understanding of citizenship has always contained moralism, myths and contradictions. In the conclusion we consider how these sorts of elements in contemporary citizenship might develop in a future influenced by post-industrialism and post-nationalism.

7
Reinventing Social Citizenship I: Post-Industrialism and New Social Rights

I

Post-industrial change and the dominant paradigm

Post-industrial change and its problems can be analysed and addressed at three interconnected political economic levels: subnational (i.e. in particular the urban), national and transnational. In this chapter I will discuss the national and to a limited extent the urban level; transnational issues will be considered in the next chapter. For my purposes here 'post-industrial change' refers to a complex of changes in the modern capitalist economy associated with: the use of new technologies; the decline of manufacturing and the rise of service employment; the increasing emphasis on consumerism; and the increasing emphasis on the need for capital (financial and technological) and labour to be 'flexible' and adaptable to changing market conditions and consumer preferences.

Some of the most negative features of post-industrial change have been clearly visible in the massive increase in unemployment and the physical deterioration in traditional 'rust-belt' industrial cities and regions of the USA, Britain and Western Europe in the late 1970s and 1980s (e.g. Bluestone et al. 1981; Bluestone and Harrison 1982; Judd and Parkinson 1990). The problems created in these heartland cities of the industrial era by de-industrialization and also by the international economy are broadly comparable in most Western societies. So too are the urban political strategies adopted to try both to react to them and, more proactively, to regenerate and restructure industrial cities' urban economies on more post-industrial (i.e. consumerist, high technology and service employment) lines. And so too are the 'post-modern' architectural, infrastructural and cultural developments which parallel these political responses and economic changes (Harvey 1989; Cooke 1990). We will consider some of these urban-level post-industrial changes in a little more detail in section II below. They are relevant to understanding the development of the new limits to social citizenship, namely the 'new poverty' and the 'underclass', since, whatever else they are, these are importantly urban problems.

At the macro level, various concepts have been applied to some or all of the complex of post-industrial changes I am concerned with. Discussions have focused on processes of 'de-industrialization' (e.g. Blackaby 1979; Bluestone and Harrison 1982; Kasarda 1989); 'restructuring' (e.g. Bagguley et al. 1990); and 'flexibilization' (e.g. Piore and Sabel 1984; Standing 1986) in the productive process and in labour markets. And various analytical perspectives have been deployed to explain them. For instance, critical social theorists have addressed the changes in terms of the decline of 'organized capitalism' into a period of endemic 'crises' (e.g. Habermas 1975; O'Connor 1987, also his 1973, 1984) and/or 'disorganization' (e.g. Offe 1985a; Lash and Urry 1987). Neo-Marxist analysts have addressed the changes in terms of capitalism's need to resolve the various contradictions and crises of its 'Fordist' (e.g. mass production, hierarchic managerialism, mass consumption) stage between 1890 and the 1970s (e.g. Aglietta 1979; Lipietz 1985; Harvey 1989; for accounts see Allen and Massey 1988; Cooke 1990). Broadly liberal analysts have addressed themselves to new forms of 'modernization' and to the development of 'post-industrial society' (e.g. Bell 1973, 1979; Gershuny 1978) and the 'information society' (e.g. Stonier 1983; NEDO 1987; Lyon 1988; Masuda 1972).

This latter liberal group tends to imply a technological determinist (or at least 'technological opportunist' – NEDO 1987) approach, a conception of the 'logic of post-industrialization' which updates the dated 'logic of industrialism' approach of

Kerr et al. (1973). From Colin Clark in the 1950s, to Daniel Bell in the 1960s and 1970s, to Alvin Toffler in the 1980s, liberal social analysts have tended to portray economic change it as something of a technologically driven 'march through the sectors' of the economy, from agriculture to manufacture to services and beyond. Early on in the debate about post-industrialization Fritz Machlup (1962) and then, later, Marc Porat (1977) produced good empirical evidence to support the picture of a long-term trend in employment distribution in the American economy as a whole away from manufacturing sectors and towards information and knowledge sectors (also Bell 1973). A comparable picture can be seen in the analysis of most Western nations and their industrial cities in the 1970s and 1980s. The 'information technology revolution' of the late 1970s and 1980s has accelerated these trends. It involves the widespread use in both manufacturing and services of the science-based high technologies of computerization, robotics and new communications technology. Arguably, the development, convergence and synergy of these technologies in the late twentieth century represents something of world-historical importance, on a par with nineteenth-century industrialization in Western Europe and the USA. Analysts such as Freeman and Soete (1987; also Bell 1979) argue strongly that this represents a new 'techno-economic paradigm', a distinctive stage in modern humanity's technological and economic conditions.

Long-term analysis and projection are not exact sciences, to say the least, and they may or may not lend much support to the personal hopes and fears about the future which usually infuse futurologists' visions. But it seems to me to be indisputable that contemporary techno-economic change is indeed of this order of importance. By contrast, what the consequences and implications are, what they *ought* to be and how they might be politically controlled or steered are of course eminently disputable. The advent of the new technologies and the beginning of their permeation not only of economic production, but also of transport, architecture, city design, politics and the home, undoubtedly give people in the advanced Western societies new powers, possibilities and freedoms. But they also *require* them to make choices if traditional social and economic organization is not simply to fall in on itself. The fact of the continuous diffusion of technological change, mainly through markets and market forces, means that policy decisions about many profound political choices and decisions about strategic aspects of contemporary social and economic organization in Western societies ultimately cannot be avoided. This is not least the case for the organization of employment, with all of its consequences for income distribution and thus for welfare (e.g. Pahl 1984, 1988).

The post-industrial capitalist economy increasingly requires various forms of flexibility from its workers and its labour supply. In the productive process employers require workers to be able and willing to be flexibly deployed between a variety of roles, while in the labour market employers ideally require a flexible supply of labour able and willing to be taken into employment and put out of work as market conditions and the trade cycle demands (e.g. Handy 1985; Piore and Sabel 1984).

The shift towards flexibilized labour uses and markets is structurally based and capable of being steered in various political directions. But the insecurity problems associated with it have been greatly accentuated by the social and economic policies of Right governments in the West in the 1980s. Trade union power, professional power, government regulation and of course the welfare state were all regarded as 'obstacles' to the efficient functioning of the national labour market and were more or less vigorously and effectively attacked as such.

The profound implications of these structural and political developments for the dominant Western paradigm of social citizenship can be seen, for instance, in Standing's analysis of British unemployment and labour market policy in the 1980s. For Standing, the 'post-1945 social consensus . . . (and) . . . the Welfare State and mixed economy' accorded citizens a number of labour rights, formulable as rights to various types of 'security' (i) in the labour market, (ii) in terms of income, and (iii) within employment. Thus labour market security was provided 'through insurance benefits and state-preserved "full employment"'. Income security was provided through 'legitimised trade unionism, minimum wage legislation and tax-benefit systems that checked the growth of income inequality', while employment security was provided (i) by controls on employers' powers to make workers redundant or dismiss them,

(ii) by accepted middle- and working-class job demarcations and other 'restrictive practices' and (iii) by health, safety and hours of work regulation (Standing 1986, p. 113).

Post-industrialism, with its de-industrialization and its labour flexibilization dynamics, raises problems for each of these aspects of labour rights and their related forms of security. And these problems are intensified by the transnational context in which states and capitalists are increasingly operating. Labour markets are becoming internationalized and nation states' powers to defend national labour rights, even where they wish to do so, are becoming increasingly curtailed. I will look at citizens' rights to 'employment security' (that is labour rights within employment) in a post-national (European) context in the following chapter.

For the rest of this chapter I want to focus on post-industrialism's implications for citizens' labour market security rights and income security rights. We can look at these areas in terms both of the new social problems post-industrialism brings and of some of the main possible policy responses to these problems. In section II we will consider citizens' rights to labour market security and in section III citizens' rights to income and income security.

II

Post-industrialism and the right to work

The implications of post-industrialism for the aggregate demand for labour or quantity of employment available are far from clear. In principle the increasing application of increasingly powerful, flexible and 'intelligent' technologies to the production of goods and services increases the productivity of labour and reduces the quantity of labour necessary to produce any given level of GNP. Furthermore, the new technologies appear to reverse the positive relationships which have long been assumed to hold (in the conventional wisdom of economics, particularly Keynesian economics) between investment and employment. With the development of practical and affordable robotic and automated systems investment seems to have more of a labour-saving than a labour-generating potential. This is certainly so in manufacturing, but it is a looming problem for routine and middle-range information-processing secretarial and managerial employment, whether in manufacturing sectors or in service sectors.

The first wave of effects of the new microelectronic technologies was felt in the late 1970s and early 1980s, coinciding with a world economic recession. It was not easy for analysts to disentangle the rise in unemployment due to the recession from that due to structural changes. Unemployment produced by 'de-industrialization' in the 'rust-belt' industrial cities of the West (in the northern USA, northern England etc.) was clearly much in evidence. But the more diversified US urban economies also showed a considerable capacity for simultaneous employment growth in the service sector (also see Standing 1986, ch. 3). By contrast, this sort of pattern took until the late 1980s to begin to emerge in the northern cities of the UK (e.g. Judd and Parkinson 1990).

These post-industrial processes of de industrialization and the shift to service employment require flexibility and often new and higher levels of skills from the workforce. They thus help to explain the development of the urban underclass of (for all practical purposes), 'non-citizens' we discussed earlier (in chapter 3 and part II). This has occurred particularly in the USA, but it has its analogues elsewhere in the post-industrializing cities and economies of the West, as we will see in the discussion of Europe in the following chapter. It will be useful at this point, then, to spell out some of the connections between post-industrial change and underclass formation in the American case. We can then consider post-industrialism's effects on employment more widely and its implications for employment policy and the right to work.

1   Post-industrialism, unemployment and underclass formation

As we saw earlier, the American poor and underclass are spatially concentrated in big cities, particularly in the Black ghettos of the traditional industrial cities of the north-east (e.g. New York, Baltimore, Boston). America's urban Black ghettos have been created by two waves of change in the structure of American capitalism, in the first instance, industrialization and subsequently post-industrialism. It is post-industrial change that helps to explain their current poverty (e.g. Bluestone et al. 1981; Bluestone and Harrison 1982; Levin 1982; Clark 1985; Block 1987a, 1987b) but before we look at this in a little more detail it is worth noting the origin of these communities in industrial change.

US Black migration and the Black segment of the urban working class were first called into existence by the forces of change involved in capitalist industrialization (e.g. Harrington 1984; Block 1987a, 1987b). On the one hand there were the 'carrots' of jobs in the industrial economy, of reasonable incomes (relative to the South) and of relative personal independence. On the other hand there was the 'stick' of agricultural unemployment (due the mechanization of southern agriculture), particularly in the 1950s and 1960s. These two processes of industrialization, one in the city and the other on the land, together produced the great waves of internal migration by southern Blacks to the northern industrial cities from the interwar years to the 1960s.

Initially, from the 1930s to 1950s, the migrants were able to establish relatively structured urban communities in spite of having to face racism in urban housing and job markets (Wilson 1987). However, the structures of these urban communities were precarious, and over time they began to be overwhelmed for many reasons, not least the sheer weight of numbers. Dramatic urban disorders and destruction resulted in the 1960s.

The modern American welfare system as we have seen was developed in this period in large part to address the various problems besetting the Black ghetto community in the 1960s and 1970s. But the growth of the American welfare state almost immediately encountered a period of economic crisis for all Western nations for which (*pace* Murray and American Neoconservatives) it had very little responsibility. These crises were produced by a variety of factors, important among them the massive impact of the oil price rises of the mid-1970s and the inflation and recession they induced. But they were also caused by the post-industrial structural changes beginning to take hold in Western economies in the same period.

To illustrate the processes of de-industrialization and the shift to services involved in post-industrial change we can now look at a relevant survey of employment trends in the major American cities from 1970 to 1980. John Kasarda's analysis (1989) allows us to see something of the nature of these changes and their divisive social effects, particularly on the poor Black urban community. Using urban-level census data Kasarda tracked the changing demand for skills and the changing distribution of employment in a number of major US cities, analysing broad types of industries (i.e. 'goods processing' or 'information processing') in terms of types of locations (i.e. city centre or suburban). We can look at an archetypal northern industrial city, Detroit, to give an example of Kasarda's general themes (see also Hill 1984 on Detroit, and data on US cities in Cummings 1988 and Judd and Parkinson 1990; also Logan and Molotch 1987).

Unskilled working-class ('blue-collar') jobs in the 'motor city', declined over the course of the 1970s by between 90,000 and 100,000 in the central city, over 53,000 of these in the production of goods such as cars. Goods-producing blue-collar jobs also declined in the suburbs by 13,000, although here there was ultimately a net gain of 16,000 jobs in service sector blue-collar jobs. Overall, the Detroit area lost 60,000 blue-collar jobs across all industrial sectors in the 1970s. However, in spite of this, the overall employment in general in the Detroit area actually increased in this period. The main growth came in the 'information processing' sectors, and it came massively in the suburbs; that is over 56,000 jobs were added in management and the professions (52,000 of these in the suburbs), together with nearly 80,000 jobs in technical and administrative support services (62,000 of these in the suburbs).

The educational and skill requirements of jobs changed and increased in line with these sorts of developments. In the past it has been possible for young people who had failed to complete high school to gain employment in the inner city. For instance, there were 200,000 such jobs in Detroit in 1970, representing nearly 40 per cent of the total inner-city workforce, but by 1980 this pool of jobs had shrunk by over 50 per cent and represented only 20 per cent of the workforce. Even the pool of jobs available to young people who had achieved high-school graduation, but who possessed no further qualifications (e.g. about 160,000 in Detroit in 1970) had shrunk by about 30 per cent by 1980. On the other hand, jobs for college graduates and those with some college experience increased substantially (i.e. 30–50 per cent) although from a smaller base. They added nearly 60,000 jobs overall and by 1980 had come to represent 5 per cent of the inner-city workforce.

The consequences of these employment trends for inner-city Black communities has been and continues to be disastrous. Black educational achievement levels have continued to rise, but White and other ethnic group levels have risen faster. This has left Blacks entering the job market in both a bad absolute position and a worsening relative position *vis-à-vis* other groups. Thus, to take inner-city Detroit again, only 26 per cent of Black males achieved some college experience or a college degree to put themselves in a position to compete for the 5 per cent of higher paying jobs in the local economy requiring high educational qualifications. At the other end of the continuum 43 per cent of Black males failed to finish high school, while an additional 30 per cent finished high school but pursued their education no further, effectively confining themselves to segments of the labour market which are shrinking rapidly.

Concomitant with this picture, the great bulk of Black male unemployment consists of people who failed to finish high school (e.g. 56 per cent in Detroit in 1980) and also of people who finished high school but went no further (e.g. an additional 30 per cent in Detroit in 1980). In addition, given the spatial shift of urban economic growth to the suburbs and poor standards of public transport, it is vital for workers and work searchers to possess a car (e.g. 90 per cent of low-skilled (no high-school degree) Black workers use cars to get to work in Detroit (Kasarda 1989, table 5)). Yet studies of households in inner-city Black areas with much poverty and high unemployment show very little car ownership (e.g. only 20 per cent in Oakland, Chicago's Southside ghetto, in 1980; ibid., p. 40). Finally, much of what new job creation has occurred in America's inner cities in the late 1970s and 1980s has been in the self-employed and small business sector. Asian ethnic groups, particularly Chinese and Koreans, have contributed notably to this development and have benefited from it. Their main resources have been family networks, family labour and a very strong work ethic, but, as we saw earlier, for whatever reason, poor and unemployed Blacks have measurably low 'work ethic' in terms of labour force participation and unemployment rates. In addition they have precious little in the way of family resources – because of the fragmentation effects of male desertion and single mothering – even to rear children, let alone to support the formation of small businesses (ibid., p. 44).

Reviewing the situation Kasarda observes:

> Advances in transportation, communication and industrial technologies interacting with the changing structure of the national and international economy have transformed [America's major] cities from centres of the production and distribution of goods to centres of administration, finance and information exchange. In the process, many blue-collar jobs that once constituted the economic backbone of cities and provided employment opportunities for their poorly educated residents have either vanished or moved. These jobs have been replaced, at least in part, by knowledge-intensive white-collar jobs with educational requirements that exclude many with substandard education. (ibid., p. 28)

The prospects for inner-city Black communities in the new post-industrial (or post-industrializing) urban economy are bleak. Kasarda sums them up as follows:

> After 1970, the bottom fell out in urban industrial demand for poorly educated Blacks . . . If greater proportions of disadvantaged Black youths do not acquire the formal education to be hired by the white-collar service industries beginning to dominate urban employment bases, their jobless rate will remain high. (ibid., pp. 35, 47)

The Neoconservatives emphasize moralistic, psychologistic and 'culture of poverty' diagnoses of America's urban poor and underclass. But, as we suggested in chapter 6, this analysis can be criticized by virtue of their studied indifference to the explanatory relevance of these kind of vitally important structural changes.

2 Post-industrialism and employment problems

In the early 1980s, British and European analysts tended to take a pessimistic view of the long-term prospects for employment in a high technology and services-based economy. They saw the problem of the formation of a permanently unemployed under-class in Western society in a manner which was comparable to that of Kasarda's and other US analysts' accounts of the American Black underclass, but which was expressed in more general and speculative terms. Arguments that an irreversible 'collapse of work' (Jenkins and Sherman 1979) was occurring, that we should bid 'farewell to the working class' (Gorz 1982) and that we should consider our future 'beyond full employment' (Clemitson and Rodgers 1981) were popular. Unemployment projections for the year 2000 included 12–14 per cent for France (Nora and Minc 1980), 18.2 per cent for the USA (Jenkins and Sherman 1981), 4–6 million (20 per cent) for the UK (Stonier 1983; Jenkins and Sherman 1979, 1981; Jenkins cited in NEDO 1987), and at least 4–5 million job losses in France, West Germany and Britain (Gorz 1982). Toffler believed 'large numbers will not find new jobs' (1985, p. 58), while according to Jenkins and Sherman, given the 'new industrial revolution based on micro electronics . . . [the] industrialised societies will not, in the future be able to provide work for all on a *continuing basis*' (1981, p. 10). Stonier declared 'Only a fool would look into the crystal ball and not tremble' (1983, p. 123).

However, these apocalyptic 'collapse of work' projections and prophecies had begun to look somewhat less credible by the end of the 1980s. This was partly due to the growth of the service sector illustrated for the USA in Kasarda's data and paralleled in Europe. It was also due to a variety of other factors including demographic changes. In most Western societies the postwar 'baby boom' has been followed by the 'baby bust' with reduced cohorts of young people entering the labour market in the early 1990s. (However, it is worth noting that this factor is likely to be counterbalanced by the continuous long-term growth of women's participation in the labour market.) Similarly, in the late 1980s the world economy and most Western economies staged something of a recovery from recession. Finally, the 'flexible' workforce (part-timers, temporary workers, home workers and the self-employed) continued to grow in most sectors in the advanced societies (for instance comprising over a third of the UK workforce in the late 1980s; NEDO 1987, p. 85; also Standing 1986; Casey 1988).

Nonetheless, none of these developments alters the probability that unemployment and/or underemployment will remain much higher in the future in the West than it has typically done throughout the postwar period. Post-industrial capitalism now has profound problems with the kind of labour market, and the kind of employment-based society, which industrial capitalism brought into being in the nineteenth and twentieth centuries.

On the basis of an authoritative survey of economic and political change in relation to the British labour market in the 1980s, Standing (1986) argues that the real underlying unemployment rate under conditions of flexibilization is higher than most governmental measures allow. Official British rates would need to be multiplied by 1.3 to get closer to the reality of 'labour slack' in the contemporary economy (1986, ch. 1 and p. 134). And he stresses the role of what I am calling post-industrial flexibilization in generating poverty, and effectively an underclass.

> The labour process of the 1980s is one of rapidly growing flexibility in labour use patterns, chronically high unemployment and underemployment, the marginalisation of large fragments of the population. . . . [A] growing segment of the working age population is chronically dependent on state benefits, alongside a growing number intermittently dependent on them, and another group likely to be tipped into dependency at almost any time. . . . [For] a sizeable proportion of the population the labour market cannot ensure secure and adequate incomes. (1986, p. 136)

Standing suggests that there are divisive dynamics in the flexibilized labour market and economy which help to generate these problems. These include the segregation of (full-time secure) 'core' categories of work and worker from variously flexibilized, fragmented and peripheral categories of work and worker. They also include a 'new form of labour-market dualism' between 'multiple-earner households' alongside 'multiple-unemployment households' (p. 38). Standing suggests that the job contacts, savings, training resources and skills in the former case and the lack of them in the latter case respectively exercise cumulative positive and negative effects over time, polarizing and inscribing employment and income inequalities between the two social categories.

It may be less desperate, anomic and chaotic than the American underclass scenario, but poverty in Britain and in Western Europe has nonetheless been renewed in the late twentieth century. Processes of post-industrial employment restructuring (i.e. de-industrialization, flexibilization and spatial relocation) comparable to those currently at work in the USA are also at work in Britain (e.g. Standing op. cit.; Blackaby 1979; Allen and Massey 1988), and, as we will see in chapter 8, in Western Europe more generally. As regards Britain, Dore (1987) takes a view on the structural post-industrial causes and consequences of contemporary poverty similar to that of Standing and other recent commentators (e.g. Field 1989, 1990). Reflecting on 'Citizenship and Employment in an Age of High Technology' and reviewing the future problems facing young people in Britain, Dore observes:

> [If they are] relegated to permanent membership in a clearly recognisable unemployed/unemployable status [and] if, in future, substantial numbers of children are *born* into that underclass with little change of getting out of it, what happens to our concept of citizenship? . . . What happens to the basic fictions which sustain our democracy? (1989, p. 319)

3 Post-industrialism, employment policy and the right to work

So far we have seen that there are major social problems of unemployment and poverty connected with post-industrial change. From a policy point of view, the issues crystallize around the problem of (1) the achievability and (2) the meaning of Keynesian 'full employment' in post-industrial conditions. Leaving aside unreconstructed Marxists, old Keynesians and free marketeers (all of whom might contest the idea that there are any really new historical conditions to consider) the main approaches to post-industrial work policy can be termed neo- and post-Keynesian.

Neo-Keynesian approaches, briefly, aim at using national and local state power to achieve something like classical postwar 'full employment'. In addition to conventional attempts to manage demand they involve the development of various proactive strategies to strengthen the 'supply side' of the economy. These approaches encompass calls for the development of such things as 'industrial' policy (e.g. a range of research and development policies, and of new technology policies); urban and regional policy; 'human resource' policy (e.g. computer literacy, skills and training policies); and infrastructure policy (e.g. new tele-communications and transport networks) (e.g. Piore and Sabel 1984; Freeman and Clark 1987; NEDO 1987; Dore 1987; Mackintosh 1986; Block 1987a, 1990; Judd and Parkinson 1990; Grahl and Teague 1990).

It is worth noting, however, that a number of advocates of those approaches (e.g. Dore, Clark and Freeman) also accept the need for radical new approaches to incomes policy in addit-ion to new employment policies, much as the post-Keynesian do. Besides these neo-Keynesian strategies other approaches to improving the supply side of the labour market and worker motivation include longstanding Left and Centrist proposals for profit sharing (e.g. Standing 1986; Esping-Andersen 1990) and for worker consultation and participation in industry (e.g. European Social Charter).

Post-Keynesian approaches to employment, those that take the view that post-industrialism involves the strong possibility of a 'collapse of work', whether in the medium or longer term, would echo André Gorz's view that: 'Keynes is dead. In the context of the current crisis and technological revolution it is absolutely impossible to restore full employment by quantitative economic growth' (1982, p. 3). 'Collapse of work' scenarios have led analysts to recommend on the one hand 'a right to useful unemployment' (Illich 1978), 'a politics of free time' (Gorz 1982) and radical work-sharing policies (e.g. Gorz 1982, 1985; Keane and Owen 1986; Handy 1985; Robertson 1985; also Cuvillier 1984). These work- and free-time-sharing policies would involve among other things reducing basic weekly hours, reducing overtime, lowering the retirement age, delaying the age of entry to the labour market for youth by massive exten-sions of education and training, accelerating exit from the labour market by lowering the age of retirement and so on. Gorz cites

French analysis which argues that the same GNP can be produced by a variety of combinations of workers and work time. For instance 'full employment', could be achieved by means of a 31-hour week for all. Or a planned mixture of full-time, part-time and temporary workers might be envisaged (e.g. the labour force might be composed of 50 per cent temporary workers (on 6 months' work), 30 per cent full-time workers on a 40-hour week, with the rest made up by part-timers (Gorz 1985, p. 120). However, post-Keynesians typically recognize that such work distribution policies would also require the radical disconnection of income from employment and the creation of a new universal guaranteed minimum income (Gorz 1982, 1985; Adler-Karlsson 1978; Rehn 1978; Keane and Owen 1986). We will explore this latter policy in section III below.

The development of labour flexibilization in contemporary Western societies indicates the fundamental problem of employment and employment policy in post-industrial conditions. Achieving what might appear to be 'full employment' with a substantially 'flexibilized' workforce does not in reality mean or achieve what traditional Keynesian-type full employment meant and achieved. Rather, it is effectively a form of work sharing and work rationing of the kind advocated by post-Keynesian 'collapse of work' theorists like Gorz, Keane and Owen. The development of flexibilization both disguises and attests to post-industrialism's underlying employment *quantity* problem, while it also threatens to build in serious employment *quality* problems in the labour market of the 1990s and beyond (e.g. Standing 1986; Casey 1988; Gershuny and Miles 1983).

Part-time and flexibilized workers have little access to 'core' full-time employment. They are effectively excluded from the 'core' and from the full rights of social citizenship attaching to such employment status. In addition, part-time and temporary employment may generate a useful addition to a family income, but it is of considerable political and social importance that this income is *not* a 'living wage'. By itself such income is generally incapable of covering even the individual worker's living expenses and necessary carework, never mind about the expenses involved in family responsibilities.

So in the era of post-industrial capitalism these sorts of income consequences of post-industrialism's most likely employment effects are not necessarily addressed by 'full (flexibilized) employment' policies, or by promoting the 'right to (flexibilized) work' alone. However these problems are claimed to be addressed, according to its advocates, by a radical approach to the reform of income distribution. This is concerned with the creation of a new social right of citizenship, namely the right to a basic income, and we can now give some consideration to this policy proposal.

III

Citizen income: an outline and a model

The dominant paradigm of citizenship assumes the existence of a material basis for citizenship. That is, as we have seen, it assumes the existence, the functioning and the co-ordination of three main institutions in modern society: (1) employment in the capitalist labour market; (2) carework in the family; (3) cash assistance and welfare services from the welfare state sufficient at least to raise citizens out of poverty. In part II, we discussed the long-term problems of two of these institutions. So we considered arguments about the ineffectiveness of the welfare state in relation to poverty and the underclass, together with arguments about the 'breakdown' of the family and the work ethic. So far in part III we have briefly considered some basic problems with the third of these institutions, namely long-term problems of employment quantity and quality (and thus problems of income distribution), due to the economic and social changes involved in post-industrialization.

Given all of these problems, then, there is clearly a crisis affecting the material basis and social reproduction of citizenship in contemporary society. One radical reformist response to these complex problems of post-industrialism is particularly relevant to my discussion. It is a response which has been in the wings for many years but which is being increasingly considered by policy analysts and social theorists of many political persuasions, particularly in Britain and Europe, although perhaps less so in the USA for reasons we will come to in a moment. The radical proposal is to create a new social right of citizenship, namely an entitlement to a guaranteed basic minimum income universally provided by the state to all citizens. Various terms have been used to refer to this income entitlement (e.g. 'social dividend', 'basic income' etc.), but I will refer to it as a right to a 'citizen income'.

The idea has attracted the interest of those concerned with the welfare and autonomy of women, children, the elderly, the disabled and the unemployed. It has attracted the interest of egalitarians and socialists on the one hand and liberals and 'popular capitalists' on the other, ecologists on the one hand and technological modernizers on the other, religious traditionalists on the one hand and futurologists on the other. To explore these various interests in and rationales for citizen income, not to mention the variety of economic calculations and administrative mechanisms by which it might be realized, would be a large undertaking and beyond the bounds of what it is useful and relevant to attempt here. For the purposes of my discussion what is needed are some outline answers to three basic questions about citizen income: (1) what is it and how might it work? (2) what are its main limitations and problems? (3) why is it claimed to be a good thing and what benefits might it produce? We can look at each of these questions in turn.

Many basic citizen income schemes have been proposed in theory over the years in a variety of countries, particularly in Britain and Europe. But few practical example have been tried out, some of the most notable being in Canada and Holland (e.g. Walter 1989, ch. 3; Jordan 1987) and in the USA, albeit in the form of 'negative income tax' (see below; also Moynihan 1973; Parker 1989). They have all involved efforts to consolidate and co-ordinate into one single scheme the various influences of the modern state on personal and family incomes, in particular through the state's tax policy and welfare systems. Currently modern states influence and redistribute income through, on the one hand, deductions from people's earned income (through income taxes, social insurance payments and various allow-able reliefs against taxation) and on the other hand through various direct payments of income and income supplements (to pensioners, the unemployed, the low paid, the disabled, and to families for their children, for their housing costs etc.).

Among the most worked-out, costed and credible schemes for citizen income currently being proposed are Hermione Parker's (1984, 1989) various Basic Income Guarantee (BIG) schemes for Britain, particularly BIG(1a) (1989, pp. 236–8; also Walter 1989, pp. 38–47) and BIG 2000 (Parker 1989, pp. 334–9). They each involve a full integration of the tax and benefits systems. While the details are specific to Britain, Parker intends the principles and strategy they embody to provide a model of the kind of policy which could be developed elsewhere, including the EC in the 1990s (Parker 1989, p. 2, and ch. 8 below). So we will focus on her schemes to illustrate the concept of citizen income in the discussion that follows.

BIG (1a) (costed for 1985–6) involves two main elements. First, there is a 'partial basic income' (PBI) for all citizens and their children (£24.00 weekly for each adult, £17.00 for each child). In addition, various categories of people such as lone parents and the disabled receive supplements to PBI while pensioners receive supplementation up to a full basic income level, £60.00 per person. Secondly, to tackle poverty in particular and since housing costs are such a large proportion of the poor's expenditure, a housing benefit is available to all citizens on an income-tested basis. At nil original (pre-PBI income) income people who are in receipt of unsupplemented PBI will get the cost of their rent, rates (now poll tax) and water rates (now water company charges) in full, together with an allowance for fuel and house maintenance costs. Housing benefit would be reduced by 50 per cent (i.e. 50 p per £1.00) of any increase on net original (pre-PBI) income (Parker 1989, table 1.2).

The PBI and BI parts of this system, since they involve unconditional and universal benefits, operate simply and automatically, either as a cash payment (to the unemployed) or as a tax credit (to the employed). Taxation and welfare bureaucracies could be reduced and their costs cut, PBI and BI being administered nationally and housing benefit locally. The scheme is designed to replace all existing personal and employers' social security payments and all personal income tax allowances (including mortgage relief and employers' and employees' relief on occupational pension scheme costs). It is thus designed to cost no *more* than the sum of these (about £90 billion in 1985/6, ibid., p. 249 and appendix I; BIG 2000 costs about £100 billion and saves £114 billion, ibid., p. 345).

It would be paid for by a combination of a new progressive tax system for personal incomes, together with a standard employer's payroll tax of 10 per cent. Personal income tax would range from 38 per cent to 44 per cent at the bottom rate (as compared currently with 39 per cent composed of 30 per cent income tax and 9 per cent National Insurance) to 60 per cent at the top rate (on incomes of £36,000 and above) (ibid., p. 239).

Because citizen income schemes require a radical change in the taxation and welfare benefits system of most modern Western societies they could only be introduced step by step over a period of time. The rest of the social system would need time to adjust and adapt to them. For instance, Parker proposes a 10-year programme (1990–2000) for the introduction of BIG 2000 (ibid., ch. 20) into Britain.

Basic income: some basic problems

Given the idealism, the wide ramifications and the large, even 'wild' (Parker 1989, p. 341), claims of the citizen income concept it would be surprising if there were not problems with it. And indeed there are many possible objections to it, both in principle and also in terms of the practicalities of the various schemes designed to embody it. This fact is readily conceded by its supporters (e.g. Walter 1989, chs 6, 7; Parker *passim*) who nonetheless obviously do not judge the objections to be overwhelming.

Citizen income policy is primarily policy for income distribution rather than for economic production, and it concedes a right to income unconditionally and (at least in some of its main versions) without reference to work. Even if the case for its distributional justice, its feasibility and its effectiveness were conceded, problems about its assumptions about *economic production* and *work* would need to be addressed. We will come to these in a moment. But first, how feasible and effective is citizen income policy likely to be?

One of the main feasibility issues is implicit in Parker's BIG(1a) scheme. As we saw earlier, this is a hybrid scheme, mixing unconditional and income-tested elements. It is a scheme mainly for a partial PBI and not a full basic income. The PBI is not enough to live on and needs to be supplemented either by further income from employment or from other provisions of BIG(1a), some of which (i.e. housing benefit) are income-tested. In her discussion Parker makes it clear time and again why her scheme necessarily had to be hybrid and partial. The reason is that a full basic income scheme is simply too expensive for any modern economy, requiring astronomic rates of taxation (e.g. 70 per cent and above) to finance it (Parker 1989, pp. 132–7 and *passim*). Also, although Parker's scheme is well worked out, Walter (1989, p. 43) notes that the idea that it would cost the state no more than the sum of all benefits and tax reliefs may significantly underestimate its real cost. For instance, income which is currently tax-relieved may not manifest itself as readily collectable under the new tax arrangements Parker proposes.

Possibly the major claim citizen income schemes make is that they are the best way to prevent poverty. Poverty in turn is strongly associated with either unemployment (or transient and infrequent employment), or 'broken families' (divorce, never married, single-parenting etc.), or both. Conversely, the best ways to prevent poverty are to encourage either active labour-market participation (and to supplement low earned incomes) or family stability and dual-parenting, or both. Basic income schemes will be definition provide an income above the poverty level. But what is their effect likely to be over time on employment incentives and family stability? If there was a major withdrawal or even a significant trend away from labour-force participation the finely balanced finances of a scheme like BIG(1a) could soon be in trouble. Tax rates would need to rise (to fund the rising housing benefit element in particular) on a stagnant or reducing base of aggregate taxable personal income. Similar cost implications would flow from a big growth in single parenting. From a rational choice point of view, the BIG(1a) scheme provides some incentive to seek employment. This would allow people at least to 'top up' PBI and to gain housing quality above that purchasable by whatever the maximal housing benefits are. But 'free-riding' would be practicable and would carry no penalty, while single-parenting might be encouraged by the full basic income and the housing benefit provided for it, and no countervailing incentive is provided to form and remain in two-parent families.

Problems of this kind arose in a series of four American experiments during the 1970s with a form of citizen income, i.e. negative income tax (NIT). NIT systems guarantee a universal minimum citizen income by setting a minimum income level above which welfare benefits are progressively withdrawn and tax begins to be paid and below which benefit is paid to top up income to the minimum level. They tend to take family (rather than personal) income as the relevant unit of assessment and they are designed to keep the demands on public expenditure down rather than to effect significant redistribution from rich to poor (Parker 1989, p. 141). They tend to incorporate a significant 'poverty trap' because of the effect of taxation at high marginal rates on near-minimum incomes. Thus they are not fully-fledged citizen income schemes in Parker's terms and arguably do not provide a real-life test of the operational effects of such schemes.

Nonetheless, the results of the American experiments involving NIT were not encouraging for the citizen income concept, to say the least. One of the main experimental variations, and certainly the longest running was the Seattle and Denver Income Maintenance Experiment (SIME/DIME) which involved about 5,000 families between 1970 and 1978. In SIME/DIME it was observed (West 1980) that husbands reduced their work effort (work hours) by 9 per cent and their wives by 20 per cent. On other sites it was observed that young single men who married during the course of the experiment (thereby taking a new family role and responsibility), reduced their work effort by 33 per cent at a time when they arguably should have been increasing it. West regarded this finding as 'important' and judged that 'the reduction in work effort may also have long-term effects on their labour supply behaviour' (West 1980, p. 588).

The effects of NIT on the family were equally disastrous. In SIME/DIME the rate of dissolution of marriages for whites receiving NIT was 36 per cent higher than for those not receiving it, while the rate for Blacks was 42 per cent up on the control group (Bishop 1980, p. 312). The experiment had begun with about 5,000 family units, but by the time it finished the members of these units, through dissolution and other factors, had created 12,000 family units (Parker 1989, p. 154). Parker argues that the particular NIT system used 'loaded all the dice in favour of marriage break-up and a string of sexual partners'. From a political point of 'NIT got too hot to handle' (ibid., p. 154). Indeed the failure of the scheme gave an impetus in the 1980s to the development of the Neoconservative familist and workfare policies which we discussed earlier (also Handler and Hasenfeld 1990, ch. 4).

Besides the basic issue of cost and feasibility there are three main problems we can raise about citizen income proposals. The first of these, indicated by the NIT experiment, is that the unconditional rights-based approach to citizen income arguably has little or nothing to say about the problem of citizens' social duties in principle, nor about its possible effects on such duties in practice. The second main problem can be called the 'panacea problem'. We came across this earlier when considering the very opposite of citizen income and its apparently duty-free work-rights, namely workfare and its apparently rights-less work duties. There we noted Wiseman's (1987a) basic question to workfare administrators, the gist of which was 'that may be alright, but what *else* are you doing?' Citizen income, like work-fare, seems to promise the solution to a lot of complex problems by means of a single policy instrument. It may or may not be feasible and effective, but it is certainly no panacea. Parker is clear, for instance, that in a full basic income scheme without housing benefit a massive amount of cheap housing would need to be produced (Parker ibid., p. 135). It is reasonable to ask whether citizen income policy would create an economic environment in which such major increases of production, and indeed economic growth and capital accumulation in general, would be likely. More to the point, there are a host of social and physical infrastructure policies, in addition to income policies, which are currently needed in the advanced Western societies to achieve both a viable post-industrial economy and also ecologically sustainable economic growth. Income policies do not address these needs.

Finally, there is the 'post-national problem' for citizen income analyses. This is simply the problem that – like much modern social science theorizing, and like much social policy and political analysis in general – citizen income studies tend to be what we might call 'methodologically nationalist'. That is they are designed on a basis which appears to take the nation state, its sovereignty and the powers of its government utterly for granted. Such schemes may be translatable into the post-national terms which are, for instance, needed to consider the future of income policy and citizens' income rights in the EC. But, despite some optimism about the possibilities, authoritative advocates of citizen income policies have not yet produced such translations.

Citizen income strategies: some bases and benefits

One of the benefits of debate about citizen income schemes is the way it has revealed common ground across the political spectrum. Thus it has revealed at least the potential for radical social reform which could be based on some sort of consensus. The underlying principles and benefits of citizen income schemes can often be expressed in both liberal individualist and collectivist terms. An important underlying principle of ethical collectivism in many of the schemes has been the idea that we are all equal inheritors of society's productive capacity and contributors to society's current production whether through full-time or part-time employment, through personal, familial or other unpaid carework, or in other ways. A citizen income thus represents a right to a 'social dividend' or an equal share in our social inheritance and social production (Jordan 1987; Walter 1989, pp. 24–5, 77–82, 153–4). Whether in these or other terms Parker (1989, pp. 125–7) notes that, among other things, citizen income schemes provide a way of simultaneously satisfying the rights to work, to individual freedom and to a means of existence, while for Walter (1989, chs 6, 7) they do the same for the classic liberal rights to liberty, equality and fraternity.

Such schemes would, of course, institutionalize citizenship principles and the social rights of citizenship to an historically unprecedented degree. For socialists they offer realizable progress towards the abolition of poverty and involuntary unemployment, together with significant income redistribution and the assertion of egalitarian and collective values (Jordan 1987; Van der Veen and Van Parjis 1985). For the New Right and Neoconservatives they offer increased individual rights, reduction in welfare-state bureaucracy and increased flexibility of labour use, together with the possibility of support for the work ethic and for the family (Friedman 1962; Minford et al. 1985; Parker 1989, parts 1, 4, chs 6, 13). For the women's movement they offer the mass of women a considerable improvement in their financial independence and security, together with a base on which to make individual choices both about relationships with male partners and about their preferred balance between employment and child care (Jordan 1987; Walter 1989, pp. 116–27; Parker 1989, pp. 76–9, 126–7).

Citizen income policies appear to hold out the promise of a single and administratively simple (Parker 1989, pp. 285–6; Walter 1989, pp. 58–9) way of addressing the various structural problems of social citizenship we have been concerned with in chapters 4 to 7, namely the simultaneous breakdown of the welfare state, the family and the capitalist labour market's income-distributing capacity in post-industrial conditions (Walter ibid., ch. 1; Parker ibid., part 1, and chs 6, 16). In terms of our two strategic issues of citizenship's limit (poverty) and material basis (post-industrialism), citizen income policies appear to have a major contribution to make to the possible solution of apparently intractable social problems, both old and new.

Earlier we considered three main problems with citizen income schemes apart from cost and feasibility. These were the duties, panacea and post-national problems, and we can now consider some responses to them. First, duties. Some leading citizen income advocates do not have an exclusive rights-bias and are aware of the importance of social duties in citizenship. Thus in his various utopian writings on post-industrial politics André Gorz stresses the importance of the social duty to work (1982, 1985, 1989). For instance: 'Each citizen must have the right to a normal standard of living; but every man and woman must also be granted the possibility (the right and the duty) to perform for society the labour-equivalent of what she or he consumes' (1989, p. 205). Also in recognition of NIT's problematic family and employment effects, and its effects on family and work obligations in particular, Parker has made various modifications to her major citizen income scheme BIG(1a). In her revised scheme (BIG 2000) she envisages redrawing the rules governing the locally administered housing benefit and emergency relief elements of BIG(1a) to incorporate a workfare-type employment test, while retaining PBI on an unconditional basis (Parker, ibid., pp. 351–2). Also she envisages reducing whatever incentive housing benefit supplies to single-household creation by tightening up on her housing benefit rules (1) to include parental incomes in the assessment of claimants under 21 years and (2) to seek maintenance from the absent parent/spouse in the case of lone parents before allowing benefit (Parker ibid., pp. 352–3).

Secondly, there is the 'panacea problem'. Complex problems usually need complex solutions. Citizen income is a policy for income distribution rather than income generation. Some of its advocates have little to say, and make large assumptions about, policy relating to production. But this may be a misleading impression. Certainly Standing has made out a strong case for citizen income on the basis of the current and future needs of modern economies for flexible labour use in production and labour market flexibility (1986, pp. 138–45). But in his terms, citizen income is only one of the 'blades of the scissors' which modernity needs to cut into its looming economic and social problems (p. 133). He recognizes that it needs supplementing – the other blade of the scissors – with new approaches to production and employment policies such as industrial policy, profit sharing etc. (also see Esping-Andersen 1990 and Pierson 1991, ch. 6 on the latter). Roberts (1983) supports citizen income as the most practical way to manage the effects of automation on employment, and this is a recurrent theme in post-Keynesian work policy analysis. In post-Keynesian analysis citizen income schemes are advocated as one part of a package of radical new measures to address the problems of sustainable economic growth and employment distribution as well as income distribution in post-industrial conditions.

No realistic assessment of the structural conditions for future citizenship or of the nature of future social citizenship is possible if the analysis is confined, virtually to the exclusion of all else, to the creation of income distribution systems and to the institutionalization of the social right to income. But equally it would appear that no politics of post-industrialism could be either complete or credible if it did not include a major reform of income (and thus welfare) policy along citizen income lines.

As we have seen, the main instruments of the dominant paradigm, namely contributory social insurance supported by the non-contributory 'public charity' of 'poor relief', have had much success with poverty among the old, but not among the young. They have failed to prevent a growth of social division, poverty and the formation of an underclass in the 1970s and 1980s because of the intrinsic weaknesses involved in their creation of 'poverty traps' and 'unemployment traps', and their direct relation to and dependence on the capitalist labour market (chs 3, 5 and 6 above). National labour markets are necessarily and perennially vulnerable to trade cycles and recessionary unemployment, particularly in an economically integrated but politically unregulated world economy. In addition, as we have seen in section II, due to long-term waves of development of mechanization, recently accelerated and qualitatively enhanced in post-industrialization, they are increasingly vulnerable to structural unemployment, core-peripheral segmentation and flexibilization of labour use.

Supporters of citizen income strategies make a powerful case that guaranteeing a right to a basic income is probably the only way in the long term to prevent these profound problems of unemployment and underemployment from generating an increasingly divisive, conflictual and morally indefensible distribution of income. The aim is to prevent poverty, rather than merely to provide relief (Moynihan 1973; Parker 1989, pp. 69–71, 224; Walter 1989, pp. 62–76). And, in addition, the aim is both to enable and also to redistribute employment in a way that is compatible both with economic growth and with personal choice under the conditions of post-industrial capitalism (Roberts 1982; Parker ibid., pp. 286–90, Walter ibid., pp. 88–94).

Finally, the post-national problem. It is true that citizen income schemes tend to be discussed and analysed almost exclusively in nation-state terms. Nonetheless, there is no reason in principle why they need to be confined to this where transnational governmental structures are developed capable of significantly influencing national policies. One of the benefits of the development of and debate about citizen income schemes currently is their potential for contributing to current policy formation in the EC. The EC's current development towards integration in economic social policy and political terms will require a major revision and harmonization of the taxation and benefits systems of member states. Citizen income strategies offer universalistic principles, a clear integration of taxes and benefits systems, relative administrative simplicity and also potential for creating common ground and political opportunities for consensus formation on social reform. If they were appropriately translated into the multinational and transnational terms necessary in the EC it is reasonable to assume that they could have a significant role to play in any major review of tax and benefit policy options for the EC over the next decade or two. Of course more will be at stake in the EC in the 1990s than new tax and benefits systems. The very notion of European citizenship will be at stake. We will consider these 'post-national' issues in more detail in the following chapter.

IV

In this chapter we have considered citizens' social rights to work and to income in the context of post-industrial social and economic change. It is clear that such structural change poses major policy problems for Western nation states in the spheres of employment, income and welfare. Traditional dominant paradigm approaches – which rely on assumptions about the effectiveness of full employment policy and of welfare state policy – are likely to run into major problems in the emerging context of post-industrial capitalism. 'Full employment', a 'living wage' (and/or 'an income adequate to raise a family'), together with a state-organized contribution-based welfare system, look set to become extremely difficult to achieve on the basis of the sort of segmented labour market post-industrial capitalism is calling into existence.

Problems of employment and income are evidently closely interrelated, and policies to tackle them by developing new social rights will similarly need to be interrelated. Post-industrial forms of poverty and non-citizenship are likely to grow, unless co-ordinated productionist and distributionist strategies can be developed. The post-industrial labour market needs to be regulated and supported in new ways, particularly in terms of equal opportunities and training. The connection between employment and income (and thus welfare) will need to be rethought. And new ways will need to be found to distribute both employment and income in terms of citizenship principles.

But, as if the problems of post-industrialism were not intractable enough, there are also the problems of post-nationalism to contend with. That is the new work, income and welfare policies which post-industrialism demands will have to be developed against the background of the other major set of structural changes in contemporary Western capitalist society. We now need to look more closely at these post-national changes and at some of their implications for social citizenship.

8
Reinventing Social Citizenship II: Post-Nationalism and New Social Rights in Europe

Contemporary social structural change is occurring along a distinctively 'post-national' political (and political economic) vector as well as along the techno-economic vector of post-industrialism. 'Post-national' change is associated with various processes of 'globalization' in contemporary economies and culture (e.g. Featherstone 1990; Hall and Jacques 1989; Sklair 1990). Post-national change is as challenging to the dominant paradigm of citizenship in general and social citizenship in particular as we have seen post-industrial change to be. In this chapter I want to focus on the historically most important example of it in the late twentieth century, namely the development of the European Community (EC). But before we turn to this a number of points need to be made.

First, it may seem incongruous to propose that modernity is marked by post-national politics and the organization of non-national polities, given the world-historical importance of events in the erstwhile Communist bloc since 1989/90. Surely the reunification of the German nation and the emergence of liberated autonomous nations and nationalities in the post-Stalinist Eastern block and within what was the Soviet Union attest to the continuing strength of the nation-state idea? However, strongly as these new tides of nationalism may run, it is reasonable to assume that they are unlikely to run for long or very effectively against the forces of globalization in the contemporary capitalist economic order. In the late twentieth century these forces are continuously eroding the economic

power and sovereignty of nation states, just as in the late nineteenth and early twentieth century they had built them up,
together with their grandiose super-national incarnations, as
competitive and militaristic 'empires'. Many social and political
analysts have acknowledged these trends recently. For instance,
Mann observes that, in the postwar period, 'the global capitalist
economy has produced more genuine internationalism, weaken-
ing nation-state divisions, than at any period in the historical
development of nation states' (1990a, p. 11). Gamble reviews
the Thatcher experiment in opening the British economy to
global capitalist economic forces in the 1980s and concludes: 'As
internationalisation proceeds one of the key questions becomes
how far national models of economic development are still
relevant' (1990, p. 90). At the same time, Held argues that,
given 'the decline of the nation state' there is a need to create
'a politics beyond the sovereign nation state' (1989, p. 204).

The case of the EC nations considered in this chapter illustrates the degree to which international models of political,
social and economic development are more relevant than
national models in the contemporary period. For instance, as
its current leadership emphasizes, the future of a reunited
Germany is more likely to lie inside the EC, albeit as the
dominant political economic force within it, than it is in attempts
at national self-sufficiency or aggrandizement. The Eastern
European nations and the ex-Soviet Union nations are economically so weak that the logic of their situation will force
them, and probably sooner rather than later, to create new post-
Stalinist political economic alliances and organizations both
among themselves (e.g. the Commonwealth of Independent
States, (CIS) project 1992) and with the West. Indeed Poland,
Czechoslovakia and Hungary could well gain some kind of
membership of the EC in the late 1990s. 'Post-nationalism' is as
much of an historical reality and predicament for the Eastern
bloc European and ex-Soviet Union countries as it is for the
West.

Secondly, I want to make it clear that 'post-nationalism' refers
not only to *trans*national political change, involving levels higher
than the nation state, such as the EC (e.g. Galtung 1973; Nairn
1977; Marquand 1989), but also to *sub*national change, involving the development of local and regional political culture and

institutions (e.g. Nairn 1977). The transnational dynamics and the subnational dynamics are intimately connected in contemporary Western politics. The fact that I focus much more on the former than the latter in this chapter should not be taken to indicate that the latter are unimportant. I will return briefly to the significance of *sub*national regionalism for the contemporary analysis of citizenship in my conclusion in chapter 9.

Finally, the pre-eminent historical importance of the Western European example of post-national political and economic change should not be mistaken for uniqueness. The world capitalist economic order is world-regional and multipolar. World-regional economic (and thus potentially political) groupings of nations exist on every continent and on the borders of every ocean, not least in the Far East. Japan's take-off to economic superpower status has been engineered on a nationalistic basis throughout the postwar period, but it is unlikely to be sustained on this basis in the long term as Japan becomes vulnerable to competition from the 'little Japans' such as Taiwan and South Korea. Greater regional economic organization looks to be as much in Japan's interest as the development of the EC is in Germany's.

With the continuous development of the world economy, existing world-regional economic groupings in the Far East, South America and Africa, and possibly also between the USA and its immediate neighbours, together with relations between these blocs look set to take on a greater importance. Each of the major blocs is likely to remain as relatively open to the influence of global financial markets and of multinational companies based elsewhere but operating in their 'economic space' as the USA, Japan and the EC currently are (e.g. Grahl and Teague 1990, ch. 4). World-regional groupings are likely to be principally concerned with the facilitation of global economic processes and with the organization of world-regional markets and their infrastructures. They are also likely to be capable of forms of protectionism and other interventions in the global economy. Such economic power and the need to control it politically may provoke some significant political restructuring beyond the nation-state level in the medium to long term. But this is unlikely to compare with the politico-economic integration achieved by the EC by the early twenty-first century.

In this chapter, then, I want to focus on contemporary Europe, not because the Eastern part of it is apparently intent on reasserting nationalism, nationalist conceptions of citizenship and the nation-state model of social and economic organization, but rather because its Western part is doing the exact opposite. The construction of the EC, then, arguably provides a forerunner and a model of post-national world-regional political arrangements which could well develop elsewhere in the world order over the course of the next century. To a large extent it is in these world regions and in the world order itself, rather than in the nation state, that the future of citizenship lies.

The discussion of 'European citizenship' and of 'European social citizenship' in the chapter proceeds in three main steps. First, I outline some of the background necessary to understand contemporary definitions and developments of European citizenship (section I). Next, I consider the problem of the social limits to such citizenship. The focus here is on the growth of poverty in Europe and its roots in social structural change (section II). Finally, I consider the social dimension of European citizenship more directly (section III) looking in particular at the currently influential concept of a Charter of Social Rights and social rights regarding employment, together with contemporary EC economic and social policies in support of such social rights.

I

European citizenship and political change

322 million Europeans have a new citizenship: one that in no way supplants their national citizenship, but supplements it . . . European citizenship . . . brings with it a whole range of rights that are guaranteed by the Community. (Commission of the EC 1987a)

1   Other Europes

Before exploring the nature of EC citizenship further, it is first worth pausing to consider that, as large as it is, the EC represents only 12 European nations. This is double the number of states which created the EC in the Treaty of Rome in 1957. With the incorporation of East Germany into the EC through German unification in 1990, with Eastern European nations wanting membership and with many non-EC Western European nations (e.g. Austria and Sweden) also wanting membership, the EC is very likely to continue to expand significantly in the 1990s and beyond. In Palmer's view, 'All recognise that the EC is going to have to enlarge in two or more phases during the 1990s to include all of Western and much of Eastern Europe' (1991a). In her Bruges speech in 1988 Margaret Thatcher drew an expansive picture of Europe to set alongside the EC. Her picture included, on the one hand, Eastern Europe, particularly Poland, Czechoslovakia and Hungary, while on the other hand, by conjuring up the image of 'a Europe on both sides of the Atlantic', it even included the USA (Thatcher 1988). Given that the EC is likely to expand in future (and without going across the Atlantic), we need to consider what more expansive conceptions of 'Europe' there than the EC, and what alternative conceptions of European citizenship they imply (Morgan 1990).

There are three such conceptions worth noting, two concerned mainly with military co-operation and thus potential citizen duties and one concerned with human and social rights. The military groupings are on the one hand NATO, particularly the European dimension of this represented by NATO's Eurogroup and by the Western European Union; this includes all EC member states except Ireland, together with Norway and Turkey. On the other hand there is the very extensive and, in a post-Cold War and post-Communist world, potentially important East-West grouping, the Convention on Security and Co-operation in Europe (CSCE). CSCE is based on a convention signed by 35 West and East European states in Helsinki in 1975.

Finally there is a human and social rights grouping which has considerable practical significance both for institutionalizing the idea of European citizenship in general and for influencing the future development of EC social citizenship in particular, as we will see in section III below. This is the Council of Europe (hereafter CE) which consists of 23 West European democracies, including all the EC states, signatories to the European Declaration of Human Rights (Helsinki 1950) and the European Social Charter (1961). Its main institutions are the European Court of Human Rights, the European Commission on Human Rights and the CE's Parliamentary Assembly of representatives of member states' national parliaments. The Court of Human Rights has been influential, particularly in a state like the UK which has no Bill of Rights or written constitution. It offers a court of appeal and redress (beyond variously inadequate national-level institutions) to defend the human rights of the weak (e.g. prisoners, mental patients and immigrants) and to control the powers of nation-state authorities (e.g. police, prison administration, government officials etc.).

2 The European Community and European citizenship

The EC's main policy-making institutions (e.g. Commission of the EC 1988b; Daltrop 1986) are the Council of Ministers (the ultimate legislative and decision-making body consisting of ministers representing the member states) and the Commission (appointed officials with considerable powers to initiate, formulate and guide the implementation of legislation and policy). In addition, there are two institutions which have an important consultative role in policy-making, together with a judicial institution. The two consultative institutions are the directly elected General Assembly (which also has some limited powers to delay Council proposals and to influence the EC's budget) (Commission of the EC 1986a, pp. 49–50) and the Economic and Social Committee (ESC) (which is a forum for employer, labour and consumer interest groups). Finally, there is the European Court of Justice set up to ensure member states' compliance with the founding treaty, the Treaty of Rome 1957, and other relevant agreements (such as amendments to the treaty, particularly the 1986 Single European Act and all EC legislation).

The EC is the world's biggest trading partner, accounting for over 20 per cent of the world's exports, and it is also the world's largest consumer market. The EC's member states' aggregate GDP in 1989/90 was nearly equivalent to that of the USA and much bigger than that of Japan (i.e. 90 per cent of US GDP and 70 per cent bigger than Japanese GDP) (Eurosynergies 1990; Commission of the EC 1989b). Importantly for social policy, it is noteworthy that a bigger proportion of EC nations' aggregate GDP is spent on welfare state/social services expenditures (about 17 per cent) than is spent in the USA (about 12 per cent) (Commission of the EC 1989b). However, as against all this, the very small scale of the EC as such and its public expenditure needs to be born in mind, accounting as it does for only about one per cent of EC members' aggregate GDP. This is small alongside the spending of the big nations like Germany, France and Britain. But nonetheless it is still a substantial sum, being equivalent to or greater than the budgets of small EC nations like Denmark or Greece (Commission of the EC 1986a). However, the EC's budget is likely to increase qualitatively as the single market develops post-1992.

The EC emerged against a background of economic reconstruction in postwar Europe (e.g. Commission of the EC 1990a). This had earlier generated a Coal and Steel Community (ECSC 1954) and it came to include an atomic energy community (Euratom 1957). The EC incorporated these industrial sector 'communities'. In its early days it represented less the creation of a 'common market in everything' and more the organization and subsiding of one particular economic sector (in addition to the energy industries), namely agriculture. Spending on the 'common agricultural policy' (CAP) in the 1980s represented over 65 per cent of the EC budget, while spending on regional policy, social policy research policy and other such important areas accounted for only about 15 per cent (Commission of EC 1986a). However, the EC's structural and social spending is planned to increase to 30 per cent of its budget in the early 1990s (Grahl and Teague 1990, p. 245).

These sorts of observations point to the weakness of the EC in developing the social conditions for a common 'European citizenship' in the 1960s and 1970s. Indeed in this period it is arguable that the Council of Europe's Court of Human Rights made more of a dent in introspective nationalist attitudes to citizens' rights than did the European Community's institutions and policies (Dean 1989; Commission of the EC 1990d). The representatives of EC citizens in the EC's Assembly had precious little power to act, as compared with the effectively unaccountable bureaucrats of the EC's Commission, while the EC as a whole had insufficient spending power and financial authority to influence the economic environment in EC member states very noticeably.

This situation began to change in the 1980s and it is still evolving. The new phase of development has in large part been an attempt to respond to trends in the world economy. The most important of these trends are those of high technology (post-industrial) production, the dominance of Japan in global consumer durables markets, the high-technology-based globalization of capital and consumer markets, the collapse of the Eastern European and Soviet economies and the gathering European ecology crisis. All of these factors have conspired to generate new needs among the European nations for European-level co-operation. Co-operation is needed in areas such as technology research and development policy, transport infrastructure policy, ecology policy and in policy to create a large enough 'domestic' European market to sustain globally viable European multinational corporations.

The EC had spent a generation talking about the achievement of a 'common market' without the leading member states feeling sufficiently pressured by economic events, even by the world recession of the mid-1970s, to make this a real priority. However, in the 1980s they began to feel and to respond to the pressures. With the appointment in 1985 of a dynamic new Commission President, Jacques Delors, they were at last prepared to make European-level co-operation a real priority and in 1986 the Single European Act was agreed. This prepared the way for a rapid movement to create a single integrated market in goods, labour and capital by the end of 1992.

These economically-based developments have been flanked by two other more politically-based developments. On the one hand the EC has felt the need to try to communicate the benefits of the single market as directly as possible to EC citizens. This is in order both to explain and to legitimate the changes. Thus a new consciousness of and public discourse about 'European citizenship' is beginning to be promoted within the EC (e.g. Commission of the EC 1985b, 1990d, 1990e). On the other hand support for quasi-federal institutions and in many quarters (not least the EC Commission) for full-blown federation (that is for a 'United States of Europe') has begun to develop (Commission of the EC 1989e; Palmer 1991c; Lodge 1987, 1991b; Gow 1991b).

One of the issues which has dominated EC politics in the late 1980s has been the debate about the minimum financial structures necessary to support an integrated EC market. The necessary market infrastructures are, as they were in the era of nation-state market building, a single currency (the ecu), a single monetary system (European Monetary Union, EMU) and a single central bank (a EuroFed on the lines of the US Federal Reserve) (Grahl and Teague 1990, ch. 3; Emerson and Huhne 1991). A politically constructed and accountable but independently operating EuroFed would be responsible for monetary policy and would seek to influence the public expenditure policies and priorities not only of the EC *per se* but also of each of the member states (Harden 1990). The 'pooled sovereignty' which such institutions create might continue to be managed by the Council of Ministers under a revised Treaty of Rome, as envisaged in the Delors timetable for economic union (Commission of the EC 1989e). However, is difficult to see how, once embarked on the creation of the new market and the financial institutions which the single market requires, it would be possible in the medium term to stop a drift, even a march, towards full political federalism in the mid- or late 1990s. This indeed is the expressed aim and timetable of EC 'federalists' such as the Commission, Germany and a good number of EC member states (e.g. Palmer 1991c; Gow 1991b). It was effectively affirmed as such, not withstanding the British government's characteristic reservation of its right to 'opt out', at the Maastricht Inter-Governmental Conference (IGC) in 1991 in the treaty agreed there on political and economic union.

Quasi-federal institutions such as a European Central Bank operating in a non-federal economic alliance would create a politically unstable situation which could not endure long. Loss of sovereignty and of democratic control of economic and monetary policy at the nation-state level would need to be compensated by the development of democratic power at the EC level. This could be achieved by giving the elected Assembly real and substantial legislative authority. By 1996 supporters of EC federalism intend to have achieved a major law-making role for the European Parliament (along with national governments' role), together with the creation of an upper revising chamber representing the EC's regions and possibly also such other

corporate interests as trades unions' and employers' organizations (e.g. Palmer 1989b, p. 57, 1991c). If this is indeed achieved
then finally something would exist which could be called a
genuine form of European political citizenship. Until then
members of EC nations are, as various Commission documents
(e.g. 1986a) put it, in a 'pre-federalist' phase. This effectively
means that they are in a phase of pre-political European citizenship, in which, as many commentators have observed, there is a
substantial 'democratic deficit' (e.g. Spencer 1990, ch. 7; Lodge
1991a).

A rhetoric of 'European Community citizenship', together
with an attempt to turn some of the rhetoric into reality, has
been an important part of the EC's revival and dynamism under
Commission President Jacques Delors since the mid-1980s. 'Pre-
federalism' is basically a pre-political phase as far as European
citizenship is concerned. But some progress has been attempted
on the civil/cultural and social/economic aspects of European
citizenship. The former was initiated by the Adonnino Report
1985 and the latter was initiated by movements involving Delors
and others to create an EC Social Charter. We will postpone
consideration of the latter until section III below; however, a
brief sketch of the former is in order here.

The Adonnino Committee on 'A People's Europe' was set up
by the Council of Ministers in 1984. It reported to them the
following year with a variety of proposals, many of which were
accepted for implementation. It was set up to consider measures
'to strengthen and promote [the EC's] identity and its image
both for its citizens and the rest of the world' (Commission of
EC 1985b, p. 5). Issues for consideration included the easing
of movement of EC citizens and goods across member states'
borders, educational exchanges and the promotion of common
symbols of EC identity. The report was not very far-reaching in
spite of its popularization of the notion of European citizenship.
Its emphasis throughout was on making speedy progress on
politically achievable policies 'of direct relevance to Community
citizens [offering] them tangible benefits in their everyday lives'
(ibid., p. 9). It aimed to begin to address the real problems of
credibility, irritation and national red tape etc. experienced by
EC citizens when travelling, looking for employment and seek-
ing new residence within the EC. Among many other things, the

report supported the introduction of such things as an EC passport, driving licence, emergency health card, EC border signs and flag, and more controversially an EC TV channel to promote 'the European message'.

The elementary nature of many of the Adonnino Report's proposals indicates the extent to which the notion of European citizenship had remained underdeveloped during the first generation of the EC's existence. Arguably, this situation began to change considerably in the late 1980s, both in terms of the substance and influence of EC civil and human rights law (e.g. Commission of the EC 1990d; also Spencer 1990 and Andrews 1991, part III) and also in terms of public awareness and interest in European citizenship. For instance, in Britain, for long notorious as one of the most insular and inward-looking EC member states, a survey (taken prior to the outburst of politicking associated with the Maastricht Treaty) indicates that over 40 per cent of British adults identify themselves as 'European' and over 70 per cent support the idea of full federalism, a 'United States of Europe' (Mintel Report 1990; also Commission of the EC 1986b; but see also Linton 1991). By 1990 the Commission felt confident enough about the concept of a 'people's Europe' to ask itself the rhetorical question: 'A flag, a passport, an anthem, are these just silly gimmicks or symbols of the banding together of peoples committed to democracy and peace?' (Commission of the EC 1990d, p. 50). In 1991, under the Maastricht Treaty of political and economic union, the concept of member-state citizens also being 'citizens of the Union' was formally inscribed for the first time (Lambert 1991).

Finally, if a federal European Community with substantial political rights of citizenship is ultimately achieved, as is anticipated by the Maastricht Treaty (Lodge 1991b), it is worth noting how its development will have diverged from what the classical social theory of citizenship might have predicted. That is, as we saw in chapter 1 T. H. Marshall's schema for the emergence of citizenship (based on British history but implicitly generalizable) saw the achievement of social rights as the coping stone completing a movement which had begun from civil rights and had then added political rights. The EC looks set to disrupt this schema by beginning with civil rights (in the EC but also in the CE; Spencer 1990), by going on to develop social rights in the early mid-1990s, but only promising the development of political citizenship through some as yet unclear enhancement of the powers of the EC Parliament beginning later in the 1990s. The significance of this reversal of stages two and three for EC social citizenship is unclear but interesting and arguable. On the one hand EC social citizenship could be held to be qualitatively much more depoliticized than that of the British model of development because, unlike the British case, its democratic basis is virtually non-existent. Or, on the other hand, it could be held to be less depoliticized because, unlike the British model, it implicitly and explicitly refers to the political domain, indeed its clear purpose is to contribute to the formation of a political community. We will return to this issue later. For the moment however we need to turn from the promise of European citizenship to its limits, namely the social problem it confronts in the growth of poverty in Europe.

II

European poverty and social change

1   Background

In chapter 3 I argued that poverty is a strategic issue for citizenship. Simply being female, or black, or old, or unemployed often consigns people to 'second-class citizenship' whether they are poor or not. But poverty, in which these dimensions often overlap in multiple layers of disadvantage and deprivation, goes further and takes citizenship to its internal limit. Thus the poor can be said to be permanently vulnerable to a form of internal exile, to exclusion (and to forms of self-exclusion) as effectively *non*-citizens. As the European Commission acknowledge 'fundamental rights are likely to remain a dead letter for the most disadvantaged of us' (Commission of the EC, 1990d, p. 19).

European citizenship and the community it implies and requires are evidently still in their infancy. Even though they are growing fast they are as yet fragile political constructs burdened by substantial, intractable and growing problems of 'second-class citizenship' and exclusion such as sexism and racism inherited from the failures of the constituent member states. And for some critical observers there are fears that the EC itself, particularly if developed in a 'neo-liberal' direction, may not only fail to tackle these problems effectively but also exacerbate them (e.g. Palmer 1989b; Grahl and Teague 1990).

Although the principle of 'equal pay for equal work' was inscribed in the original Rome Treaty in order to address the problem of women's inequality, it had little effect on the member states for at least the following two decades (arguably, it has had little effect even today; Hoskyns and Luckhaus 1989). Problems of racism and antagonism to the 16 million immigrants and migrant workers in the EC's member states are longstanding and they are growing (Webster 1990; Gow 1990, 1991b; Vulliamy 1990). At the same time the pressure on the EC of migrant labour from non-EC countries is also growing, particularly migrants from Asia and Africa (e.g. Woollacott 1991) but now also from Eastern Europe. With the EC's internal border controls being minimized after 1992, its foreign aid and immigration control policies look set to become increasingly controversial. EC foreign aid is now beginning to be shifted from African and Third World treaty partners (Lomé Convention EC associates) and towards Eastern Europe. In addition, it is possible that EC policy on immigration control could develop in a tough and potentially racist direction, giving preferential access to the nationals of white non-EC European states over (black, Asian and other) non-European states (Palmer 1990c; Spencer 1990, ch. 2; Helm 1991).

Such problems of sexism and racism are interconnected with and tend to exacerbate the basic citizenship problem of poverty. So I will focus on poverty and its roots in structural social change in this section since space precludes further exploration here of the problems of sexual and racial inequality and division also facing the EC in the 1990s. Having sketched out some of the features and causes of poverty in the EC we can then consider some of the social and economic policies aimed at tackling the problem by renewing Western European nations' existing commitment to social rights, aiming to extend them and standardize them at the supranational EC level (section III below).

2   *European poverty*

Since its first anti-poverty policies in the early 1970s the EC, unlike the USA's more 'absolute' approach, has adopted a 'relative' definition of poverty as less than 50 per cent of average EC income per head. In 1975 with a nine-state EC the poor totalled 30 million people, while by 1985, partly because of the expansion to a 12-state EC, the total stood at around 50 million people, about 14 per cent of the EC's population (Commission of the EC 1990a; also 1989e and Smeeding et al. 1990a). In their review of poverty in EC countries from the early 1960s to the mid-1970s Lawson and George (1980) note that social welfare expenditures rose over this period, up to an EC average of 24 per cent of GDP in 1975 (op. cit., table 8.2, p. 234). In spite of this, however, the post-tax share of national income accruing to the poorest 20 per cent remained remarkably constant at around 6 per cent (e.g. in the UK and West Germany) throughout this period (ibid., table 8.3, p. 236; also Lawson et al. 1984).

As we have seen earlier, poverty in modern Western society is associated with a variety of factors. These include under-class formation and work and family problems associated with such trends as (1) cultural change (e.g. family and work ethic 'breakdown'), (2) the failures of state welfare provision, (3) New Right governmental attacks on welfare, trades unions and other such labour market 'rigidities' in the USA, UK and elsewhere, and (4) post-industrial economic restructuring, structural unemployment and labour flexibilization. We considered these trends in relation mainly to the USA earlier, but they have their parallels in most of the advanced Western societies, not least the EC. We will consider EC labour-market changes and policies in a little more detail in section III below.

In his discussion of the USA's new forms of 'post-industrial' poverty Moynihan argues that 'For most of the twentieth century the social problems that beset the United States – always excluding that of race – appeared first in Europe, as did the first response . . . But we have a new set of problems, and there is no 'European' solution at hand' (1989, p. 25). But he also suggests, on the basis of international comparisons, that 'it is possible that a more universal, post-industrial pattern is emerging. Mature social insurance systems gradually eliminate poverty among the aged: but at the same time, marital instability and tenuous labour markets may leave a fair number of poor children even in prosperous countries' (ibid., p. 25).

Given all of the political, cultural and economic differences between the USA and the EC, and indeed within the EC itself, there is evidence to support the view that Europe is beginning to develop a pattern of 'new poverty' comparable to that of the USA (on Europe see Commission of the EC 1990a; Abel-Smith and Raphael 1986; Lawson et al. 1984; on the USA see above chs 3–6; on a systematic comparison between some European countries and the USA see Smeeding et al. 1990a, 1990b). An interesting recent study of this topic is that by Room et al. (1989), ' "New Poverty" in the European Community', which analyses trends in EC poverty and various structural and other explanations for them. It is relevant at this point to consider some of their main findings and arguments.

The picture drawn by Room et al. is one of a long-term growth in poverty. This is indicated (albeit roughly) by the percentage increase in numbers receiving non-insurance-based social assistance in EC countries over the period 1970–86. This increase ranges from 40 per cent in the UK to 175 per cent in Germany to over 350 per cent on the main Belgian assistance programme for the non-elderly (op. cit., table 1, p. 168). However, along with this overall growth, there has occurred a change in the composition of the poor. As in the case of the USA, insurance-based pensions have greatly reduced poverty among the elderly. For instance, in 1970 the elderly constituted 60 per cent of all poor households in the UK and 40 per cent in Germany. But by 1985 these proportions had declined to 46 per cent and 13 per cent respectively. On the other hand the unemployed have tended to grow as a proportion of the poor. For instance, from 1979 to 1983 they grew from under 1 per cent to over 25 per cent in Germany and from 15 per cent to 35 per cent in Britain (ibid., pp. 168–9; see also Achdut and Tamir 1990). However, the main group contributing to the explosive growth of social assistance recipients noted earlier is undoubtedly that of single parent families, typically single-mother families (see also Roll 1989; Hauser and Fischer 1990; Smeeding et al. 1990b). For instance, in France a benefit specifically for poor single parents was introduced in 1976; in

1981 it was paid to over 66,000 families, but by 1985 this had jumped by over 60 per cent to 108,000 families (ibid., table 1, also pp. 170, 173).

Room et al. argue that contemporary European poverty is caused by a number of 'old' and 'new' structural and cultural factors. We can consider some of the 'older' longstanding problems first. For instance, poverty is a perennial problem in the agricultural sectors of EC member states' economies, particularly in the less developed southern and Mediterranean states whose reliance upon agriculture is very substantial. Poverty is also traditionally generated by the structural and frictional dislocation induced by economic growth and urbanization in industrial capitalist societies. Finally, poverty in the postwar world of insurance-based welfare states has also traditionally tended to be produced by the welfare state's poverty and employment traps and by its various other gaps and inadequacies. In the view of Room et al. these failures of the welfare state have produced an 'underclass' throughout the postwar period. This underclass has only been added to in recent years by new forms of poverty; it has not been created *ex nihilo* (op. cit., pp. 173–4). They are suspicious of the ideological political uses of the notion of 'new poverty'. They emphasize the traditional failure of the labour market to do other than generate inequality and low-paid poverty at its bottom end and also periodically to threaten unemployment to all. Nonetheless, the picture they draw both asserts and implies the great importance for contemporary European poverty of new late twentieth-century structural and cultural factors.

The new factors are European versions of those we have already considered in the context of the USA and Western societies in general, and arguably together they constitute some of the main trends of 'post-modernity' (Roche 1992a). On the one hand there is the post-industrial economic trend to a polarized market for flexibilized 'core' and 'peripheral' labour. As we have seen, this is a market structure in which the 'peripheral' labour on offer is unreliable, poorly paid, insufficient to support families and inadequate to provide a basis for long-term insurance-based social security and pensions (ch. 7 above; also on Europe, Standing 1986 and Boyer 1988). On the other hand there is the post-modern cultural trend away from marriage and the modern nuclear family pattern (ch. 5 above; also on Europe, Roll 1989 and Hauser and Fischer 1990). This development reduces the capacity of individuals and families to care for themselves and makes them more vulnerable to periods, or long-term conditions, of dependency on welfare (Room et al. op. cit., pp. 172–3).

Room et al. also implicitly emphasize the importance of contemporary political ideology, particularly the role of New Right-influenced governments in Europe in cutting already inadequate social assistance programmes, and in failing to develop new policies and expenditures to tackle new problems. Finally, they emphasize the new situation facing the poorer southern European states (see also Grahl and Teague 1990, ch. 6; Palmer 1991b). The latter are increasingly being affected by the culturally disorganizing features of the American and northern European 'post-modern' consumer culture and the sexual and familial revolutions associated with it. This is in addition to the socio-economic disorganization typically associated with rapid industrialization, urbanization and secularization. Thus:

> In the northern countries increasing numbers of the population are resorting to social assistance; and in the southern countries, where the family and the church served traditionally as an alternative system of 'social security', rapid programmes of modernisation and urbanisation mean that growing numbers of the population are losing the security of these traditional supports and find themselves particularly vulnerable to poverty as unemployment levels rise (Room et al., 1989, p. 175)

Room et al. conclude their analysis by conceding some substance to the idea that contemporary EC poverty *is* new. In this they repeat in the European context the sort of analysis which, as we have seen when considering American society (chs 3–7) and to a much lesser extent British society (ch. 7), suggests that much of contemporary poverty and underclass formation can reasonably be argued to be historically distinctive and thus 'new'. Thus they argue:

> 'What *is* new about the 1980s is the widening of the range of the population which is subject to . . . economic insecurity. Added to this are insecurities which result from the transformation of

the family; in particular, the growing numbers of single parent families. Our social security systems seem to be incapable of coping with these two sources of insecurity . . .' (op. cit., p. 175)

Clearly, a range of new social and economic policies will be required in the EC in the 1990s to begin to address these problems of European poverty. The single market may stimulate economic growth and thus increase available resources for anti-poverty policy. And it is conceivable that in the course of harmonization of EC member states' tax and benefits systems in the 1990s the arguments for a new EC-level citizen income policy might begin to be heard. Such a policy would represent a major step in reducing poverty and promoting the social rights of EC citizenship. Time will tell whether either of these developments occur. In the meantime the most substantial current attempt to promote European social rights, and indirectly to tackle European poverty, has been that of the development of a European Charter of Social Rights. It is to this that we now turn.

III

European social rights and social citizenship

1   European social rights

In this section, and also in the concluding section (IV below), we will look at some important contemporary developments in EC social citizenship. The key issues here, of course, are the likely effects and possible implications of economic integration post-1992 on citizens' social rights and duties. These effects and implications are likely to be felt, and thus are likely to stimulate policy, in three interconnected areas: employment (see below), welfare (e.g. Abel-Smith and Raphael 1986; Teague and Brewster 1989) and income (on EC income rights and policy see Abel-Smith and Raphael 1986, ch. 2; GRAEL 1986; Jordan 1987; Parker 1989). However, it is impractical to consider reviewing each of these areas here. Employment, with the economic buoyancy and growth on which it depends, is evidently a vitally important determinant of welfare and income, setting the terms and conditions on which welfare and income rights and related distributional and social policies can be developed. And any discussion of employment rights and social rights necessarily carries an implicit reference to welfare and income rights and policies, even where these themes are not explicitly addressed. So I will focus on the area of employment rights and labour-market policies in this section.

Current movements in the EC to build social rights, particularly employment rights (i.e. rights *to* and rights *in* employment), into the EC's constitution need to be seen against the existing background of non-EC international conventions and rights relating to employment. Two organizations are relevant here, namely the United Nations' International Labour Organization (ILO) and the Council of Europe's European Social Charter. They already exert patchy and variable degrees of influence and regulation over national employment legislation and over the standards of its administration in most of the EC's member states.

ILO conventions cover a vast range of employment issues in most UN countries and when ratified they are binding in international law. Most of the basic conventions (on such things as outlawing forced labour, safety, paid vacations, protection of women and children at work etc.) have been ratified by most Western countries. But many other conventions have not been ratified. Indeed in recent years many EC states have avoided, rejected or revised conventions governing important matters such as night-work for women and young people, minimum-wage-fixing mechanisms etc. (Teague and Brewster 1989, table 1.2, p. 8, and ch. 1 *passim*). This withdrawal of enthusiasm and support for ILO conventions and rights reflects the movement in Western politics towards the New Right and the liberalization and deregulation of capital, goods and labour markets. Since this was taken furthest, both in rhetoric and policy, in the 1980s in Britain under the Thatcher governments, it is not surprising that the British have also been notable avoiders of ILO conventions (e.g. Standing 1986; Hendy and Eady 1991).

The renaissance of the EC under Delors from 1985 and the Single European Act of 1986 have prompted an intense struggle within the EC's institutions (e.g. the Council of Ministers and the Assembly) over the future of social policy and labour-market regulation in the EC post-1992 (Teague 1989 chs 4, 5; Grahl and Teague 1990, chs 1, 5). Those who wish to see a more 'maximally' structured and integrated labour market include President Delors and the Commission, the European Trade Union Confederation (ETUC), together with France and Belgium. This position is one which is conscious of the economic success and also of the economic threat of Japan with its corporatist political and economic organization. As against this the forces of 'minimalism' were led throughout the 1980s by Margaret Thatcher and the British government, together with the European employers' confederation (UNICE). This position has been inspired by the economic recovery of minimally regulated America in the 1980s.

The outcome of this particular struggle in European social policy is currently unclear (Deakin 1988; MacNeill 1988; Grahl and Teague 1990). So also is the impact on it of contemporary moves towards economic and political federalization in the EC (see section I above). Developments might stick for a period after the achievement (which looks a probability for the mid-1990s) of the *quasi*-federal stage of the creation of a European Central Bank, anticipated by the Maastricht Union Treaty of 1991. A EuroFed committed to an anti-inflationary strategy would probably operate in favour of a deregulated and highly competitive European labour market. Its aim would be to act as a brake on labour costs and thus on both 'cost push' and 'demand pull' inflation simultaneously.

On the other hand it is possible, if the Commission, Germany and others get their way, that full federalism will develop, and this is the underlying thrust of the Maastricht Treaty. Leaving Britain aside, Western Europe's political culture and institutions have long tended towards forms of liberal corporatism, whether of a social democratic or Christian (especially Catholic) kind (Grant 1985a), particularly in the postwar period, and this spirit has infused much of the work of the EC Commission (Sargent 1985). In the late 1990s a fully federal EC, even with a greatly empowered democratic core in the European Parliament, would continue to draw on this corporatist political culture. This seems to me to be in any case compatible with the major institution-building process the EC is embarked on in the 1990s. EC politics in the 1980s undoubtedly registered the influence of the New Right neo-liberal approach to politics and markets, principally that exerted by Britain, and this is compatible with that part of the 1992 market concept concerned with the removal of national obstacles and rigidities. Nonetheless, radical *laissez-faire* is likely to be a passing influence on EC development compared with continental European corporatist traditions (although see Grahl and Teague 1990, ch. 1 and *passim* for an alternative view).

Assuming economic growth in the EC, then, it is probable that more 'maximalist' than 'minimalist' versions of social and employment policies will be pursued, involving attempts to construct a regulated but flexible labour market, to 'level up' member states' welfare benefits systems and to standardize income support systems. However, as some commentators argue, even such policies as these face great political opposition and problems of avoidance from employers. They run risks of eroding labour and welfare conditions in the most developed EC nations by setting standards too low or formulating them too vaguely or impractically (Palmer 1989b, ch. 4; Weston 1991). In any case, even 'maximalist' social and labour-market policies on their own would not be able to prevent the at least short-term increases in unemployment, poverty and regional inequality which will probably accompany the initial creation of the EC-wide market. They also need to be accompanied by vigorous policies of technological and regional development and redistribution (Grahl and Teague 1990, chs 4–6; also Palmer 1989b and Standing 1986).

In the current EC debates moderates and maximalists interested in developing EC social rights have turned for precedent and support to the Council of Europe's Social Charter. This charter, signed in 1961, is less legally binding than the ILO's conventions and it contains fewer rights, many of which in any case overlap with ILO rights. Among the more important social rights the Council of Europe aims to protect are citizens' rights to work, to organize and bargain collectively, to receive vocational guidance and training, to be provided with healthy and safe working conditions and to seek work in other CE states. In addition, the CE Charter protects all citizens' welfare rights (e.g. the right to health care and assistance, to social security and assistance) both in their home state and if they are migrant workers. It also protects their family rights (i.e. their right to economic, legal and social protection for their family) (Teague and Brewster 1989, p. 10; also Harris and Jaspers in Betten et al. 1989 and Palmer 1989b, ch. 4).

The CE Charter is of considerable relevance to social rights in the EC, since most of the EC states are already covered by it. It *could* form the basis of a new, binding EC social constitution, backed by the legal authority of the EC's Court of Justice. The Court of Justice has proved to be active and influential in the social rights area (e.g. Commission of the EC 1990d), particularly in regard to equality of treatment and opportunity for men and women, both in the early 1980s (Teague 1989, pp. 105–6) and also more recently (Landau 1989; Hoskyns and Luckhaus 1989). On the other hand, if such an EC-based development were to occur, it might have adverse consequences for the Council of Europe and leave *its* Social Charter in limbo (Betten et al. 1989).

2   The Single Market 1992: employment and social rights

Commission President Jacques Delors marked the renaissance of the EC's integrative dynamic in 1985 by speaking in terms of the EC's policy goals of countering European unemployment and promoting full employment. Thus he implied the need to service a notional EC citizenship right to work (Commission of the EC 1985a). But a right to work in Western capitalist societies is an essentially fragile and vulnerable right. It is only as good as the buoyancy of the relevant economy and of labour demand in that economy. One of the fundamental justifications, then, for developing the Single Market is its potential for generating economic growth and creating jobs. So defensible projections of future labour demand and employment potential are an intellectually and politically necessary part of the case for the Single Market in terms of social policy, the 'right to employment' and thus in terms of European social citizenship.

The grounds for Delors' 1985 optimism on the employment front were subsequently presented in a number of EC Commission reports, in particular the Cecchini Report (Cecchini 1988; Commission of the EC 1988a; Palmer 1989b, ch. 1; also

Kreisky 1989). The Cecchini analysis has a negative and a positive aspect. Negatively it estimates the costs to industry of the longstanding fragmentation (and indeed increasing disintegration) of the EC's allegedly 'common market', and thus the benefits of the removal of these costs. In addition it considers positive economic benefits of the creation of a huge internal EC market. The costs of the current fragmentation of the European market between EC member states in the major industrial sectors can be illustrated by the automobile sector. This employs 7 per cent of the EC's workforce and produces 40 per cent of world car output. Different national technical regulations, tax differences, customs red tape and the denial of economics of scale add 5 per cent to the European car industry's unit costs (2.6 billion ecu), most of which could be saved by integration. The overall basic medium-term benefits of integration are calculated as an increase of 4–6 per cent in EC GDP, a deflation of consumer prices by 6 per cent, importantly an increase in employment of 1.8 million new jobs and a decrease in the EC's unemployment rate of 1.5 per cent. On mildly expansionary assumptions the employment gains could be considerably higher, i.e. 4–6 million (Cecchini 1988; Palmer 1989b, ch. 1).

However, the basis on which to build the EC's right to work may be not be as sound, at least in the *short* term, as these projections about the *medium* term suggest. Various analyses of the short-term employment effects of 1992 show them to be negative, and possibly deflationary, with overall job losses in the EC of around 500,000 (European 1990; Harper 1990a; also Rajan 1990 and Palmer 1990b). They are also likely to exacerbate the great regional inequalities in employment and wealth which already exist between the richer North and poorer South and (within the North and other industrially developed regions) between the new growth areas and the declining and de-industrializing old industrial cities and regions (RETI Report 1989; Halsall 1990; Grahl and Teague 1990, ch. 6).

In addition, there is the concern, originally expressed by Delors himself (Commission of the EC 1985a), that 'social dumping' might occur (also Commission of the EC 1990b, p. 55). That is, in an integrated market with free movement of labour, EC states with high unemployment and/or low social welfare provision could effectively 'export' their unemployed to states with lower unemployment and/or higher social welfare provision. Furthermore, low-wage states, by keeping relative wage rates down artificially, could increase exports and/or dominate their domestic markets. They would thus indirectly be exporting their own potential unemployment to other EC states. This in turn could trigger retaliatory labour cost cuts and welfare benefits cuts in these states (Teague 1989, p. 78; Daubler in Betten et al. 1989; Grahl and Teague 1990, ch. 5). It was problems of this sort that led Delors originally to press strongly for the development of a 'social dimension' to the Single Market. The 'playing field' needed to be levelled and the incentive for EC states to operate divisive strategies against each other – strategies which would almost certainly increase aggregate unemployment and waste growth potential – needed to be reduced (also Commission of the EC 1988a). We can now look at this social dimension in a little more detail.

3   The EC's Charter of Social Rights: the 'social dimension' of 1992

Speaking about the Single European Act of 1986, which provided the legal basis for 1992, Jacques Delors observed, 'All of these objectives are inextricably linked: the large market, technological cooperation, strengthening the European monetary system, economic and social cohesion and the social aspects of collective action' (quoted Betten et al. 1989, p. 103). The idea of making such major changes in such a short period of years has called for innumerable intensive planning exercises by the Commission and intense political negotiations between the member states on both the economic and social fronts. Delors had hoped that the 'social dialogue' between EC trades unions (ETUC) and employers (UNICE) might generate the substance of the post-1992 social dimension policies. But his hopes have not been fulfilled because of the lack of interest shown by UNICE in social regulation in the new market (Teague 1989, chs 4, 5, appendix 4; Grahl and Teague 1990, ch. 5). In addition, the inter-state politics over 1992 have often been acrimonious. Margaret Thatcher and the British government time and again turned their faces against more than minimum integration on the economic front. Throughout the 1980s they opposed all movements towards the creation of common EC social rights on the grounds of costs and also, allegedly, of principle (Palmer 1989b, ch. 4).

However, by 1989 at their Strasbourg IGC, the EC heads of state were in a position (with the exception of the British), to commit themselves formally to a 'Community Charter of Fundamental Social Rights' (Commission of the EC 1990b; Venturini 1989; Teague 1989; Teague and Brewster 1989). This position (again with the exception of the British) was reaffirmed at the Maastricht IGC in 1991, although not in the Union Treaty agreed there. The social rights in question are mainly rights relating to workers. They are rights *in* work and represent the 'social dimensions' of an economic market in labour (Wedderburn 1990). They do not, at this stage, include (as the CE's Social Charter does, and as Delors implied in his original 1985 speech to the European Parliament) a basic right *to* work (Commission of the EC 1985a; Betten et al. 1989, p. 103). They thus represent workers' (or citizens-as-workers') rights rather than citizens' rights *per se*, leading the Commission to ask: 'Is the citizenship [the Community] proclaims only for workers? Will it extend it resolutely to all?' (Commission of the EC 1990d, p. 50). The British response to this has indeed been 'resolute'; they have opposed any such extension. For instance, in part in deference to British objections, proposals to fix a minimum EC wage and strongly to integrate social security systems and payments were deleted from the EC's 1989 commitment to the Social Charter and to the construction of new European social rights (Usborne 1989).

On a Community-wide basis (except for Britain) the EC's Social Charter enshrines (for part-time and temporary workers in addition to full-time permanent workers) the rights to a decent wage, to maximum working hours, to join a trade union and to strike, to vocational training, to health and safety at work, to information, consultation and participation in companies by employees, to equal treatment for male and female employees and to social security. When fully implemented these rights are intended both to remove the national barriers to labour mobility within the EC and also to discourage 'social dumping' (Wedderburn 1990).

The Charter itself is not legally binding and attempts to make it so in the 1991 Maastricht Union Treaty negotiations foundered on British objections. However, the Commission's Action Programme to implement it prior to 1993 periodically brings forward elements of the Charter in the form of Directives (legally binding on EC states) or Recommendations (for voluntary implementation) for the European Parliament to scrutinize and for the Council to agree. The Charter's principles will thus be implemented over a period in the early 1990s by a mixture of binding and voluntary regulation. The European Court of Justice's interpretations of both the Directives and the basic EC Treaties (1957 and 1986, together with their references to social rights) are likely to play an important role in determining the nature of European citizens' social rights in the 1990s.

The first draft Directive brought forward in 1990 (Palmer 1990a) concerned social rights for part-time and temporary workers. As we have already seen they form a substantial (25–33 per cent) sector of the labour force, and a growing one in all post-industrializing economies. In addition, they provide most of the new job opportunities – not to mention most of the social problems of low pay and insecurity – for groups such as women, young people and ethnic minorities. So, both in economic and social terms, part-time and temporary workers are a new and strategically important sector to incorporate in modern social-rights provisions (health and safety, night work and shift work restrictions etc.).

The draft Directive was damningly criticized by the Thatcher government (Palmer 1990d). This is not surprising, since the British government even treats as anathema as basic a social right as the right to strike – at least in Britain. (It is ironic, given its support for Solidarity, that the Thatcher government deemed this right to be perfectly legitimate in Stalinist Poland.) The inclusion of this in the EC Charter merely 'Europeanizes' a right which has long been established in many of the national constitutions of the EC's member states. But for the Thatcher government, even this was declared to be unacceptable. The then Employment Minister, Norman Fowler, denounced the Charter proposals on the eve of the Strasbourg IGC in 1989 as 'a threat to jobs'. He declared: 'The right to strike conflicts with our national traditions. Since 1906 there has been no right to strike in Britain but [only] a limited immunity [from prosecution] for those who organise strikes' (quoted Palmer 1989a). Given this, the British reaction to the EC Charter's Directive creating a new set of social rights for part-time and temporary workers was predictable. Margaret Thatcher, faced with the requirement to enrol all those working more than eight hours a week in the UK's National Insurance scheme, furiously denounced it as 'mad' and as 'one of the worst examples I have yet seen of bureaucratic meddling' (quoted Milne 1990, also Usborne 1989).

With less passion but equal intransigence, a subsequent Employment Minister, Michael Howard, repeated Fowler's spoiling tactics on the eve of the 1991 Maastricht IGC. He criticized EC Charter proposals on maximum work time (48 hours/six days per week) and minimum paid leave (four weeks), among other reasons for their costs to employers and thus their threat to jobs (Brown and Usborne 1991). The new Prime Minister, John Major, claiming a new post-Thatcherite position of pragmatic rather than ideological objection to the Charter (White 1991), nonetheless, succeeded in excluding social policy from the Maastricht Union Treaty. Since the other EC member states are committed to pressing on with implementation of the Charter irrespective of Britain's objections, it is more accurate to see Major's 'achievement' as a marginalization of Britain in the contemporary development of EC social policy (Usborne et al. 1991) and social citizenship.

It can be reasonably argued that it was Thatcher's badly mistaken judgements about the politics of contemporary citizenship (i.e. her nationalism, her attack on local government powers and rights, her enforcement of local tax duties and her rejection of European-level political identity and rights) which brought about her political downfall. British governments in the 1990s are unlikely to wish (or indeed to be allowed by their political and economic context) to repeat the Thatcherite romance with 'little Englandism'. Whatever their political complexion, they are likely to be, or in the case of Conservative governments to appear to be, positive about the EC and about the further development of Euro-citizenship.

However, some formidable problems need to be faced by

each and every member state if their rhetoric about Euro-citizenship is to be turned into reality. The Single Market project could well exacerbate the growth both of the 'new poverty', by promoting deregulation and exploitative forms of flexibilization in the new European-wide labour market, and of existing and new forms of regional inequality. Promotion of the Social Charter, as limited as it is (Piachaud 1991), and of further social rights of Euro-citizenship, looks likely to be the most minimal policy needed to ensure a wide dissemination of the benefits of economic growth promised by the Single Market project and to minimize and control its social costs.

IV

Conclusion: European social rights and social duties

Western concepts of politics and of citizenship have their historical origins in the European political experience. That experience has involved the construction of political communities, of states and citizenship at every level from the level of the city (e.g. ancient Greece and Renaissance Italy) to that of the nation (post-medieval Europe, particularly nineteenth-century Germany and Italy), to that of the empire (ancient Greece and Rome, post-medieval Europe, particularly Spain and Britain). So the contemporary structural complexity which began to emerge in the 1980s, while it represents a great change from the oversimplifications of political and cultural identity of the nation-state era, is, from a deeper historical perspective, nothing essentially new. Europeans in the 1990s will continue to be simultaneously both united and divided in their political loyalties and identities much as they always have been, in spite of the veneer of nationalism, according to the three factors of *locality* (the ethnicity and 'nationhood' of city and region), *nationality* and *Europeanness*. But post-1992, economic, social and possibly political integration and federalism, a United States of Europe, will give historically unprecedented form to this traditional complexity of political experience, and it will allow it to be expressed and reinvented in unpredictable ways.

A feature of the post-industrial and post-national world

emerging in the late twentieth century has been the simultaneously increasing importance of both transnational-level and subnational-level (global-local) political economic systems and processes. In the EC context this has been illustrated by the simultaneous growth in size and importance of the transnational EC level itself and also of EC regions at the subnational level. Both levels offer people forms of general citizenship and of social citizenship in addition to their national citizenship.

Circuits of citizenship capable of bypassing the nation-state level were created with the Treaty of Rome – circuits on the one hand between EC citizens (and interest groups) and the EC political and legal institutions, and on the other hand between the latter and local (urban and regional) governments. These circuits and relationships have often been filtered and detoured through the national government level. But there is every probability that increasingly in the post-1992 era they will become relatively independent of the national level and will grow in scale, complexity and importance.

These political and social changes will require a rethinking not only of traditional national citizenship but also of the nature and balance of rights and duties of individuals and collectivities within and between all three of the political levels: local, national and European, (Bryant 1991). This new complexity in the circuits of citizenship has implications for the future of social citizenship in Europe. To conclude this chapter we can illustrate some aspects of the new complexity in terms of EC employment policy and issues about duties as well as rights which are connected with it.

In multi-level democratic systems, each level is ultimately accountable to and derives its legitimacy from differently defined electorates. Thus it is necessary to develop our modern individualistic language and discourse about politics and citizenship to provide a space for more corporate entities and actors alongside individuals and national governments. In the European context the effective 'citizens' of the EC since its inception have been the 'member states', that is the collection of national corporate actors negotiating agreements and taking decisions democratically among themselves through the Council of Ministers. As noted earlier, Delors' attempt to extend this corporate citizenship and to give a social policy-making role to the 'social partners' of ETUC and UNICE, the workers' and employers' organizations, has not so far been particularly successful (Teague 1989; Grahl and Teague 1990, ch. 5). Nonetheless, this illustrates the importance of thinking in corporate as well as individual terms about the EC post-1992 (Commission of the EC 1990b, pp. 11–14).

Subnational EC regions (e.g. Scotland in the UK, the Lander in Germany, the Basque regions in Spain and France etc.) are increasingly likely to seek their own collective voice and distinctive representation within or beyond national political party structures in the EC's Assembly. As its name indicates, the Federal Republic of Germany, which is the strongest supporter of European political union and of legislative power for the European Parliament, already has substantial experience of operating a successful decentralized political constitution built on regional autonomy and distinctive regional representation in central government.

Thus models are available for developing a Europe of 'member regions' as well as of 'member nation states', and for developing it in political terms in addition to and beyond the economic and social terms in which EC 'regional policy' has traditionally tended to be considered (Grahl and Teague 1990, ch. 6). Such a political and structural commitment by the EC to regionalism may well be necessary in any case in order to make a reality out of the concern for regional economic and social inequalities expressed in the notion of an 'EC regional policy'. But this is particularly so given the internationalization of the world economic system and the increasing space it provides for the growth and operation of powerful large-scale multinational corporations (MNCs).

Whether they are non-European (i.e. American, Japanese) or, as the European Commission and many federalists hope, European, Europe's vast post-1992 market will attract and foster the growth of both 'domestic' and 'foreign' MNCs. Regions' abilities to influence their own economies will be reduced as both Euro and non-Euro MNCs grow in the EC market in the 1990s. MNCs already wield great and unaccountable powers to disregard individual nation states in their decision-making about location, investment, environmental effects etc. Indeed in the medium and long terms, in a post-1992 EC, such economic powers and rights (sovereignty) as nations currently retain which can be used to contain MNCs will need to be removed in order to be handed over to a democratically empowered EC Federal Assembly (assuming that this is built as planned by the federalists by the mid- late 1990s).

However, the corollary of this acquisition of economic power and *de facto* rights in EC economic space by and over regional economies, in particular by MNCs, whatever their origin, is that the EC will need to enforce a range of social and environmental duties and obligations on MNCs (Pearce 1990), particularly at regional level. MNCs' and other employers' duties as corporate actors to individual EC citizens as employees are already being institutionalized in the Community via the Social Charter. But something comparable will need to be developed in respect of the relations *between* corporate actors, in particular the environmental and economic rights of Europe's regions claimable against private (e.g. MNCs) and public organizations.

Subnational regional social citizenship (e.g. Dicken 1988; also Nairn 1977 re British regionality) as well as transnational citizenship is an important aspect of the situation of citizenship in the post-national era. So too is the theme of corporate social citizenship. In the next and final chapter I will return to these issues and to other elements of the new agenda for the social theory and political practice of contemporary citizenship.

9
Rethinking Social Citizenship: Rights, Duties and Capitalism

Social change forces us to rethink what we take for granted (Gellner 1964). In this book I have suggested that late twentieth-century social change is having this effect on our conventional wisdom and our dominant paradigm assumptions about social citizenship. We have seen that as a result of social change in the 1980s and 1990s, social citizenship is being rethought on the Right by Neoconservative moral reformers (chs 4–6), in the Centre by welfare pluralists and work and income reformers (chs 2, 7), on the Left by European social democrats and corporatists (ch. 8) and in the 'new social movements' by ecologists, feminists and others (ch. 2). We have considered a number of main themes in these diverse processes of rethinking social citizenship. So we have looked at (1) *new limits* of social citizenship in the 'new poverty' and in 'underclass' formation; (2) the moral character and *moral complexity* of contemporary social citizenship in terms of its mix of new (and old) rights and duties and its risks of de-politicization; and (3) the new (sub- and transnational) *structural complexity* of social citizenship in a post-national world etc. Evidently a complex new field and set of agendas is currently emerging for rethinking both the politics and the sociology of social citizenship.

To organize my concluding overview of this field and of the rethinking necessary in it, I will first consider the idea, initially proposed by Neoconservatism, that in a number of respects, some positive and some negative, dominant paradigm social citizenship and its social rights can be held to be myths (section

I below). Next I want to review some issues in the relation between capitalism and social citizenship. T. H. Marshall originally saw the relationship as a 'war', but one in which the welfare state and its system of social rights would 'civilize' capitalism's more barbarous tendencies (ch. 1 above). Given the failures of the welfare state, arguably a new social contract is needed between capitalism and its host societies. So it will be useful to consider briefly some of the longstanding and new dynamics in the capitalism–social citizenship relation, particularly regarding health and education rights and duties (section II below).

Finally, as I suggested in chapter 2, a 'discourse of duty' as well as of rights has emerged across the political spectrum in the contemporary period, and in part II I developed a critique of the Neoconservative version of this discourse of duty with its over-emphasis on familial and work duties. In this concluding chapter I want to affirm the vital importance of an understanding of social duties in modern society both to counter its various anomic and destructive tendencies and, indeed, to enable it to have some hope of surviving long-term (see also Walzer 1985 and Wolfe 1989 on social obligation). To highlight the theme of duties I will look briefly at general personal and inter-generational social duties in section III, and at personal, corporate and state duties regarding health and education in section II. Of course highlighting duties in this way should not be taken to imply that they can be understood apart from rights, or vice versa, a point I have been at pains to emphasize throughout my discussion. But perhaps the social rights that duties imply are myths. Before discussing duties more directly we first need to consider what might be involved in such a view of rights.

I

Myths of social rights

By calling an idea or ideal a 'myth' we can intend to do at least two very different things. On the one hand we can intend to discredit it by implying that it is without much foundation or empirical substance, or otherwise insubstantial and unreal; on the other hand we can intend to credit it with a certain kind of social and existential reality. Myths such as popular and traditional beliefs are socially real and powerfully effective as such, while, in addition, 'myth' can refer to ideas which we can call existentially real, ideas that people feel it personally necessary to believe 'in spite of reality'. Thus, common citizenship – like human beings' trust in each other, or their hope in the future and in human possibilities – is a notion which helps to make present reality at least *appear* to be what it all too rarely is in reality, namely potentially just, rational and bearable.

In postwar Western society 'social citizenship' (together with its associated ideas of social rights, equal membership status, social justice etc.) has been a myth in at least these two positive senses. First, it has been a socially real and popular (and now 'traditional') belief. It has, in Dore's terms, been one of 'the basic fictions which sustain our democracy' (1987, p. 319; also above ch. 7, p. 175). Indeed it was an objective of postwar politics and policy to construct it and promote it as such. Secondly, it has also been a personally and existentially real moral trust and political hope for many citizens in modern Western polities. We will have more to say about these positive senses later. Nonetheless, it is evident that social citizenship can also be regarded as a myth in more negative and discrediting senses of the term, as we can now consider (for a relevant discussion of the importance of myths and symbols in social policy see Handler and Hasenfeld 1990).

An extreme critique of the very idea of social citizenship, and not just of the version of it I have referred to as the 'dominant paradigm', is implied in the views of the New Right. These hold that any state beyond the minimal and any form of citizenship much beyond the civil (and *possibly* also the political) is morally groundless and indefensible and in that sense mythic, (above ch. 4; Nozick 1975; Paul 1982; Roche 1988b). Of course neo-libertarian discourse is full of readily discernible myths of its own (myths of the 'state of nature', asocial individuals, economically rational individuals etc.) so no great store need be set by this critique.

Neoconservatism accuses the welfare state of creating perverse incentives to dependency and poverty. It charges the dominant paradigm's prioritization of social rights with misrepresenting the socio-economic and moral realities of life in modern liberal capitalist societies. On this view the dominant paradigm has thus constructed myths which mystify reality, which need to be rolled back to reveal reality and which need to be restructured to take account of it. Nonetheless, unlike the New Right, the Neoconservative critique of social citizenship does not imply that the idea is an empty and discreditable myth. On the contrary, as we saw, the idea is understood to be rooted in popular and traditional cultural beliefs about work and family obligations. In fact, given the erosion of these cultural beliefs, and given the Neoconservatives' critique of modern decadence and their support for policies of moral reform, it is clear that they are committed precisely to (a version of) the mythic status of social citizenship. That is, their policy involves the promotion of what they deem to be creditable myths (i.e. ideals, values) about social citizenship and its duties, however discrepant these may be with contemporary familial and employment patterns and norms.

Finally, the dominant paradigm of social citizenship and its instrument, the welfare state, could be criticized in terms of myth in two respects, namely as being founded on myth and also as being a promoter of myth. First, it is founded on the existence of social rights which are rarely built into national political constitutions in any full, explicit and unequivocal way. So, while the political and civil dimensions of citizenship *are* formal, tangible and thus 'real' features of modern nations, the social dimension is more mythic in the sense of usually being less formalized, much more ambiguous and a matter of recurrent political controversy.

Secondly, the perennial claims of the welfare state and its supporters are that the problem of poverty (not to mention other less extreme forms of social inequality) can be solved and that the extension and servicing of social rights by the state is the best way to solve it. These claims can, to some extent, be said to be myths; as we have seen above and as both Right and Left analysts have observed about the welfare state in the USA, Britain and other European nations poverty has persisted and grown in modern society. The welfare state has not been as effective in reducing it, at least in the 'industrial era', as policies of employment creation and economic growth have been.

However, these criticisms can be countered and it can be argued that neither social citizenship nor the defeat of poverty are myths in these senses. First, it is arguable that there is nothing in principle to stop social rights from being translated into more comprehensive guarantees in modern nation states. In addition, it would appear that nation states are drifting in this sort of direction at the *international* level, that is, throughout the postwar period but particularly in recent decades, nations have been acceding to a proliferating web of international covenants, treaties and courts governing global and world-regional social, economic and ecological affairs (Roche 1988f). Also, in Europe at least, strong efforts are currently being made to begin to develop a new constitutional basis for social rights in member states of the EC.

Secondly, while the failures of the welfare state are no doubt legion, nonetheless (as we saw, in our discussions of the arguments of Glazer, Moynihan and Murray in part II), even its Neoconservative critics agree that it has at least one success against poverty to its credit; that is, it has been responsible to a considerable extent for the historic achievement of a reduction in poverty among the mass of the elderly in recent decades. Whatever its various failures, the claim of supporters of the dominant paradigm of postwar social policy, that the welfare state *can* be effective as an instrument of anti-poverty policy, evidently cannot be dismissed wholesale as rhetoric and myth as Neoconservatives are wont to argue.

These sorts of criticism of the dominant paradigm are thus less hard-hitting than they might appear. Nonetheless, my discussion *has* raised a number of deeper moral/political problems (part II) and structural/historical problems (chs 7, 8) for the dominant paradigm. First, *the moral/political problems*. I have suggested that the dominant paradigm tends to overemphasize citizens' rights as against their duties. It thereby, wittingly or not, effectively tends to sponsor and disseminate a morally questionable 'duty-free' conception of citizenship. In addition, along with the welfare state and social policy in general, and also along with Neoconservatism, the dominant paradigm tends to over-emphasize the discrete character of social citizenship; that is, it tends to treat it in relative isolation, disconnected from the civil and political dimensions of citizenship. In each of these respects, and whether wittingly or not, it could be argued that one of the major problems with the dominant paradigm's version of social citizenship is that effectively it tends to sponsor and disseminate a duty-free and depoliticized myth of social citizenship.

Secondly, *the structural/historical problems*. Here three main points can be made. The first is that the dominant paradigm involves a conception both of history as social progress and also of the history of citizenship as effectively completed; or at least it implies that the beginning of the end of major social problems is in sight, given the creation of a system of social rights serviced by an active and interventionist state social policy, or welfare state. These sorts of ideas are most clearly expressed in T. H. Marshall's outline history of citizenship rights in Britain, which pictures the development of first civil, then political, then social rights from the sixteenth to the twentieth centuries (see ch. 1 above).

Whatever the pleasing evolutionary logic of this story, it takes on something of the character of a myth when compared with the details of group and class struggles over citizens' rights and when compared with the variety of alternative sequences which, equally plausibly, could be read into the record of British history. The use of this story as a model – whether for interpreting the historical record of other very different nations or, worse, for planning the development of the state and of citizenship in other very different nations – underscores its status as myth, an academic myth and to some extent an ideological and political myth as well.

In the contemporary period we are seeing histories of citizenship unfold which are inexplicable in terms of Marshall's evolutionary schema. As we have seen, social rights and social citizenship in contemporary Europe are being developed prior to effective political rights and political citizenship. Or again, after generations of virtually exclusive (and thus radically depoliticized) social citizenship, the post-Stalinist countries of Eastern Europe and of the old Soviet Union are only now struggling to simultaneously achieve genuine civil and political rights, and thus genuine citizenship.

The second main point to be made about structure/history, is as follows. The dominant paradigm, as we have seen, was developed in a particular historical context. In this context a whole set of social assumptions could reasonably be made: about national industrial capitalism; about national politics, economic management and social planning; and about common national values and family systems. But the development of post-industrial and global capitalism, of post-national politics and of (post-)modern cultural change undermines each of these assumptions. Thus the institutions and policies based on them are increasingly open to question, and increasingly appear unrealistic, groundless and in other ways essentially mythic.

The third main point to be considered derives from this second point: it is that the conception of nationhood and national identity on which modern notions of citizenship and its social rights and duties depend is itself a myth. Contemporary post-national social change, as for instance in the case of the EC, is, in a sense, recreating the kinds of partial, overlapping and complex political identities and memberships, from local to supranational polities and communities which characterized pre-modern, pre-nation-state society. Nationhood and national citizenship always was a myth which oversimplified the complex roots and forms of social membership and identity. And contemporary change increasingly reveals it to be so. In discussing post-national change we concentrated on the transnational issues of European citizen identity and European social rights. But as we also noted in chapters 7 and 8, the subnational levels of city and region, particularly the former, are also of increasing importance in modern society. City or locality is the sphere of the familiar, the predictable and the face-to-face (home, family, friends) in a world of transience and anonymity, of distant and abstract forces and threats. City or locality offers a 'home territory', 'place of origin' and thus a tangible spatial form of social identity and membership. It also offers a physical arena, public space, in which social differences, inequalities and divisions can be dramatically enacted and symbolized (announced and denounced, celebrated and ridiculed etc.).

Modernity's global ecological crisis and its cultural crisis (e.g. its anti-traditionalist disconnection from the past) and the threats they pose to locality only serve to heighten its perceived importance. They cultivate the ground for a politics of local conservation, of stewardship and of social duties to the local natural, urban and cultural 'heritage'. Finally, as compared with the national and international spheres, locality is a sphere of relatively tangible politics, visible power structures and actions with some traceable effects. One of the most important imperatives in contemporary urban politics has been generated by post-industrial change and particularly felt in the de-industrializing 'rust-belt' cities and urban areas of Western societies in the 1970s and 1980s. That imperative is 'to restructure or die' (e.g. Bagguley et al. 1990; Harvey 1989; Cooke 1990). Proceeding through such things as 'local partnerships' and 'growth coalitions' between private and public sectors, the new urban politics has a unique urgency and political dynamism (Judd and Parkinson 1990; Cummings 1988; Roche 1992b). Where it is effective and successful it is likely to result in the strengthening of local political identity against the claims of simplistic nationalism (Stewart and Stoker 1989; Cooke 1990).

The upshot of these three main structural/historical points is that any future theoretical or political agenda concerning citizenship in general and social citizenship in particular will undoubtedly need to take account of the various influential modern myths connected with social rights and of citizenship's intrinsically mythic characteristics. We can now consider some of the structural/historical issues noted here in a little more detail by reviewing some of the longstanding and contemporary dynamics in the relationship between social citizenship and capitalism.

II

Capitalist change, social citizenship and duties

1 National functionalism and capitalism

In chapter 1 I suggested that the dominant paradigm of social citizenship was developed in the postwar West through various forms of 'national functionalism'. This concept refers to the functional interdependence or symbiosis which was developed and maintained between the major societal sectors (namely the economy, polity and culture) and their systems of institutions in modern society. Another way of referring to this type of societal arrangement is to see it as a *de facto* 'national social contract'. The contract was formed between democratic nation states and the nationally based and organized industrial capitalist economies to which they played host. Welfare and social citizenship, both the welfare state and the welfare market, were central to this accommodation. Capitalism would undertake to deliver employment and income (and thus market-based welfare), in return for various state services. The state would undertake to produce and reproduce a relevantly skilled and healthy labour force (via an educational and welfare state). It would also undertake to maintain the cultural, institutional and physical infrastructure of the market and of social life in general at local/urban and national levels.

T. H. Marshall had early on pointed to the inevitably dialectical character of the societal arrangements involved in the development of the welfare state and the institutionalization of the social rights of citizenship. He acknowledged the underlying tension or 'war' between capitalism on the one hand and democratic citizenship and social justice on the other as many analysts have done since (e.g. Bowles and Gintis 1986; Walzer 1985). Nonetheless, he also implied that the accommodation between capitalism and democracy (via the state's development of a 'welfare state' on behalf of the 'nation') in the postwar period represented an event of historic and lasting significance for modern Western society. The 'war' could be controlled, the warriors pacified and capitalism 'civilized'.

However, as we have seen throughout this book, evidently the 'war' is not over. It has been renewed by the forces of ideological change and of social structural change. The dialectics of capitalism and citizenship have been renewed and their relationship needs to be rethought. The 'problem of social citizenship', particularly the internal limit problem of poverty, remains an important and recurrently controversial focal point in contemporary politics. In the terms I have been using to conceptualize the structural context of social citizenship, the 'national functional' system and the 'national social contract' are both breaking down under the pressure of social change.

Looking to the future, it is reasonable to assume that a large part of the future politics of social citizenship will be concerned, as suggested in chapter 7, with attempts to repair these arrangements at the nation-state level (also Jordan 1987; Walzer 1985). In addition, as suggested in chapter 8, new sorts of functional and social contract arrangements at local and world-regional/ global levels (e.g. Galtung 1980; Dilloway 1986) are likely to be sought for and to develop.

Capitalism and the market system, relative to any other system, generate high standards of welfare for the mass of the West's population. But, particularly in the recently fashionable unregulated form, they also generate severe diswelfares for marginalized groups, and social inequalities and ecological costs for all. Markets certainly embody some important principles of civil society (e.g. rights to privacy and private property, contractualism). They may also be managed so as to remain compatible with political (democratic) and social citizenship principles. But this requires close monitoring, regulation and where necessary 'fixing' by democratic political power to prevent the emergence and abuse of monopoly economic power, to provide equality of opportunity and so on. In addition, as Walzer (1985) argues, for capitalism and market organization to remain compatible with social and political citizenship, clear and principled limits need to be developed and enforced, banning commodification and market-making in many spheres (building on such obvious spheres as the governmental process itself, human life itself etc.).

It is possible, but by no means certain, that, out of the disorganization of capitalism–society relations in Western societies in the late twentieth century a new *modus vivendi* might be achieved. Arrangements roughly comparable to the 'national social contracts' of the dominant paradigm could emerge sooner or later. But if they do, then they will necessarily be much more structurally complex in terms of sub- and transnational levels than before. In addition, importantly, they will also be more structurally complex in terms of providing a much larger, clearer and legitimate role for markets along with the other elements of the 'mixed welfare economy', elements which too long have been hidden in the shadow of the welfare state.

They will also be more explicitly morally complex than

dominant paradigm arrangements. These latter arrangements at least appeared to encourage one-dimensional, de-moralized and depoliticized conceptions of social citizenship in terms of social rights claims and the status of welfare clienthood. At the same time, by casting social citizenship as a mainly citizen–state process, they also tended to downplay citizen–citizen and citizen–capitalist corporation relations. In the modern period social rights claims have been made as much against other citizens (usually relatives and usually female) and capitalist corporations (albeit with varying degrees of success), as they have been made against the state (also with varying degrees of success). The public attention given mainly to political struggles concerning the latter in much of the twentieth century misrepresents the importance of the underlying 'civil society' processes of rights–duties exchanges in the familial and voluntary sectors and of duties enforcement on capitalists in the productive process, in markets and the economic sphere in general.

To revert to the 'figure–ground' terms in which we pictured it in chapter 1, in contemporary and future versions of a new social contract we are likely to see much more of social citizenship's civil society 'ground', and, by comparison, relatively less of the 'figure' (or now, given sub- and transnationalism, the figure*s*) of the state servicing of welfare rights. To illustrate these possibilities and issues we can look briefly at two topics of importance for an expansive and progressive conception of social citizenship, namely education and health. Capitalism's general technological dynamic and its current post-industrial restructuring using information technology have important implications for contemporary and future patterns of social rights and duties concerning education and health. We can look first at education.

2   Post-industrial change and education

In chapter 7 we considered major structural changes in contemporary 'post-industrial' capitalism. These involve changes in the labour market and in income distribution. They also involve the emergence of new forms of poverty and social polarization, and of the need in the advanced Western societies for a major rethinking and reform of employment-distribution policies and income-distribution policies. But in addition it is also clear that post-industrialism calls for an equally major rethinking, reform and renewal of education policy and its associated rights and duties.

In a number of respects, education is an interestingly ambiguous area as far as dominant paradigm conceptions of social citizenship go. The notion that all citizens have absolute rights to education, particularly literacy, and that the state has the duty to service those rights (or to see to it that parents service them), was long fought for and is now a long-established axiom across the political spectrum. Although radical Neoconservatives like Charles Murray (1984) may claim that the 'welfare state' ought to be wound up, they make no such claims for public support for education. All citizens and capitalists are assumed to have tax-paying duties to support some version or another of educational rights for all.

In the education process the state 'grows' its future citizenry as much as young people 'grow' themselves and their future identities. The process for young people is thus morally and ontologically formative, but in political terms it is pre-political or more accurately meta-political. It is *for*, not by, citizens (unlike adult and lifelong education which is eminently and richly political in principle; e.g. Freire 1976). It involves social rights claims against the state. But the servicing of these rights typically takes the form of the rigorous and legal imposition of social duties (of school attendance etc.) on the young, and also upon their parents (to ensure attendance at school, or at least some acceptable form of education). In addition, in Western society, the notion of a right to education is associated with a culture and ideology of self-development, and with the work ethic. It is thus associated with duties to develop one's talents and abilities to their fullest extent and, to a lesser extent, to train for the labour market, and to use efficiently whatever opportunities and resources are available for these purposes. There is also an assumption that once a talent or skill has been developed there is a certain obligation on its possessor to use it. Nonetheless, from a societal perspective, capitalists' toleration of increased tax-duties to help finance citizens' rights to education is of comparable importance to citizens' acceptance of the various duties education involves in understanding the development of postwar education.

Education (or at least schooling) has been part of the development of the national social contract between industrial capitalism and the state in the West since the mid-nineteenth century. The functionality of the arrangement has been evident to all concerned, whether supporters (e.g. Parsons 1959) or critics (e.g. Bowles and Gintis 1976). However, in the 1970s and 1980s this functionality began to break down. The mass secondary and tertiary education systems developed in Western societies in the postwar period have been reasonably successful in inculcating at least a functional literacy and relevant work skills in the mass of their populations. But post-industrial capitalism requires different skills and attitudes from workers than industrial capitalism did (e.g. Hopson and Scally 1981, chs 1, 2 and *passim*).

From a 'logic of capitalism' (or at least a 'logic of national capitalism') point of view an effective capitalist 'information and service economy' cannot be constructed with a labour supply that is either (1) unskilled in *both* oral and written communication (and other relevant social skills), or (2) unskilled in computers and other information technologies ('IT illiterate') or (3) unskilled in both (e.g. NEDO 1987; Toffler 1980, 1985; Robins and Webster 1989). However, for a variety of ideological and organizational reasons and causes, postwar state-based schooling systems have been unable and unwilling to develop oral and social skills. Also, they have a poor record in developing science and technology interests and skills in at least half of their constituency (i.e. girls). In many countries they have proved incapable (at least in the first decade in which computers and other information technologies have been widely diffused) of changing sufficiently rapidly and flexibly to be able to inculcate mass IT literacy among young people in the 1980s. The task of developing such literacy in the mass of the adult population, including workers, has hardly begun.

Such a lack of education and skills in this period (as in other periods since the late nineteenth century), evidently presents 'industrial' and now 'post-industrializing' capitalist economies with labour supply problems and crises comparable to many they have had to face since the late nineteenth century. They have solved these problems in the past both by developing in-house industrial-sector-based training systems and also by tolerating tax increases to fund state education and training. This particular aspect of the 'social contract' between capitalism and the polity is likely to be renewed in the post-industrial period since, at the very least, it is in the long-term interests of capitalists to do so. The knowledge and skills content of education and training, the balance in funding and provision between private corporations and the state/individual tax-payers, the place of education and training in the benefits packages and company strategies of corporations are all beginning to change to meet the needs of industrialists and employers for a socially skilled, IT literate and flexibly specialized labour supply.

The politics of social citizenship here require that the vocational dynamic be bridled and ridden for political and cultural gain. Rights and duties to know and to develop life skills need to be protected in the post-industrial social contract with capitalism (as much as they had to be in the industrial social contract) from reduction to training and work duties. Some hope that this reduction might be avoided exists by analogy with industrial capitalism's interest in mass literacy. Once cultivated, the skills of literacy were put to a variety of political and cultural uses other than purely economic ones. Literacy was (and remains) strongly connected with the development of democracy and thus with the development of political rights, both in principle and historically (Goody and Watt 1963; Freire 1976; Williams 1965).

There are evidently major problems facing citizens in the development of 'the information society' about surveillance and the threat to privacy involved in the secret compilation and circulation of personal data by state agencies and private corporations using IT's potential (e.g. Lyon 1988). But it is likely that this will be countered to some extent by the development of demands for (rights to) greater informational transparency and reciprocity within and between capitalist and state organizations. Information technology (Toffler 1980, 1985; NEDO 1987) and mass IT literacy make such developments possible, although, of course, they by no means make them inevitable. Western governments in particular might find themselves under even greater pressure than they are already under to concede and service new rights to information about government and its policy-making processes, and new rights of access for individuals to personal data concerning them and held by government agencies.

The achievement of mass IT literacy and mass science and technology literacy, not to mention effective oral skills among the majority (e.g. bi- and multi-lingualism, confident communication with non-familiars, questioning and interviewing skills, etc.), are the kinds of things needed to restore the economic functionality of the 'education rights-servicing system' from the point of view of capitalism. Such changes might, from this perspective, restore the labour-market benefits capitalism seeks by its toleration of tax duties to help support the system. Of course, the changes may not be made and the functional breakdown and crisis may persist. While a 'capital logic' can be legitimately discerned in much of modern history and social change, the contemporary situation and contemporary change are too unstable and uncertain to present any guarantees that a new form of social contract and functionality can be re-established. Time will tell. But if they were achieved, besides the narrow economic functionality such changes might produce, they could, in a longer and more optimistic view, produce important if unintended cultural and political benefits. They may turn out to be as useful and important for twenty-first-century citizenship and democratic politics in general as the achievement of literacy has been in the twentieth century.

3   Technological change and health

The drive to gain a competitive edge in existing markets and/or to create new and unique products (and thus to monopolize their markets) through technological development and mechanization has been part of the 'logic of capitalism' since its inception. This was one of the main factors inspiring both the Industrial Revolution and the successive waves of technological developments and new 'techno-economic paradigms' this unleashed from steam to electricity and beyond (e.g. Freeman and Soete 1987). And it lies behind the development of information technology and post-industrial economics in recent decades. However, throughout the modern period the technological intensification and extension of capitalist production and distribution processes has been fraught with health, safety and environmental risks and costs for workers, consumers and localities.

Workers' social rights to protection from the damaging effects of production processes, and employers' duties to protect them, have been a continuous topic of political and trade union struggle and conflict from the early days of industrial capitalism in the early nineteenth century. By contrast, the development of consumers' social rights and localities' environmental rights to equivalent protection (e.g. from the damaging effects of both production and consumption processes, and capitalists' duties to protect them from these effects) have historically attracted much less political attention, at least until the last third of the twentieth century. An important part of the 'national social contract' struck between capitalism, the nation state and citizens in the modern period was thus initially worked out over capitalists' basic social duties to service workers' basic social rights to physical protection in the production process. In most Western nations this occurred as a result of the pressure of trades unions, social reformers, enlightened capitalists and medical professionals. With the important exception of late nineteenth-century Germany and Bismarck's welfare state, it occurred largely in advance of and independent of moves to create an explicit 'welfare state' (e.g. Pierson, 1991, table 4.4 and ch. 4 *passim*). The 'welfare state', then, could be understood as the developed twentieth-century version of this emerging national social contract between capital, labour and the state over the social conditions appropriate for the capitalist production and accumulation process.

But even after the welfare state had been achieved it remained the case that consumers' social rights and localities' environmental rights to protection against the damaging effects of capitalist production and consumption processes (together with the state's and capitalist's duties to service those rights) were not recognized and institutionalized to anything like the same extent. They were not recognized parts of the national social contract, the welfare state/welfare capitalism system, constructed in most postwar Western societies.

Capitalism's technological dynamic has led modern society's production processes (material extraction, material creation, energy creation, commodity production etc.) to become continuously more indebted to increasingly powerful science-based high technologies throughout the twentieth century and particularly in the postwar period. So the national social contract around workers' health rights and capitalist and state duties continues to need, as it always has done, to be updated and renewed in response to technological change. But in addition, in recent decades the politics of social citizenship have been taken up by new political movements, principal among them the ecology movement and consumers' rights movements. It is now much better recognized than ever before that citizens' modern social rights should be understood to include rights to such things as healthy foods, safe transport systems and unpolluted environments, particularly local environments but also more generally. These social rights, as with workers' health and safety rights, impose social duties upon corporate capitalist and state employers. And like workers' rights they also require that the 'national social contract' between capitalism and the citizen community be continuously updated and renewed in line with changes in products and in production and distribution processes.

It is also worth noting a further implication of capitalism's technological dynamic for social citizenship. This relates to the changing balance of rights and duties in the personal sphere in the contemporary period. That is, the point needs to be stressed that citizens in a capitalistically influenced society owe social duties to each other regarding the unhealthy and polluting effects of their own consumption.

The modern capitalist economics and societies of the West have promoted historically unprecedented levels and rates of growth of consumer expenditure. For the mass of their citizens they are 'affluent societies' pervaded by a 'consumer culture' and a culture of market choices. Such a high consumption regime evidently carries with it considerable risks to the health of consumers themselves (e.g. via reckless, excessive or addictive forms of consumption such as those involving tobacco, alcohol, unhealthy foods etc.). In addition, by their consumption choices, consumers can and do damage the health of other people (e.g. through alcohol-induced violence, reckless driving etc.), and the urban and country environment (e.g. through car exhausts, waste dumping, littering etc.). As a result, citizens in the affluent consumer societies of the West are increasingly faced with the need to change their lifestyles.

The need for such a change towards more healthy, sustainable and responsible lifestyles is a recurrent theme in contemporary politics and represents a new form of the politics of social citizenship. There is a certain, albeit currently limited, popular recognition of affluent societies' economic and ecological responsibilities to Third World nations. But it is arguable that ultimately the main pressure to make a significant change in Western lifestyles derives from a recognition of rational self-interest. A movement to control affluence and the effects of affluent lifestyles may appear to be exclusively altruistic, enabling (or more likely requiring) people to honour the social duties of public health and safety. But nonetheless, in addition, a coincidence of public interest and rational self-interest is conceivable here for the following reason. One of the more rational and effective ways for people to secure their own social rights (e.g. personal and public health and safety) is precisely for them to honour new social duties (i.e. to curb and change their own unhealthy, risky and ecologically damaging consumption).

A significant part of the contemporary and future politics of social citizenship is thus likely to be concerned with developing this awareness (both altruistic and, equally important, rationally self-interested) among citizens and also among capitalist corporations. To the extent that this development occurs, it will constitute a renewal of the tacit social contracts which have long existed in modern society both among citizens, and also between the democratic state and polity on the one hand, and the capitalist economy on the other. And, to the extent that it occurs, such a development will contribute to the renewal of both the concept and the politics of social citizenship in Western society in the coming decades.

III

Social duties and citizenship

1 Personal social duties and citizenship conditions

As we saw in part II, Neoconservatism focuses on the personal and cultural sphere of social citizenship and emphasizes (indeed *over*emphasizes) personal duties and responsibilities. However, leaving the overemphasis aside, the new 'duties discourse' in contemporary politics seems to me to be highly appropriate to modern social conditions. The duty emphasis is not one which can be, will be or ought to be simply reversed (see also Walzer 1985 and Wolfe 1989). This is even more so if our conception of social citizenship is broadened, as I have suggested it should be, to refer to the social conditions (and poverty limits) of citizenship in general. I have throughout this book emphasized the economic aspects of these conditions (work, income etc.). But what might be called the personal and cultural aspects of these social conditions of citizenship (i.e. family, education, local community etc.) are equally important.

In the previous sections I suggested that there is an evident and increasing need to control the negative consequences of capitalist economic growth for these sorts of spheres, along with the sphere of public and personal health. Consequently in future it is likely that the social rights and duties involved in these spheres will receive a much greater emphasis in the politics of citizenship than they have traditionally received in the dominant paradigm and in the social policies stemming from it. One principal concern will undoubtedly involve the imposition of a new generation of social duties upon capitalist corporations from global to local level. But, as is also evident in the case of health, an equivalent concern must be with the development of public education, rational self-interest and personal responsibility, together with new law where necessary to enforce personal responsibility.

Personal and cultural spheres such as those of family, education and local community are spheres in which there is a strong requirement for adult citizens to honour social duties in some senses 'prior' (both existentially and logically) to the claiming and exercising of citizens' rights. Some of the most relevant social duties here are those of care (e.g. parental care of children, but also including self-care), behavioural control (e.g. violence–control within families, but also including self-control) and development (e.g. the education of children but also particularly self-development) (see also Finch 1989).

To emphasize moral (and thus social) duties in this way is to register the continuing cultural importance of Enlightenment rationalism as an ideological framework for the West and for modern society. The Enlightenment heritage does not only consist of the theory of human rights and of citizens' rights that we associate with the American and French Revolutions, with writers such as Tom Paine (1979) (whose *Rights of Man* appeared in 1791), and with the contemporary politics of human rights. It also consists of the theory of personal responsibility and moral duty, a theory given its most profound articulation in the moral philosophy of Immanuel Kant (e.g. 1965, original 1797).

Kant's version of the theory is probably too abstract and unrealistic for contemporary conditions. Nevertheless, his notion that the idea of duty can be a rational idea rather than merely a non-rational traditional idea remains of great importance for modernity in my view. Moral duties tend to be understood as deriving either from mere conformity to social norms (e.g. Durkheim and other forms of sociologism) or from an ideal of altruism (e.g. many forms of Christianity and socialism). It seems to me that they would be better understood as deriving, in rationalistic (but non-Kantian) terms, from peoples' enlightened self-interest (Roche 1989).

Consider the performance of duties of self-care and of self-control, and the socialization of children to recognize these duties. These are obvious yet fundamental examples of the important potential for coincidence between, on the one hand, rational self-interest and, on the other, what is 'socially useful' (or, to put it more strongly, what is necessary for a society to claim to be 'civilized'). In the potentially anomic conditions of modernity and post-modernity the rationality and ontological importance of such social duties seem to me to need to be better understood and appreciated (Roche 1989, 1990b, 1992a; Wolfe 1989). Social duties are the business of whole societies and of corporate actors as well as of individuals, as I have indicated throughout my discussion. In the next and final section we will return briefly to these more collective forms of social duty, and particularly, in an historical frame of reference, to those involved in the relations between generations.

2 Collective social duties and citizenship conditions

In part II and also in chapters 7 and 8 above we considered the three main dimensions of social change in modern Western society, namely cultural, economic and political change. American family structures (*re* cultural change), British and American employment structures (*re* economic change) and European social policies (*re* political change) were the main examples given to illustrate each of these dimensions. Social change of one kind or another, whether incremental, cyclical, discontinuous or accelerative appears to be endemic in the 'modern' (and particularly the contemporary) social formation (Toffler 1970). It renders modern societies 'historical' in a radical sense; that is, they are incessantly required to reinterpret and reconstruct their collective versions of their 'past', 'present' and 'future'. Modernity's accentuated temporal consciousness is one of its unique cultural features when compared with all other periods of human social life.

There are many profound implications for the sociology and politics of modern society and Western culture in this recognition of its uniquely historical character which it would be inappropriate to begin to explore in a conclusion such as this (Roche 1989, 1990a). However, in this section we can briefly note *one* of those many implications, an implication which seems to me to be of particular importance for the contemporary understanding of social citizenship, its possibilities and its problems. This is the new salience of inter-generational relations in modern culture and politics (and indeed also in modern moral philosophy; e.g. Parfit 1986, part IV).

The dominant paradigm of social citizenship, including Marshall's version of it, rests on unspoken and usually barely recognized temporal assumptions. It tends to take it for granted that the only issues worth considering are those connected with the social rights and welfare needs of the contemporary set of generations. In the dominant paradigm of most postwar politicians, social policy-makers and social policy analysts, the notion that future generations as yet unborn need to be taken into account in terms of social/distributional justice is notably absent. Nothing reveals the outdated character of the dominant paradigm more than this. For understandable historical reasons, as a child of its times, it developed no serious or substantial concept of the social rights of future generations. Nor, it should be said, does Neoconservatism's concept of social duty recognize this temporal limit and the importance of going beyond it. Neoconservatism arguably goes beyond present generations' rights and duties by emphasizing the claims of tradition and thus of the past. But, aside from this, the Right has no relevant concept of the claims of the future *per se*, other than in terms of such things as privatized conceptions of personal inheritance (e.g. Nozick 1980).

The social rights of future generations is an issue which has been placed firmly on the contemporary political agenda by the ecology movement (ch. 2 above, also Roche 1988d). Thus such rights, for some agreed national or global population figure, could be argued to include those of an environment which is at least no less healthy and life-supporting than the one the present generation currently enjoys. They could also be argued to include reserves of economic resources sufficient to support a quality of life which bears some reasonable comparison to the one the majority of people in contemporary Western societies currently enjoy. Major national and international debates, political struggles and policy-making initiatives will undoubtedly be needed over the coming decades to make anything very clear and concrete out of any such notions of inter-generational social rights as these. Nonetheless, in the contemporary period, no analysis of the problems of social justice and social equality, nor any political programme to address them can now be said to be comprehensive and well grounded which does not take full account of such problems of inter-generational resource distribution.

This underscores the inadequacy of the dominant paradigm's mainly social-rights-based picture of social citizenship. Evidently to acknowledge the social rights of future generations is to call on present generations to recognize and accept considerable new social duties. The academic and political agendas for social citizenship in the 1990s and beyond will undoubtedly emphasize that 'rights imply duties'. To argue for the social rights of future generations is necessarily to argue for considerable new social duties and constraints to be accepted by present generations with no possibility of compensation or reciprocation by rights claims against future generations. It will require substantial political rethinking and renewal across the political spectrum to digest this particular implication of the development of new social rights. The new inter-generational social context for politics which is needed in our era is likely to pose a major challenge to the theory and practice not only of contemporary social citizenship but of modern politics in general.

IV

The period in which it was possible to conceive of citizenship in general and social citizenship in particular in national and welfare-state terms is clearly coming to an end. New positive myths and ideals of citizenship rights are developing, such as those involving notions of 'the Earth's rights', the 'rights of the unborn' and 'world citizenship'. They both enrich and complicate the more conventional modern myths and ideals relating to citizenship, such as those involving notions of human equality, of place and territorial identity, of nation and of heritage.

The new agendas for politics and also for social theory and research regarding social citizenship in the 1990s and beyond must, of course, continue to be concerned with nationally defined social citizenship and with the future of the welfare state. But they also need to be sensitive to these new developments. With this in mind I have suggested in this book that both the contemporary politics and the social analysis of social citizenship need to be rethought by confronting citizenship's essential moral and structural complexity. The development of social citizenship has always involved political mobilization and conflict, and the future doubtless will be no different in this respect. But the new lines of conflict are unlikely to be as clearly drawn as in the past since they are likely to reflect these forms of complexity.

To address the challenges of the 1990s and the early twenty-first century both the politics and the study of social citizenship will need to go beyond the nation state and the welfare state. They will need to grasp the emerging *structural complexity* and the new post-industrial and post-national dynamics influencing social citizenship, from familial and local levels to the transnational level and the inter-generational sphere. The far-reaching implications of these dynamics for the generation and transmission of poverty and social inequality, that is for the institutionalization of 'non-citizenship' and 'second-class citizenship' in modern (and 'post-modern') society, will need to be much better understood than they currently are in social policy and social research.

The *political and moral complexity* of social citizenship will also need to be much better understood than it currently is, both in theory and in practice. This form of complexity arises in part from the fact that, in all sorts of ways in our political and moral experience, rights and duties both conflict with and also imply each other. My discussion suggests that in the period of history Western societies are now entering, the dominant paradigm's institutionalization of social rights claiming will need to be fundamentally reconsidered. The various claims that social duties, both old (e.g. parental) and new (e.g. ecological), make on us all, both individually and collectively, will now need to be fully recognized. A new generation of social rights appropriate to changing structural conditions will need to be fought for and developed. And finally a new approach to social rights, which explicitly connects them with obligations and responsibilities (for instance as empowering resources and conditions for the latter), needs to be developed. This political and moral complexity of social citizenship has not been adequately appreciated whether by the dominant paradigm or its main (Neoconservative) critique since, as we have seen, each of them tends to promote unrealistic one-sided and one-dimensional views of citizenship politics and social policy.

Common citizenship is the most important form of membership and identity in modern societies – societies which, in many other respects, increasingly present themselves to people as fragmented, divisive and anomic. Given this situation, it is understandable why the idea of citizenship and the discourse of citizens' duties are beginning to emerge as highly significant terms of reference in contemporary Western politics and ideological debate. In this book I have focused on two of the most significant attempts by the Right (USA) and the Centre/Left (EC) to reform and reinvent Western social citizenship in the contemporary period. My account of this rethinking suggests that a realistic sociology of modern citizenship needs to address itself to understanding the changing social conditions of citizenship, in particular, on the one hand, the dynamics of post-industrial and post-national vectors of change in contemporary capitalism, and, on the other, the social nature and lifeworld of 'modern' human beings, modernity's versions of 'the human condition'.

My account also suggests that, given these social conditions, supporters of a progressive approach to the politics of social citizenship will need to rethink the absolute priority they have traditionally given to social rights in ideological debate. They will need to reconsider the moral and ideological claims of personal responsibility, of parental and ecological obligations, of corporate and inter-generational obligations, and so on. The politics of citizenship has for generations formulated its goals, fought its battles and found its voice in the discourse of rights. In the late twentieth century it also needs to be able to speak, to act and to understand itself in the language of citizens' personal responsibility and social obligation, in the discourse of duties as well as of rights.

Bibliography

Abel-Smith, B. and Raphael, M. (1986) *Future Directions for Social Protection*, Action Group 'Science and Society', Athens.

Achdut, L. and Tamir, Y. (1990) 'Retirement and well-being among the elderly', ch. 5 in Smeeding et al. 1990a.

Adler-Karlsson, G. (1978) 'The Unimportance of Full Employment', IFDA Dossier 2 (International Foundation for Alternative Development) Nyon, Switzerland.

Adonnino Report *see* Commission of the EC 1985b.

Adorno, T. et al. (1950) *The Authoritarian Personality*, Harper, New York.

Aglietta, M. (1979) *Theory of Capitalist Regulation: The US Experience*, New Left Books, London.

Alcock, P. (1989) 'Citizenship and Welfare Rights', *Critical Social Policy*, 26, autumn, 32–43.

Algie, J. (1975) *Social Values, Objectives and Action*, Kogan Page, London.

Allen, J. and Massey, D. (eds) (1988) *The Economy in Question*, Sage, London.

Anderson, B. R. (1987) 'The quest for ties between rights and duties – A key question for the future of the public sector', in Evers, A. et al. *The Changing Face of Welfare*, Gower, London.

Anderson, E. (1989) 'Sex codes and family life among poor inner-city youths', *Annals of the American Academy of Political and Social Science*, January, 59–78.

Anderson, M. (1978) *Welfare: The Political Economy of Welfare*

Reform in the United States, Hoover Institute Press, Stanford.

Andrews, G. (ed.) (1991) *Citizenship*, Lawrence and Wishart, London.

Auletta, K. (1983) *The Underclass*, Vintage, New York.

Bacon, R. and Eltis, W. (1976) *Britain's Economic Problem*, Macmillan, London.

Bagguley, P. et al. (1990) *Restructuring: Place, Class and Gender*, Sage, London.

Bane M. J. (1978) 'Family policy in the United States', Joint Center for Urban Studies, MIT/Harvard, Cambridge, Mass.

Bane, M. J. and Ellwood, D. (1986) 'The Impact of AFDC on Family Structure and Living Arrangements', *Journal of Labour Research*, (cited in Ellwood and Summers 1986).

Barbalet, J. M. (1988) *Citizenship*, Open University Press, Milton Keynes.

Barrett, M. and McIntosh, M. (1982) *The Anti-Social Family*, New Left Books, London.

Baudrillard, J. (1988) *Selected Writings*, Polity Press, Cambridge.

Bean, P. and MacPherson, S. (eds) (1983) *Approaches to Welfare*, Routledge, London.

Bell, D. (1973) *The Coming of Post-Industrial Society*, Basic Books, New York.

Bell, D. (1976) *The Cultural Contradictions of Capitalism*, Heinemann, London.

Bell, D. (1979) 'The Social Framework of the Information Society', in Dertouzos and Moses (eds) 1979.

Bell, D. (1980) 'Liberalism in the Postindustrial Society', ch. 12 in his *Sociological Journeys*, Heinemann, London.

Bell, D. (1989) 'American exceptionalism' revisited: the role of civil society', *The Public Interest*, 95, 38–56.

Bendix, R. (1964) *Nation-Building and Citizenship*, John Wiley, New York.

Benn, T. (1991) 'The Commonwealth of Britain Bill', *Guardian*, 20 May.

Berger, P. (1987) *The Capitalist Revolution*, Wildwood House, Aldershot.

Berger, P. and Berger, B. (1983) *The War over the Family*, Hutchinson, London.

Besharov, D. and Quinn, A. (1987) 'Not all female-headed families are created equal', *The Public Interest*, 89, 48–56.

Betten, L. et al. (eds) (1989) *The Future of European Social Policy*, Kluver, Deventer/Boston.

Beveridge, W. (1942) *Social Insurance and Allied Services*, HMSO, London.

Beveridge, W. (1960) *Full Employment in a Free Society*, (2nd edn) Allen and Unwin, London (original 1944).

Beveridge, W. (1948) *Voluntary Action*, Allen and Unwin, London.

Bishop, J. (1980) 'Jobs, Cash Transfers and Marital Instability', *Journal of Human Resources*, 15, summer, 301–34.

Blackaby, F. (ed.) (1979) *Deindustrialisation*, Heinemann, London.

Bleaney, M. (1985) *The Rise and Fall of Keynesianism*, Macmillan, London.

Block, F. (1987a) 'Rethinking the Political Economy of the Welfare State', ch. 13 in Block et al. 1987b.

Block, F. et al. (1987b) *The Mean Season: The Attack on the Welfare State*, Pantheon Books, New York.

Block, F. (1990) *Post-Industrial Possibilities*, University of California Press, Berkeley.

Bluestone, B. et al. (1981) *Corporate Flight: The Causes and Consequences of Economic Dislocation*, Progressive Alliance, Washington.

Bluestone, B. and Harrison, B. (1982) *The Deindustrialization of America*, Basic Books, New York.

Bowles, S. and Gintis, H. (1976) *Schooling in Capitalist America*, Routledge, London.

Bowles, S. and Gintis, H. (1986) *Democracy and Capitalism*, Routledge, London.

Boyer, R. (1988) *In Search of Labour Market Flexibility: European Economies in Transition*, Clarendon Press, Oxford.

Bremner, R. (1986) *American Choices: Social Dilemmas and Public Policy since 1960*, vol. I, Ohio State University Press, Columbus.

Brindle, D. (1990a) 'State of war on fathers who shirk duty', *Guardian*, 8 February.

Brindle, D. (1990b) 'When truancy hits the family income',

Guardian, 8 February.

Brindle, D. (1990c) 'Thatcher years "failed to roll back the welfare state"', *Guardian*, 13 December.

Brown, C. and Usborne, D. (1991) 'Howard softens stand on EC social policy', *Independent*, 4 December.

Brown, J. (1988) *In Search of a Policy: The Rationale for Social Security Provision for One Parent Families*, National Council for One-Parent Families, London.

Brown, J. (1989) *Why don't they go to work? Mothers on benefit*, HMSO, London.

Bruce-Briggs, B. (ed.) (1979) *The New Class?*, Transaction Books, New Brunswick, N. J.

Bryant, C. (1991) 'Europe and the European Community 1992', *Sociology*, 25, 2, 189–207.

Burghes, L. (1987) *Made in the USA: Workfare*, The Unemployment Unit, London.

Burton, J. (1987) *Would workfare work?*, University of Buckingham, Bucks.

Butler, S. and Kondratas, A. (1987) *Out of the Poverty Trap: A Conservative Strategy for Welfare Reform*, The Free Press, New York.

Carballo, M. and Bane, M. J. (1984) *The State and the Poor in the Nineteen Eighties*, Auburn House, Boston.

Carlson, A. (1987) 'Facing Realities: Reply to Gilder', *The Public Interest*, 89, 33–5.

Casey, B. (1988) *Temporary Employment*, Policy Studies Institute, London.

Cawson, A. (1982) *Corporatism and Welfare*, Heinemann, London.

Cecchini, P. (ed.) (1988) *The European Challenge 1992: The Benefits of a Single Market*, Wildwood House, Aldershot.

Clark, C. (1957) *The Conditions of Economic Progress*, (3rd edition) Macmillan, London.

Clark, D. (1985) *Post-Industrial America*, Methuen, London.

Clemitson, I. and Rodgers, G. (1981) *A Life to Live: Beyond Full Employment*, Junction Books, London.

Commission of the EC (1985a) 'The Thrust of Commission Policy' (by Jacques Delors), *Bulletin of the European Communities*, Supplement 1/85, EC, Luxembourg.

Commission of the EC (1985b) 'A People's Europe' (Addonino Report Parts I and II) *Bulletin of the European Communities*, Supplement 7/85, EC, Luxembourg.

Commission of the EC (1986b) *The European Community's Budget*, European Documentation 1/86, EC, Luxembourg.

Commission of the EC (1986b) *Europe as seen by Europeans 1973–86*, Eurobarometer, Documentation 4/86, EC, Luxembourg.

Commission of the EC (1987a) 'New Rights for the Citizens of Europe', *European File* 11/87, June/July, EC, Luxembourg.

Commission of the EC (1987b) 'Equal opportunities for women', *European File*, 10/87, May, EC, Luxembourg.

Commission of the EC (1988a) *Europe without frontiers: completing the internal market*, (2nd edn) European Documentation, EC, Luxembourg.

Commission of the EC (1988b) *Working Together – The Institutions of the European Community* (by E. Noel), EC Official Publications, Luxembourg.

Commission of the EC (1988c) *The Social Dimension of the Internal Market*, Social Europe Series, ed. no. 3, EC, Luxembourg.

Commission of the EC (1989a) 'The European Community and Human Rights', *European File*, 5/89, April, EC, Luxembourg.

Commission of the EC (1989b) *Europe in Figures*, EC Official Publications, Luxembourg.

Commission of the EC (1989c) 'A Community of Twelve: Key Figures', *European File*, 3–4/89, March, EC, Luxembourg.

Commission of the EC (1989d) *The Fight Against Poverty*, Social Europe Supplement 2/89, EC, Luxembourg.

Commission of the EC (1989e) 'The Delors Report' on Economic and Monetary Union, EC Official Publications, Luxembourg.

Commission of the EC (1990a) *Poverty in the European Community: a survey* (Poverty 3, Poverty Action Programme), EC Official Publications, Luxembourg.

Commission of the EC (1990b) *1992 – The Social Dimension*, (4th edn) European Documentation, EC, Luxembourg.

Commission of the EC (1990c) *Europe – A Fresh Start: The*

Schumann Declaration 1950–1990, European Documentation, EC, Luxembourg.

Commission of the EC (1990d) *A Human Face for Europe*, European Documentation, EC, Luxembourg.

Commission of the EC (1990e) 'Vision of a Europe Marching in Step: European political union, Italian EC Presidency Report' (reported, *Guardian*, 22 November).

Cooke, P. (1990) *Back to the Future: Modernity, Postmodernity and Locality*, Unwin Hyman, London.

Cooper, D. (1967) *Psychiatry and Anti-Psychiatry*, Tavistock, London.

Cummings, S. (ed.) (1988) *Business Elites and Urban Development*, SUNY Press, Albany.

Cuvillier, R. (1984) *The Reduction of Working Time*, International Labour Office, Geneva.

Dahrendorf, R. (1968) *Society and Democracy in Germany*, Weidenfeld and Nicholson, London.

Dahrendorf, R. (1990) 'Decade of the citizen: an interview with Dahrendorf' J. Keane, *Guardian*, 1 August.

Daltrop, A. (1986) *Politics and the European Community*, (2nd edn) Longman, London.

Deakin, S. (1988) 'Towards a Social Europe?', *Low Pay Review*, 35, 12–17.

Dean, M. (1989) 'The five per cent solution: the Council of Europe's human rights agenda' *Guardian*, 5 May.

Delors Reports *see* Commission of the EC 1985a and 1989e.

Dertouzos, M. and Moses, J. (eds) (1979) *The Computer Age: A Twenty-Year View*, MIT Press, Boston, Mass.

Dicken, P. (1988) *One Nation? Social Change and the Politics of Locality*, Pluto, London.

Dilloway, J. (1986) *Is World Order Evolving?*, Pergamon, Oxford.

Dixon, J. and Scheurrell, R. (eds) (1989) *Social Welfare in Developed Market Countries*, Routledge, London.

Donzelot, J. (1980) *The Policing of Families*, Hutchinson, London.

Dore, R. (1987) 'Citizenship and Employment in an Age of High Technology', *British Journal of Industrial Relations*, 25, 2, 201–25.

Doyal, L. and Pennell, L. (1983) *The Political Economy of*

Health, Pluto, London.

Duncan, G. (ed.) (1984a) *Years of Poverty, Years of Plenty*, University of Michigan, Ann Arbor.

Duncan, G. et al. (1984b) 'The Dynamics of Welfare Use', in Duncan 1984a.

Duncan, G. and Coe, R. (1984) 'The Dynamics of Poverty', in Duncan 1984a.

Duncan, G. and Hoffman, S. (1984) 'Recent Trends in the Relative Earnings of Black Men', in Duncan 1984a.

Durkheim, E. (1964) *The Division of Labour*, Free Press, New York. (original 1893)

Eberstadt, N. (1988) 'Economic and Material Poverty in the U.S.', *The Public Interest*, 90, 50–65.

EC *see* Commission of the EC.

Ehrenreich, B. (1987) 'The New Right's Attack on Welfare', in Block et al. 1987b.

Ellwood, D. (1986) 'The Spatial Mismatch Hypothesis: Are there teenage jobs missing in the ghetto?', in Freeman and Holzer 1986a.

Ellwood, D. and Summers, L. (1986) 'Is Welfare really the problem?', *The Public Interest*, 83, 57–77.

Elshtain, J. B. (1981) *Public Man, Private Woman*, Princeton University Press, Princeton.

Emerson, M. and Huhne, C. (1991) *The ECU Report*, Pan, London.

Esping-Andersen, G. (1990) *The Three Worlds of Welfare Capitalism*, Polity Press, Cambridge.

European, The (1990) 'Industry's winners and losers in new markets of Europe', *The European*, 13 July.

European Community (EC) *see* Commission of the EC.

Eurosynergies (1990), quoted, *Guardian*, 6 August.

Featherstone, M. (ed.) (1990) *Global Culture: Nationalism, Globalisation and Modernity*, Sage, London.

Field, F. (1989) *Losing Out: The Emergence of Britain's Underclass*, Blackwell, Oxford.

Field, F. (1990) 'Britain's Underclass: Countering the Growth', ch. 2, in IEA 1990.

Finch, J. (1989) *Family Obligations and Social Change*, Polity Press, Cambridge.

Finlayson, G. (1990) *Citizen, State and Social Welfare in Britain*

1830–1990, Oxford University Press, Oxford.

Flynn, N. (1989) 'The "New Right" and Social Policy', *Policy and Politics*, 17, 2, 97–109.

Fraser, D. (1984) *The Evolution of the British Welfare State*, (2nd edn) Macmillan, London.

Freeman, C. and Clark, J. (1987) 'Quantitative analysis of the future of UK employment', in Freeman and Soete 1987.

Freeman, C. and Soete, L. (eds) (1987) *Technical Change and Full Employment*, Blackwell, Oxford.

Freeman, R. and Holzer, H. (eds) (1986a) *The Black Youth Unemployment Crisis*, University of Chicago Press, Chicago.

Freeman, R. and Holzer, H. (1986b) 'The Black Youth Unemployment Crisis: Summary of Findings', in Freeman and Holzer 1986a.

Freire, P. (1976) *Education: The Practice of Freedom*, Writers and Readers Publishing Cooperative, London.

Friedman, M. (1962) *Capitalism and Freedom*, University of Chicago Press, Chicago.

Friedman, M. and Friedman, R. (1980) *Free to Choose*, Penguin, London.

Friedmann, R. et al. (eds) (1987) *Modern Welfare States: A Comparative View of Trends and Prospects*, Wheatsheaf Books, Brighton.

Furniss, N. and Tilton, T. (1979) *The Case for the Welfare State*, Indiana University Press, Bloomington.

Galtung, J. (1973) *The European Community: A Superpower in the Making*, Allen and Unwin, London.

Galtung, J. (1980) *The True Worlds: A Transactional Perspective*, Free Press/Macmillan, New York.

Gamble, A. (1985) *Britain in Decline*, (2nd edn) Macmillan, London.

Gamble, A. (1988) *The Free Market and the Strong State: the Politics of Thatcherism*, Macmillan Educational, Basingstoke.

Gamble, A. (1990) 'Britain's Decline: Some Theoretical Issues', in Mann 1990b.

GAO (General Accounting Office) (1984) 'Proposed Mandatory Workfare Program: Questions from CWEP', GAO/PEMD-84-2, 2 April, US General Printing Office, Washington.

GAO (1985) 'Evidence against proposed changes to AFDC Work Program', GAO/HRD-85-92, 27 August, US General

Printing Office, Washington.

Garfinkel, I. and McLanahan, S. (1986) *Single Mothers and their Children: A New American Dilemma*, Urban Institute, Washington.

Gellner, E. (1964) *Thought and Change*, Weidenfeld and Nicholson, London.

Gellner, E. (1983) *Nations and Nationalism*, Blackwell, Oxford.

Gershuny, J. (1978) *After Industrial Society?*, Macmillan, London.

Gershuny, J. and Miles, I. (1983) *The New Service Economy*, Praeger Publishers, New York.

Giddens, A. (1985a) 'Class, sovereignty and citizenship', in his 1985b.

Giddens, A. (1985b) *The Nation State and Violence*, Polity Press, Cambridge.

Gilbert, N. (1983) *Capitalism and the Welfare State*, Yale University Press, New Haven.

Gilder, G. (1982) *Wealth and Poverty*, Buchan and Enright, London.

Gilder, G. (1986) *Men and Marriage*, Pelican, Gretna, Louisiana.

Gilder, G. (1987) 'The collapse of the American family', *The Public Interest*, 89, 20–5.

Glazer, N. (1982) 'Reform Work not Welfare', in Paul and Russo 1982.

Glazer, N. (1988) *The Limits of Social Policy*, Harvard University Press, Cambridge, Mass.

Glazer, N. (1990) 'The Limits of Social Policy', *Dialogue*, 87, 1, 34–40.

Glennerster, H. (ed.) (1983) *The Future of the Welfare State*, Heinemann, London.

Goodin, R. et al. (1987) *Not Only for the Poor*, Allen and Unwin, London.

Goody, J. and Watt, I. (1963) 'The Consequences of Literacy', *Comparative Studies in Society and History*, 5, 3, 27–68.

Gorz, A. (1982) *Farewell to the Working Class: an Essay on Post-industrial Socialism*, Pluto, London.

Gorz, A. (1985) *Paths to Paradise: On the Liberation from Work*, Pluto, London.

Gorz, A. (1989) *Critique of Economic Reason*, Verso, London.

Gough, I. (1979) *The Political Economy of the Welfare State*, Macmillan, London.

Gouldner, A. (1979) *The Future of Intellectuals and the Rise of the New Class*, Seabury Press, New York.

Gow, D. (1990) 'German rage increases with rise in foreigners', *Guardian*, 13 April.

Gow, D. (1991a) 'Germans "forget their foreigners"', *Guardian*, 27 March.

Gow, D. (1991b) 'Kohl sets out timetable for a United States of Europe', *Guardian*, 16 May.

GRAEL (1986) *The Guaranteed Basic Income and the Future of Social Security*, Green-Alternative Link, European Parliament, EC Publications Brussels/Luxembourg.

Grahl, J. and Teague, P. (1990) *1992 – The Big Market: The Future of the European Community*, Lawrence and Wishart, London.

Grant, W. (1985a) 'Introduction', in Grant 1985b.

Grant, W. (ed.) (1985b) *The Political Economy of Corporatism*, Macmillan, London.

Gueron, J. (1986) 'Work for people on welfare', *Public Welfare*, winter, 7–12.

Habermas, J. (1975) *Legitimacy Crisis*, Beacon Press, Boston.

Habermas, J. (1979) *Communication and the Evolution of Society*, Heinemann, London.

Habermas, J. (1987) *The Theory of Communicative Action*, vol. 2, Heinemann, London.

Hall, S. and Held, D. (1989) 'Citizens and Citizenship' in Hall and Jacques 1989.

Hall, S. and Jacques, M. (eds) (1989) *New Times*, Lawrence and Wishart, London.

Halsall, M. (1990) 'Euro-expansion costs North-west jobs', *Guardian*, 31 December.

Halsey, A. H. (1986) *Change in British Society*, (3rd edn) Oxford University Press, Oxford.

Handler, J. and Hasenfeld, Y. (1990) *The Moral Construction of Poverty: Welfare Reform in America*, Sage, London.

Handy, C. (1985) *The Future of Work*, Blackwell, Oxford.

Harden, I. (1990) 'Sovereignty and the Eurofed', *The Political Quarterly*, 61, 4, 402–14.

Harper, K. (1990a) 'Trade union movement and the impact of the single market', *Guardian*, 31 August.

Harper, K. (1990b) 'Work-for-benefit pilot schemes planned for six areas next year', *Guardian*, 30 October.

Harrington, M. (1963) *The Other America: Poverty in the United States*, Penguin, London.

Harrington, M. (1984) *The New American Poverty*, Holt, Rinehart and Winston, New York.

Harris, J. (1977) *William Beveridge: A Biography*, Clarendon Press, Oxford.

Harrison, M. (ed.) (1984) *Corporatism and the Welfare State*, Gower, London.

Harvey, D. (1989) *The Condition of Postmodernity*, Blackwell, Oxford.

Hasenfeld, Y. and Hoefer, R. (1989) 'USA social services and social work under Reaganism', in Munday 1989.

Hatch, S. and Hadley, R. (1981) *Social Welfare and the Failure of the State*, Allen and Unwin, London.

Hauser, R. and Fischer, I. (1990) 'Economic well-being among one-parent families', ch. 6 in Smeeding et al. 1990a.

Hayek, F. (1973) *Law, Legislation and Liberty*, vols 1 and 2, Routledge, London.

Hayek, F. (1986) *The Road to Serfdom*, Ark/RKP, London.

Hegel, F. (1967) *The Philosophy of Right*, Oxford University Press, Oxford. (original 1821)

Held, D. (1989) 'The Decline of the Nation State', in Hall and Jacques 1989.

Helm, S. (1991) 'There's no room at the EC', *Independent*, 1 October.

Hendy, J. and Eady, J. (1991) 'Creeping assault on workers' rights', *Guardian*, 9 August.

Heseltine, M. (1989) 'Why I believe in workfare', *Reader's Digest*, March, 43–6.

Hill, R. (1984) 'Transnational Capitalism and Urban Crisis: Detroit', in Szelenyi, I. (ed.) *Cities in Recession*, Sage, London, 1984.

Hill, R. (1988) 'Cash and Non-Cash Benefits among Poor Black Families', ch. 21 in McAdoo, H. 1988.

HMSO (1990) *Encouraging Citizenship: Report of the Speaker's*

Commission on Citizenship, HMSO, London.

Hopson, B. and Scally, M. (1981) *Lifeskills Teaching*, M'Graw-Hill, London.

Hoskyns, C. and Luckhaus, L. (1989) 'The European Community Directive on Equal Treatment in Social Security', *Policy and Politics*, 9, 321–35.

Hughes, M. (1990) 'European Court's decision heralds equal pensions ages', *Guardian*, 19 May.

Hurd, D. (1988) ' "Active Citizenship" and Law and Order' (speech to Tory Party annual conference, reported in Sharrock, D. and Linton, M. (1988) 'Electronic tags hailed as part of assault on "dependency culture"', *Guardian*, 13 October).

IEA (Institute of Economic Affairs) (1990) *The Emerging British Underclass*, IEA, Health and Welfare Unit, London.

Illich, I. (1976) *Limits to Medicine*, Penguin, London.

Illich, I. (1978) *The Right to Useful Unemployment*, Marion Boyars, London.

Jacques, M. (1988) 'Alternative British citizens by the left quick March', *Sunday Times*, 16 October.

Jacques, M. (1991) 'Charters riddled with hollow promise', *Sunday Times*, 7 July.

James, O. (1990) 'Crime and the American Mind' *The Independent*, 21 May.

Jenkins, C. and Sherman, B. (1979) *The Collapse of Work*, Eyre Methuen, London.

Jenkins, C. and Sherman, B. (1981) *The Leisure Shock*, Eyre Methuen, London.

Jessop, B. (1988) 'Regulation theory, post-Fordism and the state' *Capital and Class*, 34, 147–68.

Johnson, N. (1987) *The Welfare State in Transition: the Theory and Practice of Welfare Pluralism*, Wheatsheaf, Brighton.

Johnson, T. (1972) *Professions and Power*, Macmillan, London.

Jones, B. (1982) *Sleepers, Awake: Technology and the Future of Work*, Wheatsheaf, Brighton.

Jordan, B. (1987) *Rethinking Welfare*, Blackwell, Oxford.

Jordan, B. (1989) *The Common Good*, Blackwell, Oxford.

Judd, D. and Parkinson, M. (eds) (1990) *Leadership and Urban Regeneration*, Sage, London.

Judge, K. (1987) 'The British Welfare State in Transition', ch. 1

in Friedmann et al. 1987.

Kagan, S. et al. (1987) 'Shaping child and family policy', ch. 23 in Zigler et al. 1987.

Kant, I. (1965) *The Metaphysical Elements of Justice*, Bobbs-Merrill, New York. (original 1797)

Kasarda, J. (1989) 'Urban Industrial Transition and the Underclass', *The Annals of the American Academy of Political and Social Science*, 501, January, 26–47.

Katz, M. (1986) *In the Shadow of the Poorhouse; A Social History of Welfare in America*, Basic Books, New York.

Kaus, M. (1986) 'The Work Ethic State', *New Republic*, 7 July.

Keane, J. and Owen, J. (1986) *After Full Employment*, Hutchinson, London.

Keniston, K. (ed.) (1977) *All our Children: The American Family Under Pressure* (The Keniston Report, Carnegie), Harcourt Brace Janovich, New York.

Kerr, A. (1986) *The Common Market and How it Works*, (3rd edn) Pergamon, Oxford.

Kerr, C. et al. (1973) *Industrialism and Industrial Man*, (2nd edn) Penguin, London.

King, E. (1987) *The New Right*, Macmillan, London.

Kirp, D. (1986) 'The Californian Work/Welfare Scheme', *The Public Interest*, 83, 34–48.

Kreisky, B. (ed.) (1989) *A Programme for Full Employment in the 1990's: Europe*, Pergamon Press, Oxford.

Kristol, I. (1985) 'Skepticism, meliorism and The Public Interest', *The Public Interest*, 81, 31–41.

Laclau, E. and Mouffe, C. (1985) *Hegemony and Socialist Strategy*, Verso, London.

Ladner, J. (1988) 'The Impact of Teenage Pregnancy on the Black Family: Policy Directions', ch. 20 in McAdoo, H. 1988.

Lambert, S. (1991) 'Beyond the little red passport to Euro-citizenship', *Independent*, 22 November.

Landau, E. (1989) *The Rights of Working Women in the European Community*, EC Official Publications, Luxembourg.

Lasch, C. (1980) *The Culture of Narcissism*, Abacus, London.

Lash, S. and Urry, J. (1987) *The End of Organised Capitalism*, Polity, Cambridge.

Lawson, R. and George, V. (eds) (1980) *Poverty and Inequality in Common Market Countries*, Routledge, London.

Lawson, R. et al. (eds) (1984) *Responses to Poverty*, Heinemann, London.

Leacock, E. (ed.) (1971) *The Culture of Poverty: A Critique*, Simon and Schuster, New York.

Le Grand, J. (1982) *The Strategy of Equality*, Unwin Hyman, London.

Leiby, J. (1978) *A History of Social Welfare and Social Work in the United States*, Columbia University Press, New York.

Lekachman, R. (1969) *The Age of Keynes*, Penguin, London.

Lemann, N. (1986) 'The Origins of the Underclass', *Atlantic Monthly*, June.

Lerman, R. (1986) 'Do Welfare Programs Affect the Schooling and Work Patterns of Young Black Men?' ch. 11 in Freeman and Holzer 1986a.

Lerman, R. (1988) 'Middle Class and Underclass', *The Public Interest*, 91, 111–13.

Levin, M. (1982) *Ending Unemployment: Alternatives for Public Policy*, University of Maryland Press, Baltimore.

Levitas, R. (ed.) (1986) *The Ideology of the New Right*, Polity Press, Cambridge.

Linton, M. (1991) 'Britons' attitudes to EC', *Guardian*, 21 June.

Lipietz, A. (1985) *Mirages and Miracles; The Crises of Global Fordism*, Verso, London.

Lister, R. (1990a) 'Women, Economic Dependency and Citizenship', *Journal of Social Policy*, 19, 4, 445–67.

Lister, R. (1990b) *The Exclusive Society: Citizenship and the Poor*, Child Poverty Action Group, London.

Lodge, J. (ed.) (1987) *European Union: The European Community in Search of a Future*, Macmillan, London.

Lodge, J. (1991a) 'European Union and the "Democratic Deficit"', *Social Studies Review*, March, 149–53.

Lodge, J. (1991b) 'Blinded by the f-word', *Times Higher Education Supplement*, 27 December.

Logan, J. and Molotch, H. (1987) *Urban Fortunes: The Political Economy of Place*, University of California Press, Berkeley.

Loney, M. et al. (eds) (1987) *The State or the Market*, Sage, London.

Lyon, D. (1988) *The Information Society*, Polity Press, Cambridge.

McAdoo, H. (ed.) (1988) *Black Families*, (2nd edn) Sage, Newbury, California.

McAdoo, J. (1988) 'The Roles of Black Fathers in the Socialization of Black Children' in McAdoo, H. 1988.

Machlup, F. (1962) *The Production and Distribution of Knowledge in the United States*, Princeton University Press, Princeton.

Mackintosh, I. (1986) *Sunrise Europe: the dynamics of information technology*, Blackwell, Oxford.

McLanahan, S. and Garfinkel, I. (1989) 'Single Mothers, the Underclass and Social Policy', *The Annals of the American Academy of Political and Social Science*, 501, January, 92–104.

MacNeill, K. (1988) 'Social Europe: the potential and the pitfalls', *Low Pay Review*, 35, 18–23.

MacNicol, J. (1990) 'Nightmare on Easy Street: the myth of the underclass', *Times Higher Education Supplement*, 29 June.

Magill, R. (1989) 'United States of America: Welfare System', in Dixon and Scheurrell 1989.

Mann, M. (1987) 'Ruling Class Strategies and Citizenship', *Sociology*, 21, 3, 339–54.

Mann, M. (1990a) 'Empires without Ends', in Mann 1990b.

Mann, M. (ed.) (1990b) *The Rise and Decline of the Nation State*, Blackwell, Oxford.

Marquand, D. (1989a) 'The subversive language of citizenship', *Guardian*, 2 January.

Marquand, D. (1989b) 'The Irresistible Tide of Europeanisation' in Hall and Jacques 1989.

Marshall, T. H. (1963) 'Citizenship and Social Class' (original 1950) in his *Sociology at the Cross Roads*, Heinemann, London.

Marshall, T. H. (1972) 'Value problems of welfare-capitalism', *Journal of Social Policy*, 1, 1, January, 18–32; and in Marshall 1981.

Marshall, T. H. (1977) 'Voluntary Action' (1964), ch. 16 in *Class, Citizenship and Social Development'*, University of Chicago Press, Chicago, 1977.

Marshall, T. H. (1981) *The Right to Welfare*, Heinemann, London.

Marshall, T. H. (1985) *T. H. Marshall's Social Policy*, (5th edn, with A. Rees) Hutchinson, London.

Marx, K. (1970) *Critique of Hegel's 'Philosophy of Right'*, Cambridge University Press, Cambridge (original 1843).

Marx, K. and Engels, F. (1969) *Basic Writings on Politics and Philosophy*, ed. L. Feuer, Fontana, London.

Masnick, G. and Bane, M. J. (1980) *The Nation's Families 1960–1990*, Auburn House, Boston.

Massey, D. (1990) 'American apartheid: Segregation and the making of the underclass', *American Journal of Sociology*, 96, 329–57.

Masuda, Y. (1972) *The Social Impact of Computerisation*, Kodansha, Tokyo.

Mead, L. (1986) *Beyond Entitlement: The Social Obligations of Citizenship*, Free Press, New York.

Mead, L. (1988a) 'The New Welfare Debate', *Commentary*, 86, 44–52.

Mead, L. (1988b) 'The Potential for Work Enforcement', *Journal of Policy Analysis and Management*, 7, 2, 264–86.

Mead, L. (1988c) 'Jobs for the Welfare Poor', *Policy Review*, winter, 60–9.

Mead, L. (1988d) 'The Hidden Jobs Debate', *The Public Interest*, 91, 40–58.

Mead, L. (1989) 'The Logic of Workfare', *The Annals of the American Academy of Political and Social Science*, 501, 156–69.

Merton, R. (1968) *Social Theory and Social Structure*, Free Press, New York.

Mills, C. W. (1970) *The Sociological Imagination*, Penguin, London.

Milne, S. (1990) 'Charter, "would cut new jobs"', *Guardian*, 6 August.

Minford, P. (1984) *State Expenditure: A Study in Waste*, supplement to *Economic Affairs*, 4, 3, April/June.

Minford, P. et al. (1985) *Unemployment: Cause and Cure*, Blackwell, Oxford.

Minford, P. (1987) 'The role of the social services: a view from the New Right', in Loney et al. 1987.

Mintel Report (1990), quoted, *Guardian*, 7 February.

Mishra, R. (1984) *The Welfare State in Crisis*, Harvester/ Wheatsheaf, London.

Morgan, R. (1990) 'Continental Divides', *Times Higher Educational Supplement*, 5 January.

Morris, R. (1987) 'Rethinking Welfare in the United States', ch. 3 in Friedmann et al. 1987.

Moynihan, D. P. (1965) 'The Negro Family: The Case for National Action', in Rainwater and Yancey 1967.

Moynihan, D. P. (1973) *The Politics of a Guaranteed Income*, Random House, New York.

Moynihan, D. P. (1989) 'Towards a post-industrial social policy', *The Public Interest*, 96, 16–27.

Munday, B. (ed.) (1989) *The Crisis in Welfare*, Harvester/Wheatsheaf, London.

Murray, C. (1984) *Losing Ground*, Basic Books, New York.

Murray, C. (1986) 'No, welfare isn't really the problem', *The Public Interest*, 84, 2–11.

Murray, C. (1988a) 'The coming of custodial democracy', *Commentary*, 86, 19–24.

Murray, C. (1988b) *In Pursuit of Happiness and Good Government*, Simon and Schuster, New York.

Murray, C. (1989) 'The Underclass', *Sunday Times Magazine*, 26 November, 26–45.

Murray, C. (1990a) 'Underclass', ch. 1 in IEA 1990.

Murray, C. (1990b) 'In pursuit of happiness', *Dialogue*, 87, 1, 41–8.

Nairn, T. (1977) *The Break-up of Britain*, New Left Books, London.

NEDO (National Economic Development Council) (1987) *IT Futures – IT Can Work*, NEDO, London.

Nora, S. and Minc, A. (1980) *The Computerisation of Society*, MIT Press, Cambridge, Mass.

Novak, M. (1987a) 'Welfare's "New Consensus": Reply to Gilder' *The Public Interest*, 89, 26–30.

Novak, M. et al. (1987b) *The New Consensus on Family and Welfare*, American Enterprise Institute, Washington.

Nozick, R. (1980) *Anarchy, State, and Utopia*, Blackwell, Oxford.

Oakley, A. (1974) *The Sociology of Housework*, Robertson, London.

O'Connor, J. (1973) *The Fiscal Crisis of the State*, St Martin's Press, New York.

O'Connor, J. (1984) *Accumulation Crisis*, Blackwell, Oxford.

O'Connor, J. (1987) *The Meaning of Crisis*, Blackwell, Oxford.

Offe, C. (1984) *Contradiction of the Welfare State*, Hutchinson, London.

Offe, C. (1985a) *Disorganised Capitalism*, Polity Press, Cambridge.

Offe, C. (1985b) 'Work: the Key Sociological Category?', in Offe 1985a.

O'Neill, J. (1987) *Five Bodies*, Cornell University Press, Ithaca.

Pahl, R. (1984) *Divisions of Labour*, Blackwell, Oxford.

Pahl, R. (ed.) (1988) *On Work*, Blackwell, Oxford.

Paine, T. (1979) *The Rights of Man*, Dent, London (original 1791).

Palmer, J. (1989a) 'UK isolated on Charter for Workers', *Guardian*, 31 October.

Palmer, J. (1989b) *1992 and Beyond*, Commission of the EC, Luxembourg.

Palmer, J. (1990a) 'Uneasy silence is broken after Social Charter's sound and fury', *European*, 15 June.

Palmer, J. (1990b) 'EC warned that poorer members must be helped', *Guardian*, 4 September.

Palmer, J. (1990c) 'Europe shuts its doors to the desperate', *Guardian*, 24 January.

Palmer, J. (1990d) 'Work hours clash looms with Brussels', *Guardian*, 26 July.

Palmer, J. (1991a) 'Rush to join EC prompts Nordic rethink on future', *Guardian*, 30 April.

Palmer, J. (1991b) 'EC Partners may get more aid', *Guardian*, 15 May.

Palmer, J. (1991c) 'Political union casts shadow over accord', *Guardian*, 1 July.

Parfit, D. (1986) *Reasons and Persons*, Oxford University Press, Oxford.

Parker, H. (1984) *Action on Welfare*, Social Affairs Unit, London.

Parker, H. (1989) *Instead of the Dole*, Macmillan, London.

Parker, J. (1975) *Social Policy and Citizenship*, Macmillan, London.

Parsons, T. (1959) 'The School Class as a Social System', *Harvard Educational Review*, 29, fall, 297–318.

Parsons, T. (1964) *The Social System*, Free Press, New York.

Parsons, T. (1970) *The System of Modern Societies*, Prentice-Hall, New Jersey.

Pascal, G. (1983) 'Women and Social Welfare', in Bean and MacPherson 1983.

Patten, J. (1988) 'Active Citizens', *Sunday Times*, 11 December.

Paul, E. et al. (eds) (1984) *Human Rights*, Blackwell, Oxford.

Paul, E. and Russo, P. (eds) (1982) *Public Policy*, Chatham House, New Jersey.

Paul, J. (ed.) (1982) *Reading Nozick*, Blackwell, Oxford.

Pearce, F. (1990) ' "Responsible Corporations" and Regulating Agencies', *The Political Quarterly*, 61, 4, 415–30.

Philpott, T. (1988) 'Charles Murray – A Guru Losing Ground?', *Community Care*, 19 May.

Piachaud, D. (1991) 'A Euro-charter for confusion', *Guardian*, 13 November.

Pierson, C. (1991) *Beyond the Welfare State. The New Political Economy of Welfare*, Polity Press, Cambridge.

Pimlott, B. (1988) 'Opposition citizens unite!', *Guardian*, 24 October.

Pinker, R. (1979) *The Idea of Welfare*, Heinemann, London.

Pinker, R. (1981) Introduction in T. H. Marshall 1981.

Piore, M. and Sabel, C. (1984) *The Second Industrial Divide*, Basic Books, New York.

Piven, F. and Cloward, R. (1971) *Regulating the Poor*, Vintage Books, New York.

Piven, F. and Cloward, R. (1987) 'The Contemporary Relief Debate', ch. 2 in Block et al. 1987b.

Plant, R (1988a) 'Citizenship and Society', *New Socialist*, 58, 7–9.

Plant, R. (1988b) *Citizenship, Rights and Socialism*, Fabian Society, London.

Plant, R. et al. (1980) *Political Philosophy and Social Welfare*, Routledge, London.

Popper, K. (1966) *The Open Society and its Enemies*, vol. 2, (5th edn), Routledge, London.

Porat, M. (1977) *The Information Economy*, US Department of Commerce, Washington.

Porritt, J. (1984) *Seeing Green*, Blackwell, Oxford.

Rainwater, L. and Yancey, W. (eds) (1967) *The Moynihan*

Report and the Politics of Controversy, MIT Press, Cambridge, Mass.

Rajan, A. (1990) *1992, A Zero Sum Game*, The Industrial Society, Birmingham.

Rehn, G. (1978) 'Towards a Society of Free Choice', Swedish Institute for Social Research, Stockholm.

Reischauer, P. (1989) 'The welfare reform legislation: Directions for the future' in Cottingham, P. and Ellwood, D. (eds) *Welfare Policy for the 1990s*, Harvard University Press, Cambridge, Mass., 1989.

Reisman, D. (1977) *Richard Titmuss: Welfare and Society*, Heinemann, London.

RETI Report (1989) *Socio-Economic Consequences of the Single Market in the Traditional Industrial Regions of Europe*, RIDES-IRES, Université Catholique de Louvain, Louvain, Belgium.

Ricketts, E. and Sawhill, I. (1988) 'Defining and measuring the underclass', *Journal of Policy Analysis and Management*, 7, 2, 316–25.

Rimlinger, G. (1971) *Welfare Policy and Industrialisation in Europe, America and Russia*, John Wiley, New York.

Roberts, K. (1982) *Automation, Unemployment and the Distribution of Income*, Centre for Work and Society, Maastricht.

Robertson, J. (1985) *Future Work*, Gower/Temple Smith, Aldershot.

Robins, K. and Webster, F. (1989) *The Technical Fix*, Macmillan, London.

Roche, M. (1973) *Phenomenology, Language and the Social Sciences*, Routledge, London.

Roche, M. (1984) 'Citizenship and Social Theory: T. H. Marshall and beyond', Sociology Working Paper, Department of Sociological Studies, University of Sheffield.

Roche, M. (1987) 'Citizenship, Social Theory and Social Change', *Theory and Society*, 16, 363–99.

Roche, M. (1988a) 'On the Political Sociology of the Lifeworld', *Philosophy of the Social Sciences*, 18, 2, 259–63.

Roche, M. (1988b) 'The New Right and Citizenship', Policy Studies Centre (PSC) Working Paper, University of Sheffield.

Roche, M. (1988c) 'Feminism and Citizenship', PSC Working Paper, University of Sheffield.

Roche, M. (1988d) 'Ecology and Citizenship', PSC Working Paper, University of Sheffield.

Roche, M. (1988e) 'Work, Income and Citizenship', PSC Working Paper, University of Sheffield.

Roche, M. (1988f) 'Global political institutions: a context for "world citizenship"?', PSC Working Paper, University of Sheffield.

Roche, M. (1989) 'Historicality and Citizenship', PSC Working Paper, University of Sheffield.

Roche, M. (1990a) 'Time and Unemployment', *Human Studies*, 13, 1, 1–25.

Roche, M. (1990b) 'Motherland or Motherhood: Neoconservatism and citizenship duties', *New Socialist*, October/November, 10/12.

Roche, M. (1992a) (forthcoming) 'Rethinking Social Citizenship', Proceedings of the XIIth World Congress of Sociology, New Classes and Social Movements Section, International Sociological Association, Madrid.

Roche, M. (1992b) (forthcoming) 'Mega-Events and Micro-Modernisation: On the Sociology of the New Urban Tourism', *British Journal of Sociology*, September.

Roll, J. (1989) *Lone Parents in the European Community*, Family Policy Studies Centre, London.

Room, G. et al. (1989) ' "New Poverty" in the European Community', *Policy and Politics*, 17, 2, 165–76.

Room, G. (1979) *The Sociology of Welfare*, Martin Robertson, Oxford.

Rose, M. (1985) *Re-Working the Work Ethic*, Batsford, London.

Rothbard, M. (1982) 'Welfare and the Welfare State', in Paul and Russo 1982.

Runciman, W. G. (1966) *Relative Deprivation and Social Justice*, Routledge, London.

Sargent, J. (1985) 'Corporatism and the European Community', in Grant 1985b.

Scott, A. (1990) *Ideology and the New Social Movements*, Unwin Hyman, London.

Scott, P. (1987a) 'Back to the Future: American Neoconservatism', *Times Higher Education Supplement*, 6 February.

Scott, P. (1987b) 'Viewed from the Right: Kristol and Glazer', *Times Higher Education Supplement*, 13 February.

Scott, P. (1987c) 'Empirical measures for a sympathetic tendency: Bell and Moynihan', *Times Higher Education Supplement*, 20 February.

Segalman, R. and Marsland, D. (1989) *Cradle to Grave: Comparative Perspectives on the State of Welfare*, Macmillan, London.

Sharff, J. (1981) 'Free enterprise and the ghetto family', *Psychology Today*, 15, 4.

Sheehan, S. (1976) *A Welfare Mother*, Mentor, New York.

Shorter, E. (1977) *The Making of the Modern Family*, Fontana, London.

Skidelsky, R. (ed.) (1977) *The End of the Keynesian Era*, Macmillan, London.

Sklair, L. (1990) *Sociology of the Global System*, Harvester/Wheatsheaf, Brighton.

Smeeding, T. et al. (1990a) *Poverty, Inequality and Income Distribution in Comparative Perspective*, Harvester/Wheatsheaf, Brighton.

Smeeding, T. et al. (1990b) 'Income poverty in seven countries', ch. 3 in Smeeding et al. 1990a.

Spencer, M. (1990) *1992 and All That: Civil Liberties in the Balance*, Civil Liberties Trust, London.

Standing, G. (1986) *Unemployment and Labour Market Flexibility: The UK*, International Labour Office, Geneva.

Steele, S. (1990) *The Content of Our Character; A New Vision of Race in America*, St. Martin's Press, New York.

Stewart, J. and Stoker, G. (eds) (1989) *The Future of Local Government*, Macmillan Education, Basingstoke.

Stonier, T. (1983) *The Wealth of Information*, Thames/Methuen, London.

Swann, A. de (1988) *In Care of the State*, Polity Press, Cambridge.

Taylor, D. (1989) 'Citizenship and social power', *Critical Social Policy*, 26, 19–31.

Teague, P. (1989) *The European Community: The Social Dimension*, Kogan Page, London.

Teague, P. and Brewster, C. (1989) *European Community Social Policy*, IPM, Wimbledon.

Testa, M. et al. (1989) 'Employment and Marriage among Inner-City Fathers', *The Annals of the American Academy of*

Political and Social Science, 501, 79–91.

Thatcher, M. (1988) 'Heirs to Europe: the Bruges Speech', *Guardian*, 21 September.

Titmuss, R. (1963) *Essays on the Welfare State*, Allen and Unwin, London.

Titmuss, R. (1970) *The Gift Relationship*, Allen and Unwin, London.

Toffler, A. (1970) *Future Shock*, Pan, London.

Toffler, A. (1980) *Third Wave*, Pan/Collins, London.

Toffler, A. (1985) *Previews and Premises*, Pan, London.

Townsend, P. (1975) *Sociology and Social Policy*, Penguin, London.

Townsend, P. (1979) *Poverty in the United Kingdom*, Penguin, London.

Travis, A. (1991) 'Labour brings its own Charter to market', *Guardian*, 4 July.

Travis, A. and Hencke, D. (1991) 'Major's Charter negotiates Whitehall obstacle course', *Guardian*, 11 July.

Turner, B. (1986) *Citizenship and Capitalism*, Allen and Unwin, London.

Turner, B. (1990) 'Outline of a Theory of Citizenship', *Sociology*, 24, 2, 189–217.

Urry, J. and Lash, S. (1987) *The End of Organised Capitalism*, Polity Press, Cambridge.

Usborne, D. (1989) 'Social Charter softened after UK objections', *Independent*, 21 November.

Usborne, D. et al. (1991) 'EC leaders agree union deal', *Independent*, 11 December.

Van der Veen, R. and Van Parijs, R. (1985) 'A Capitalist Road to Communism', *Theory and Society*, March.

Venturini, P. (1989) *1992: The Social Dimension*, EC Official Publications, Luxembourg.

Vincent, A. and Plant, R. (1984) *Philosophy, Politics and Citizenship*, Blackwell, Oxford.

Vulliamy, E. (1990) 'Carnival "joke" turns out to be a nation's tragedy', *Guardian*, 13 April.

Walker, D. (1986) 'S. M. Lipset: Trotskyist of the New Right', *Times Higher Education Supplement*, 17 January.

Walter, T. (1989) *Basic Income*, Marion Boyars, London.

Walton, R. G. (1982) *Social Work 2000*, Longman, London.

Walzer, M. (1985) *Spheres of Justice*, Blackwell, Oxford.

Weale, A. (1983) *Political Theory and Social Policy*, Macmillan, London.

Webb, B. (1948) *Our Partnership*, Longman, London.

Weber, M. (1964) *The Theory of Social and Economic Organisation*, Free Press, New York.

Weber, M. (1970) *The Protestant Ethic and the Spirit of Capitalism*, Unwin, London.

Webster, P. (1990) 'National Front seeps into political cracks', *Guardian*, 13 April.

Wedderburn, W. (1990) *The Social Charter, European Company and Employment Rights: an outline agenda*, The Institute of Employment, London.

Weir, M. et al. (eds) (1988) *The Politics of Social Policy in the United States*, Princeton University, Princeton, N.J.

West, R. (1980) 'The Effects (of N.I.T.) on Young Nonheads (of families)', *Journal of Human Resources*, 15, 587–8.

Westergaard, J. and Resler, H. (1976) *Class in a Capitalist Society*, Penguin, London.

Weston, C. (1991) 'Health and safety go into the melting pot', *Guardian*, 1 June.

White, M. (1991) 'Social charter rift puts deal in balance', *Guardian*, 10 December.

Wicks, M. (1987) *A Future for All: Do we need a Welfare State?*, Penguin, London.

Wicks, M. and Kiernan, K. (1990) *Family Change and Social Change*, Family Policy Studies Centre, London.

Williams, R. (1965) *The Long Revolution*, Penguin, London.

Williams, K. and Williams, J. (1987) *A Beveridge Reader*, Allen and Unwin, London.

Wilson, E. (1977) *Women and the Welfare State*, Tavistock, London.

Wilson, J. Q. (1985) 'The rediscovery of character: private virtue and public policy', *The Public Interest* , 81, 3–16.

Wilson, W. J. (1987) *The Truly Disadvantaged*, University of Chicago Press, Chicago.

Wilson, W. J. (1989) 'The Underclass', *The Annals of the American Academy of Political and Social Science*, 501, January, 182–192.

Wilson, W. J. and Wacquant, L. (1989) 'The Cost of Racial

and Class Exclusion in the Inner City', *The Annals of the American Academy of Political and Social Science*, 501, January, 8–25.

Wiseman, M. (1987a) 'How workfare really works', *The Public Interest*, 89, 36–47.

Wiseman, M. (1987b) 'Obligation and Welfare Policy', *Policy Sciences*, 21, 97–107.

Wolfe, A. (1989) *Whose Keeper? Social Science and Moral Obligation*, University of California Press, Berkeley.

Wolfenden, J. (1978) *The Future of Voluntary Organisations* (The Wolfenden Report), Croom Helm, London.

Woollacott, M. (1991) 'Beating a path to the citadel: mass migration from the poor world', *Guardian*, 10 June.

Young, H. (1991) 'Unbound by a bill of rights', *Guardian*, 11 July.

Young, M. (1962) *The Rise of the Meritocracy*, Penguin, London.

Zigler, E. et al. (eds) (1987) *Children, Families and Government: Perspectives on American Social Policy*, Cambridge University Press, Cambridge.

Index